D0636897

lost in care

lost in care

THE TRUE STORY OF A FORGOTTEN CHILD

JIMMY HOLLAND
WITH
STEPHEN RICHARDS

JOHN BLAKE

Published by John Blake Publishing Ltd,
3, Bramber Court, 2 Bramber Road,
London W14 9PB, England

www.blake.co.uk

First published in hardback in 2005

ISBN 1 84454 161 4

British Library Cataloguing-in-Publication Data:

A catalogue record for this book is available from the British Library.

Design by www.envydesign.co.uk

Printed in Great Britain by Creative Print and Design (Wales),
Ebbw Vale, Gwent

3 5 7 9 10 8 6 4 2

Papers used by John Blake Publishing Ltd are natural, recyclable products made from wood grown in sustainable forests. The manufacturing processes conform to the environmental regulations of the country of origin.

But I found a family that loves me the way I love them.
And for my late uncle James 'Macky' MacLeer

Contents

Foreword	ix
Prologue	xi
Introduction	xvii
Abandoned as a Baby	1
Product of the System	5
Look Back in Anger	29
Off to Sunny Govan and Then the Big Hoose	41
The Road to Hell	53
Goodbye to the Bar L (The Hate Factory)	63
Westend Ned with No Bed	71
The Sullen Majesty of a Young Offenders Institution	85
This is a Man's World	101

Smacked Up 111
Man in a Suitcase 121
Hostage Takers Demand Rubber Dolls and Planes to Ibiza 133
Man-eater Survival 149
Smacking it up at a £2m Trial 165
Double Hostage Siege Drug Hell in Glenochil and Perth Prisons 179
Jingle Bollocks at the High Court 195
The Bar L Wendy House isn't for Kids 207
Screwbirds and Killing the Junkie 213
Shoot to Kill Prison Siege – Back to the Wendy House 219
Holland Takes a Hostage for a Sausage Roll 231
Transitional Suicide 257
The Seven Oafs of Glenochil Hate Factory 261
In and Out of the Wendy House like a Fiddler's Elbow 269
Suicide isn't Painless … It Kills 279
Screwing the Screwbirds and the Shotts Riot 285
Attempted Murder of Four Prison Officers 293
Kangaroo Trial 297
Epilogue 309

Foreword

They say you've never lived until you've been imprisoned, and I can vouch for that. But there is a flipside to that equation: when you've been to prison, living a normal life afterwards can be hell.

With that in mind, once freed from incarceration, I believe you can turn your life around by virtue of something profound happening to you, which I suppose has happened in Jimmy Holland's life ... although he's currently still behind bars.

There's no argument, Jimmy was once considered one of the most violent inmates held in the Scottish penal system. A multitude of incidents, including prison sieges, criminal damage, hostage-taking incidents, assaults and threats to kill, all while behind bars, must make Jimmy unequalled in the annals of Scottish prison history as the most violent prisoner ever! I do not give Jimmy that tag of violence lightly, as I too faced an attempted murder charge and, at one of my trials, I was once dubbed the most dangerous man in Scotland.

The same remarkable incident that helped turn my life around is now occurring in Jimmy's life. Someone believes in him enough to make him want to turn away from the devastation that the world of violence holds.

Channelling his energy into becoming a successfully published author has been no mean feat for Jimmy. You can count the number of successful living prison authors in Scotland on both hands. Now Jimmy is a member of this most select club.

I was able to turn my life around by virtue of channelling my negative energies into writing and winning awards for my first publication, *It's Criminal*, which I wrote while behind bars. Now that I'm free, I can concentrate on writing crime thrillers and more true-crime books.

The road to freedom, from my experience behind bars, is paved with obstacles; Jimmy has certainly had more than his fair share of these, but he's well on his way to freeing himself from the constraints of prison life and fully able to concentrate on his writing.

Good luck, Jimmy,
James Crosbie

Prologue

This book is full of Glaswegian slang words and jail words, and I've written some of them down here for you, so you can understand the words I'm using. I'll also give you an example of Eggy Pater.

EGGY PATER

Jeggimy means 'Jimmy', you can use this in any name at all, like 'Steggevie' for Stevie, 'Sceggott' for Scott, 'Treggacey' for Tracey, and 'Seggandra' for Sandra.

When Eggy is spoken very fast, it's very hard to understand to an untrained ear. This way of talking has been used for years in prison to outwit the prison officers. I'm now going to write down a sentence in eggy, then translate it for you.

Hegger, heggave yeggou geggot egga veggisit thegg neggight?

Here, have you got a visit the night?

Now I'm going to put the words I'm using in this book into the proper context for you, so you'll understand the words and abbreviations in English.

Glossary

A HIT – sticking a needle in your arm, leg or neck to inject heroine
BAM – when one person calls another person an idiot
BANG TO RIGHTS – caught red-handed
BANG-UP – put in a segregation unit
BANGER – a handgun or shotgun
BEAST – someone who rapes children or women, or sometimes a man who hits his wife
BENNY – Benzedrine (amphetamine sulphate)
BENT – to call someone a poof
BLACKPOOL TOWER – getting a shower in prison
BURN – putting heroin on the foil and holding a lighter underneath it
CHAVI – what Glasgow people call boys from Edinburgh
CID – Criminal Investigation Department
CIVI (or Civvy) – civilian

CIVICHARGE – police come in
CLARET – blood
COKE – powdered form of cocaine
CON – prisoner over the age of twenty-one
COPPER – name for a policeman or policewoman
CREEPING – burgling houses while the owners sleep
DAFTY – someone who makes out he's something that he really isn't
DAGGER – homemade jail knife
DARKIES' LIPS – chips
DEAR JOHN – when you or your bird send a letter to say that it's finished between you
DC – detention centre
DIFS (DFs) – Dihydrocodeine (Codeine) painkillers and anti-depressants
DIGGER – segregation unit
DINGY – a liar
DIVVY – share
DOWNERS – Valium, mogadones, in fact, any sleeping tablets
DUFF – jail cake that mostly goes with custard
DRUMMY – prison
ES – ecstasy tablets
FREDDIE KROUGAR – sugar
GETTING DONE – means someone is going to stab someone else
GHOSTED – moved to another prison at short notice
GLESGA – Glasgow
GRASS – when one person tells the screws or police on you
HASH – dope, weed, blow – all the same thing
HMYOI – Her Majesty's Young Offenders Institution
HOLY GHOST – toast

JAGGING – injecting
JELLIES – Tamazipam, sleeping tablets that people, myself included, would jab into the arms
JOBBYED – shit your pants
KIT – heroin
LIFTED – arrested
MARS BAR – someone's scar on his face or body
MISTYS (Morphine Sulphate) – MST tablets for cancer
MOHAMMED ALI – swally of drink or drugs
MOLOTOV COCKTAIL – homemade petrol bomb
PETER THIEF – a peter's another name for a prison cell. No one likes a peter thief
PLUG YOU – stabbing someone with a knife
POISON – people talking behind your back
PP9 – a large square battery, quite heavy and often used as a weapon when put into a sock
PROCURATOR FISCAL (PF) – prosecutor
PTI – physical training instructor
ROCKET – someone that tells someone else to do the dirty work for them
ROCKS – crack cocaine
ROOL AS – that's a civilian charge, waiting for police to come in and charge you
ROOL BO – the governor puts you on this to keep you in segregation
SPS – Scottish Prison Service
SCREW – prison warden
SCREWBIRD – female prison warder
SCREWING – burgling (or sexual intercourse, whichever you prefer)
SLABPIE – jail steak or mince pie

SLASHING – someone runs a razor down someone's face
SLOPPING OUT – emptying out of ablutions from cell bucket into sluice
SMACK – heroin
SNORTING – that's when you have to snort the drug up your nose
SPEED – Amphetamine Sulphate
STIFFY – someone's sending someone else a secret letter in prison
TARIFF – if you give someone tobacco and if the person cannot pay it back, you get a tariff
TAX – someone bullying someone else for his drugs or canteen food
TEMS – Temgesic tablets, usually prescribed for back pains
TOOL – homemade jail razor melted on to a toothbrush
TURN – to rob a shop, bank, post office, shoplift, house break, anything for money
UP FOR IT – someone that's not scared of anyone in or out of prison
WEAGIE – what Edinburgh boys call boys from Glasgow
WHITE MOUNTAINS – jail mashed potato
WHO'S HOLDING? – someone asking, 'Who's got drugs?'
YO – young offender
YOI – Young Offenders Institution
YP – prisoner under the age of twenty-one

These are the most common words used in Glasgow and in Scottish prisons. I hope they are of some help to you in understanding what is written when I use colloquialisms. Enjoy the read.

Introduction

I'm Jimmy 'Boy' Holland, the worst motherfucker, some say, in the British penal system. I'm thirty-four years old, and have spent all but a few months of my life in children's homes, foster care, young offenders institutes and prisons. I've experienced just about every drug that can be injected, snorted or swallowed. Crime also figures quite heavily in my life. My story is one of being state raised ... here it is.

Some kids get a fair crack of the whip, being born into a loving and caring family, raised with kindness and having the best in them brought out by virtue of loving and attentive parents. But this type of upbringing is alien to me. Getting any love out of me is like pulling teeth. The dice of life hasn't rolled in my favour right from the start. At only two weeks old, I was placed into the care of the anachronistic Scottish Social Work System. With unremitting cruelty, this stark upbringing by the state has moulded me into a feared, drug-crazed man of violence and has continued to do so all the way from the maze of children's homes right through to the network of Scottish prisons, from the notorious Barlinnie Prison (Bar L) all the way through to the austere penal establishment of the infamous Special Unit at HM Prison Shotts and, at the time of writing, HMP Perth, where I'm currently serving nine years for armed robbery. The earliest release date I'm looking forward to is 2007, unless I win parole or an appeal.

When it comes to armed robbers and prison hostage takers, my intensely touching story isn't the normal run-of-the-mill story you're used to reading about. I wasn't driven by a passionate greed to become filthy rich. I just needed to satisfy my drug addiction. As well as being a chronic drinker and gambler, my father stole the money for the food and battered my mother. I remember him lying in a drunken stupor in our house, in Springwells, Blantyre. My father's respect for women was akinto the way he respected us, his children ... like shit on the sole of his shoe. Although I was put into social-work care, for some strange reason my two brothers were allowed to stay with that cowardly brute of an excuse for a man. My mother, unknown to me, successfully pleaded with the social services to get me back home. But, after only a short stay with my parents, I was off, and would not see my mother again until thirty-one years later.

But I don't want to use emotional metaphors that might move you to think that I led a worse life than I actually did, as I've no reason to hoodwink you. I don't seek your sympathy vote, but I do seek an end to this sort of upbringing for those who come after me.

I'm not proud of a lot of things in my life. This book isn't written to glorify any violence or drug taking, as I hope that it can do some good against the bad that's been done by me and the people I've done it with. Hopefully, this book will clear up some of the lies and myths that have surrounded the incidents portrayed herein and the mistakes I've made. I really would like this book to be a guideline for all systems: social work, convicts, police and prison services, and drug and addiction workers.

You may find this book disturbing for its accounts of children under the age of fourteen, so a lot of the names have been changed to protect their privacy. I've also added fictional names and places in certain events so that no one need be associated with the things I'm going to tell you.

Yours,

James 'Jimmyboy' Holland

CHAPTER ONE

Abandoned as a Baby

I arrived in this crazy, mixed-up world at twenty-four minutes to six in the morning on 10 December 1970. To all, I was a happy, bouncing bundle of joy, tipping the scales at six pounds and seven ounces. My birth was to be a memorable one for my mother, as I wasn't the easiest of births.

My father, Albert, was conspicuous at my birth by his drunken absence – he was nowhere to be seen. Apparently, he was out of his head on booze, laid out in a drunken stupor in our house in Blantyre, Glasgow. Dad was a chronic drinker and, if that wasn't enough, he was a gambler too. He treated kids the same way he treated women: like shit on the sole of his shoe on a frosty morning. My two brothers would have to huddle together in their single bed, clinging to each other for warmth and comfort because my father had gorged himself on drink with the money that was to pay towards the rent and fuel. I now know from records that I was put into social care at only a few weeks old, but the strange thing was, my two brothers were allowed to stay with that brute of a man.

My mother pleaded with the social services to get me back home, but my homecoming didn't last long because my father soon boozed away the food money. He then gave my mother a battering.

She bawled at him, 'I'll not be here when you come back!'

He tersely replied, 'Fuck off, the lot of you bastards!'

My mum, who was called Liz, took us around to her sister's and asked her to take in my brothers, Albert and John, on a short-term stay. She then took me with her, but she had nowhere to seek shelter, fairly typical for our area in 1971. She ended up leaving me on the steps of the hospital I was born in. Her reason: 'They would look after you better than I could.' It would be another thirty-one years until I saw her again, when I had that eerie encounter with her in the courtroom. When I got back to the cells, under the courtroom, I had mixed emotions. I felt like crying and screaming, all at the same time. I blamed her for the way I'd turned out and for the many failings within my flawed life. Where had she been all my life? On the other hand, when I now consider what her life must have been like, to lose her three kids, I feel sorry for her.

Anyway, to cut a long story short, after progressing through the annals of Scottish social work and penal history, I was told that my mother had died of cancer just after giving birth to me. But I now know that to be total bullshit, as I saw my mother when I got my sentence on 15 April 2002, in courtroom number five of Glesga High Court. I didn't even know who she was when she shouted my name, 'James, James.' I looked around and saw a frail old woman. My head was in bits as I tried to identify her, but nothing came to mind. At the end of the day's events, she came down and told me that she was my mother, Elizabeth. She put her hand over the protective glass; that was the very first time I had seen her in thirty-one years.

In the meantime, I was passed from pillar to post, and they created a problem child. Soon enough, I was familiar with most of the children's homes and foster-care centres in Scotland.

CHAPTER TWO

Product of the System

FLEMINGTON HOUSE CHILDREN'S HOME

Flemington House Children's Home is in Udingston, Lanarkshire. Udingston is most famous for the Tunnocks biscuit factory. The children's home was about two miles from the train station, and was set in one acre of its own fairytale, woodland grounds. The house was a Victorian building with a multitude of bedrooms, twenty in all. I was clueless to the fact that this was a state-run children's home. I was there with my two brothers, along with thirty resident children, ranging in age from two up to sixteen.

I can clearly remember one of the boys from that time called Scott, who was my best pal. He had an older sister, who was the same age as my eldest brother, John, around about seven or eight years old. A house fire had orphaned Scott and his sister. Both Scott and I did everything together; we were inseparable, even in the infants' form at school.

All the boys in my dorm had one thing in common: we all suffered with enuresis – wetting the bed. When the nightshift woman came round to check us to see if we'd wet the bed, my eyes filled with tears and I burst out crying in fear of being hit. Gently, the nightshift lady's arms unfolded and she lifted me out of my soaked bed and tucked me in under her arm, like a mother goose protecting one of her goslings, close to her warm, protective bosom. Her soothing chants soon put me at ease. She asked me what was wrong, and I told her I'd jobbyed my pyjamas. She told me not to be a silly Billy. 'You don't need to cry,' she soothed. Her name was Bunty. I grew to love her. Instead of being physically abused, I was getting a fair share of loving cuddles from this middle-aged woman, who had the softest and kindest heart I've ever known someone to have. When Bunty held me in her bosom, I knew no one could hurt me; I was safe, until I was moved again.

The cook, Martha, would often give us a big bowl of chocolate. It may not sound much, but please believe me, if you had only tried sweets once or twice in your life up to this point, it was a big deal. You can imagine the delight and smile it put on our chocolate- or cream-covered faces.

Leading up to Christmas, there was talk of Santa. But I'd never even heard of Santa. Bunty, tried to explain, 'He brings little angels like you presents.'

I quizzed, 'How does he know me?'

Bunty replied, 'Santa knows everyone.'

I blurted out, 'But he can't like me, because I jobby my bed!'

Bunty comforted, 'That's how you're special.' She then asked, 'If you could get anything at all off Santa, what would it be?'

I asked for a fire engine and sweets. Bunty exclaimed in delight, 'Santa will get you that, but you and Scott will need to leave out a bowl of milk and some carrots for Rudolph.'

'Who's Rudolph?' I asked.

Bunty told me in confidence that Rudolph was Santa's reindeer and that he helped pull all the children's toys in the world over the snow. I couldn't wait.

In readiness for Rudolph, Scott, Martha, Bunty and I picked out four of the biggest carrots from a bag in the kitchen, which we then washed. We found a big bowl that we used to lick the cream out of, which we filled with milk. We put the bowl along with the carrots under the Christmas tree, with all the other children's offerings. Then Bunty and Martha came in and washed us, put us to bed and read us a story, before kissing us good night. On their way out they said, 'When you wake up, Santa will have been.'

Sure enough, when the morning came the presents were there. Thirty screaming children were running about playing with their toys with mouthfuls of sweeties. For a kid who hadn't had much of a life, it was the best day imaginable. But the happiness didn't last long. The next day, my brother John burst my head open. He asked me for a shot of my fire engine, to which I said 'No', so he picked it up and hit it off my head. Blood was streaming down my face. Bunty came in and picked me up, held me in her bosom and patched up my head with a damp cloth and plasters. Meanwhile, my other older brother, Bert, who was very protective of me, hit Scott over the head with one of his football boots, with the result that all hell broke loose.

Nevertheless, I was close to both my brothers, so it broke my heart when, a year and a half later, they were both taken back to stay with my father. I gave them a kiss and cuddle each and asked them to take me with them. My oldest brother explained with sadness in his eyes, 'We can't. I wish we could, but we can't.' As they were driven off, I ran as fast as my little legs could carry me to Bunty's skirt. I grabbed it, never wanting to let it go. Bunty's welcoming arms, once again, reached out toward me, and she lovingly plucked me up, pulled me towards her and smothered me with love and affection.

But I myself only had sixth months left at Flemington House, as one day I was to be moved, out of the blue, to another children's home, one from which you could be fostered or adopted. I was crying and crying, beside myself with grief because I loved Bunty and Scott, and I didn't want to leave. Bunty told me she would come and see me with Scott at weekends. I was only five or years old. Bunty made me a picnic take with me, and Scott gave me one of his teddy bears. Little did I know it at the time, but I wouldn't see Scott, Bunty or Martha for another nine years.

RIGPARK CHILDREN'S HOME, LANARK

As I gazed out of the window, the gravel path roared as it was crushed into submission under the wheels of the car that was taking me towards a menacing-looking medieval castle with two huge and terrifying turrets that seemingly reached out towards me. I imagined that I was the gravel and the wheels of the car were the social-care system. The building scared the shit out of me – it was like something straight out of a Stephen King novel. Compared to the last place, this was on a far bigger scale. There were massive trees like giant bogeymen.

I was jolted out of my miserable, dreamlike state by the abrupt stopping of the car. A man in his late twenties was standing ominously in a nearby doorway.

'Hello, Dave,' the social worker in the front of the car said to this unpromising-looking character.

'Hiya,' the man replied. 'How was your journey through?'

'Not too bad, the roads were empty,' replied the driver.

'And you must be James?' Dave asked me.

I was both scared and shy. All I could do was nod my head in the affirmative.

'Well, let's get you inside,' he said.

When I entered the building, it was like something straight out of a Stephen King movie. In the middle of the hall, there was an old cobwebbed chandelier and a giant wood-panelled oak staircase. The hall was a dark, dimly lit place with big old oil paintings hanging from every space available on the walls. The wallpaper was made of velvet.

'Right, James, come into my office,' Dave requested.

His office was filled with bright light from the sun spilling in through the massive windows.

Dave continued, 'James, I would like you to meet Susan.' He introduced me to a woman who couldn't have been any older than twenty-five. She was very attractive with shoulder-length brown hair. I don't know why, but I just knew I would like this woman.

'Hello, James,' Susan greeted.

I croakily managed a dry 'Hello.'

'I'll be your key worker, James,' Susan announced. 'Come on.' She beckoned with her hand. 'I'll show you around the place and your room.'

She took me by the hand, through room after room. The place was even bigger than I had thought. My bedroom was different from what I was used to, as it only had two beds in it, whereas before I had been in a dormitory with four other boys. I was, however, still scared of Dave, so blurted out to Susan about my bed-wetting problem because I didn't want him to hit me. She chirpily told me not to worry about that. As it turned out, my fears about Dave were utterly unfounded, and he ended up being like a father to me. He was engaged to Susan, and they ran Rigpark Foster Home together.

A couple of weeks after I settled in, I found out that there was a nearby special-needs school for handicapped children. One of the girls from the home, called Wilma, attended this school. She was a beautiful person, who I soon grew very close to. Her parents had abandoned her because she had learning difficulties. Even though she was fourteen years old, she had the mental age of a six- or seven-year-old. But I didn't care, as to me she was like a big sister. To see her break out into a mile-wide smile was very rewarding to me.

During the six months I was there, Wilma and I were inseparable, and we did everything together. The home had stables for horses, even though there weren't actually any horses. But there was a pony, three sheep, a dog and chickens. That was the first time I'd been close to animals and I've loved them ever since. The pony was called Neeps, and was Wilma's favourite. Dave and Susan more or less let Wilma own it. We were only allowed to bring Neeps out of the stables when Susan and Dave were with us, but we could collect the eggs from the hens every morning without any of the staff being with us.

I didn't know it, but I was to be fostered out to a family in Carstairs Junction, which is about seven miles from Rigpark, in Lanark. For legal reasons and to keep their names out of this book, I'll call them Mr and Mrs McCalum. Over a two-month period, Jean and Jack McCalum came to visit me. I soon grew to look forward to them visiting me on a Saturday afternoon.

They took me to New Lanark Cotton Mills and The Falls of Clyde, the picture house. Then they asked me how I felt about staying with them over a weekend. I asked if I could bring Wilma, but Dave and Susan said I couldn't. That hurt me, but I went anyway and, I must say, I enjoyed it. Back then, Carstairs was a major train stopover for London, and I enjoyed seeing all the trains passing. Soon, I was spending most weekends with the McCalums. I met a boy called Gordon who was around the same age as me and had a couple of brothers and sisters. Eventually, Dave and Susan asked me if I would like to stay with the McCalums full-time, to which I said 'Yes'. Unbeknown to me, my two brothers were also going to be fostered to the McCalums.

CARSTAIRS JUNCTION

My new foster parents, Jean and Jack, came to the front door of their modest council house. I'll never forget Jean and Jack's address, the number and street name are clear in my mind. As the car pulled up to the door, my eyes were transfixed on the sight of my two older brothers scampering out of the front door. I was so glad to see them, and was totally surprised! I later found out that they only lasted four weeks with my father after leaving Flemington House. They had since been back in care in homes all over Lanarkshire. Seeing them again, for the first time in two years or so, was magical.

Bert and John pulled open the back door of the car and gave me a cuddle. The McCalums had taken John and Bert on full-time two weeks before I got there. Bert pulled me by the hand into my new bedroom where there were three beds. 'Look, James,' Bert exclaimed with excitement and a big smile across his face, 'you and John have got this bedroom to yourselves, isn't that great?'

I eagerly nodded my head up and down in agreement.

We all settled into our new home in no time. Within the first week of being there, we started Carstairs Junction Primary School. I went into year one with my new pal, Gordon. My brother, Bert, went into year four and John went into year seven. For the first three to six months, I only attended school for half a day. Jean would pick me up and take me home where I would get my favourite lunch of toast and lemon curd and half a mug of milk. I don't know what it was, but I would always fall fast asleep for a couple of hours after my lunch.

School was going great, as was my friendship with Gordon. We used to do some mad, schoolboy pranks. One of our favourites was to stand under the metal staircase at playtime so we could get a good look up the girls' and the teachers' skirts. Once ensconced in class, we would taunt the girls by goading them, 'You've got pink pants on' or 'You've got green pants on.' We'd be really nasty by saying to the girls in year two or three that used to bully us that we'd seen up their skirts and they'd jobbed their pants. At this, all the other girls and boys would taunt and chant in unison: 'JOBBY PANTS! JOBBY PANTS!' That episode led to my first chastisement from my foster mum, Jean, as the girl we mocked eventually told the teacher. The teacher pulled Gordon and me into the headteacher's office where we were told that our respective mothers would be getting notified about our little escapade.

When Jean got me home, she wasn't too happy. She slapped my bottom, told me I wasn't to get any supper and sent me to bed. Little did I know it at the time, but that was just the start of it. Somehow that first beating unlocked the demon in her. She soon started lashing out at me, more and more indiscriminately. Over the next year and a half, I grew to detest her being near me due to her viciousness. She was also very cruel about my bed-wetting. She would make me stand in the bath, and would smear the wet sheets all over my body and then whack my bottom with a wooden Scholl sandal.

I don't know what she got out of it, but it just strengthened my resolve and made me more determined not to cry. As a consequence, she would pound me harder and harder with a fiercer frenzy of blows. My brothers didn't agree with what this brutal woman was doing to me, but they couldn't really help me escape from my daily diet of beatings. I rebelled against my wicked foster mother in the only way I could – by proxy.

I would run away from school with Gordon and smash milk bottles and oil down on the roads so people on motorbikes and cars would skid and crash. One day, a motorbike rider came sliding off, and went like a rocket along the ground into the woods on the other side of the road. It was brilliant to see him fall off his bike. We just never gave any thought that this was a prank with disastrous consequences. It turned out the rider was a nurse who worked up in Carstairs Mental Hospital. Soon enough, the police came round to the school, and marched Gordon and me to the head's office where Jean, the rider, a policeman and Gordon's mum were all sitting down.

It turned out that we'd been spotted spreading the oil on the road by a woman in one of the houses across from the woods. We got a stiff telling-off from the teacher. The policeman was called Mr Taylor, and he told us we were silly boys for doing such a stunt. That telling-off was distasteful, and would have been sufficient to put me off doing such pranks for the rest of my life. I say the word 'would' with great trepidation, as this was not to be my final telling-off for my transgressions. But that wasn't an end to the matter, as, when Jean got me home, she gave me the worst beating I had ever suffered. For a child of this age to be disciplined in such a physical way was bound to leave indelible marks on their mind. To further add insult to injury, I was also told not to play with Gordon.

My foster dad, Jack, was however the antithesis of my foster mum, as he had a warm heart. He would take me out for walks when he was exercising his greyhound. The dog, Jules, was lovely and had a gold coat. He could run like the wind. Keeping and racing greyhounds was Jack's pastime.

During one of these walks with my foster dad, about 30 November 1976, an incident was to happen that made Jack's blood run cold. Out of the blue, he told me to start running home. A siren was sounding.

I didn't know what he meant. There was panic in his voice.

'Why, Dad?' I asked, puzzled.

'Because,' he said, 'the bad men will get you if you don't run home!'

I ran as fast as my little legs would carry me. We made it home within five minutes from the opening of the woods. When we got home, Jean was red in the face.

'Oh! Thank God,' she bawled when she set eyes on Jack and me. 'Thank God.'

I started crying, wondering what was wrong. Jean calmed me, 'Oh, you don't need to cry.'

She told me to get washed and to put my pyjamas on. When I went into the living room, Bert and John were already washed and in their pyjamas. We were all puzzled as to what was going on.

When I heard the sound of the siren, I didn't know what it meant, but Jack did, as he'd lived in Carstairs all his life. The police were now going around the streets with the blue lights flashing from the tops of their patrol cars. They were shouting out via a loudspeaker, 'Please do not leave your house, keep all doors and windows locked and do not answer your doors to anyone.'

It must have been something bad for all this to happen. The

warning was blasted out at regular intervals all night. My two brothers and I slept in the living room with Jean and Jack, and for the first time in my life, as long as I could remember, I never wet the bed. I don't know if it was from fear of wetting the carpet or wetting my two brothers, because we were all on the one double mattress.

The next day, I learned to my horror the reason for the panic. Two madmen had escaped from Carstairs Mental Hospital and had killed a nurse, a fellow patient and a policeman. The policeman was George Taylor, who had come to the school to tell Gordon and me off for putting oil on the road. I guess I was still too young for it all to sink in, but, over the years, it sunk in all right. I later learned that one of the madmen, named McCulloch, had spent half his prison life in the seg block because he was classed as dangerous. He and his partner had meticulously planned their escape from Carstairs. They were involved in helping to build some of the props for a Christmas show, and they had secretly made fake nurses' uniforms to assist in their escape bid.

During their escape, they had killed the double murderer Ian Simpson with an axe. Apparently, Simpson had tried to save the life of one of the hospital recreation officers, Neil McLellan. The madmen then went over the hospital's barbed-wire perimeter where they stabbed the policeman, Mr Taylor, before making off with his car.

After they were both caught and sentenced to life imprisonment, McCulloch was sent to Peterhead Prison and the other escapee Mone to Perth Prison. Unbeknown to me, our paths would cross by virtue of my eventual incarceration. I have since heard that McCulloch has been sent to Saughton in Edinburgh, and is now acting as an agony aunt for his fellow cons! Robert Mone, from Dundee, was originally banged up in Carstairs after he took hostage a class of teenage girls and shot dead their pregnant teacher.

After that, I couldn't stop wetting the bed. It got so bad that I was sent back to Rigpark Children's Home with Dave, Susan and Wilma. About six months later, I got moved to Carluke Children's Home with my brothers.

CARLUKE CHILDREN'S HOME

I was moved on once again like a piece of unwanted lost luggage. The first thing to catch my eye about Carluke was its sheer size. It was massive. The outside of the building was a brilliant white, and the rays of sunshine were bouncing off it. The place shone like a star in the night sky: it was blinding.

I followed my social worker around like a lost sheep into the main part of the building. An old lady greeted me.

'Hello, you must be James?' she said.

'Yes, Miss,' I shyly answered back, not knowing where to look.

She stood with a straight back, and her hair was neat and tidy. She was immaculately dressed and was wearing the biggest pair of glasses I'd ever seen.

'I am Mrs Brown, the head of this children's home. I hope you can settle down in here, James,' she said with an air of grace.

The cat had my tongue: I didn't know what to say.

Catching me off guard, she enquired, 'Are you hungry? You look as if you could be doing with a good feed.'

I started crying my eyes out. I turned to my social worker and bawled, 'I want to see my big brothers, please.'

'I'm sure you can,' he promptly told me, 'but Mrs Brown hasn't finished talking with you yet, James.'

'I am sure the rest can wait until later,' Mrs Brown finished.

She picked up a phone on a big new wooden desk and dialled a number. Some two minutes later, a young woman with blonde hair entered the office. Her name was Anne, and she took me by the hand and speedily led me from the office, asking me if I liked chips.

'It's OK, James, I'll not bite you.' Her words were like the warmth of a ray of sunshine. 'Has the cat got your tongue?' she asked.

For the first time that day, I broke out into a smile.

'Oh, look at you,' Anne proclaimed, 'you can smile after all.'

Immediately after, I heard a familiar voice, saying, 'Jimmy, Jimmy.' As soon as I recognised it as the voice of Albert, my big brother, I let go of Anne's hand and darted off towards him. I started crying again. When would my tears finally stop, after all, I'd been crying all of my life!

'Don't cry,' he soothed, 'you're all right now, you're with me and John.' I asked him where John was.

'He's at school,' Bert smiled.

I started to gather my composure, smiled back and said, 'School?'

'Yes, we go to school in this home,' Bert said in a funny voice that always made me snigger. 'Come on, I'll show you our room,' he continued.

So off we dashed, hand in hand, to explore my big brother's bedroom.

When we finally reached the bedroom, after whizzing up five flights of stairs and along a corridor, we were out of breath. The place was spotless and everything inside the room was brand new. My brother asked me if I liked it. 'Where does John sleep?' I asked Bert, because I wanted to feel close to John as well.

'Oh, he's got his own room at the other end of the

corridor,' Bert told me. 'This is mine and your room, with all its new furniture.'

I jumped on to the bed that Bert had said was mine and, straight away, I could feel that familiar rustle of the rubber sheet – the safety sheet under the blankets. Just at that moment, Anne, came in and said, 'There the two of you are! I've been looking for you. Come on, I've made you some chips.' Then off we went, back down the seemingly endless flight of stairs to the kitchen for our chips.

When we had finished our chips, my eldest brother, John, was just coming in from school.

'All right, Lug?' John spouted.

He called me 'Lug' because I've got a big ear and a small ear. He knew I hated that nickname. But I just nonchalantly shrugged off his sarcasm and ran towards him to give him a brotherly cuddle. He half-pushed me away in horror, embarrassed that his youngest brother was trying to cuddle him in front of all of his new pals. A sea of faces had started to come in, all of which I would soon get to know. There was Willie, Danny, Duck and Bin, and a few girls, called Ann, Linda, Angela and Rosemary. They all came in from school at the same time, trouncing off the bus that used to drive them there and back.

Time flew for the rest of the day. I met most of the other kids from the children's home. That night, I got put in a bath and was washed by Anne. After drying me, she put me in my pyjamas and into bed. After reading me a story out of a kid's book, she kissed my head and got up to walk out.

My brother's bed was empty, as Bert didn't need to come to bed for another two hours as he was ten years old.

A woman in her mid-forties came into the room and turned on the night-light. To say I lay in my bed like a frightened rabbit caught in the glare of a car's headlights would be an understatement: I was scared stiff!

'Is your bed wet?' she asked me in a lovely soft voice.

'I'm sorry, I'm very sorry,' I mustered.

'Oh don't be sorry, love,' she reassured me, taking off the bed covers.

My pyjamas were stuck to my legs and bottom. I had started crying.

'SSSssshhhh or you'll wake your brother, come on, follow me,' she whispered. I soon found out that this angel-like figure was called Betty. She stripped me, washed me down, dried me, put me in a clean set of pyjamas and changed my bedding. In Rigpark Children's Home, I would have had to stay wet all night, so this caring regime was new to me. It turned out that there was a machine under my blanket that detected whenever I had wet the bed. After giving me a comforting hug, Betty tucked me back into my clean new bed. I soon fell fast asleep.

The months started to fly by, and it wasn't long until I started my new school, Carluke Primary, where I met some pals that have remained life long friends. I still have a memory that comes flooding back to me every time I think of the school. It all started on the weekend when me and my best pal Barry were down the woods, just jumping the stream like any other boys of our age. Rather foolishly, I tried to jump off the wall that towered above the stream, which was some fifteen feet high. I must have thought I was Superman! I came tumbling off the wall like a soused Humpty Dumpty, landing face and head first into the fast-running stream. If it wasn't for Barry helping me out of the stream, I don't think I'd be here today. Anyway, he pulled me out to the bank, where I sat stunned, shaken and soaking wet. I tried to put on a brave face for my best pal, signalling that I was OK, but I ended up crying with the pain that was surging through my body. To my surprise, I hadn't broken any bones, but had only grazed my arms off the rocks and boulders that were discarded in the stream.

But that wasn't the end of the day as far as I was concerned. I told Barry that we were going to see through our plan to collect frogs and frogspawn from the old pond that lay deep in the woods. So off we went, with me soaking wet. Every time I took a step behind Barry, my feet would squelch in my cheap school shoes. I knew that the staff in the home would go mental at me for being wet, but in my head, I didn't care because I was having such a great time. Thoughts of being told off soon left my head as we eventually reached the old pond. Local legend had it that, at night, a green-coloured female ghost haunted the place. But it was the middle of the summer, with the sun blazing down and not a cloud could be seen in the sky – we weren't scared.

Barry would pull up old boulders and moss-covered logs of wood to try and discover some frogs. I can still vividly remember the feel of the frogs, their moistness and the way their heads stuck straight out of their bodies, as they had no necks. The male frogs had slightly larger feet than their female counterparts. I found one which had really big feet; I called him 'Bigfoot'. Over the next two hours of hungrily scampering around in search of these elusive amphibians, we had collected about twenty frogs and had filled an old paint tin with frogspawn. We felt as if we had the crown jewels.

Once back at Barry's house, Barry's mum came out and told me to take off my clothes so she could dry them. She was a lovely woman who, God bless her, is no longer with us.

Barry's dad was a keen hunter. He kept ferrets and a couple of hunting dogs in kennels. Looking back on some of the cruel things we used to do makes me feel I was someone else. With great pain, I can still recall how Barry and I lobbed a couple of frogs in with the ferrets, who pounced on the frogs and chewed them to bits. We stood watching, open mouthed. Looking back, I know that these barbaric acts would make any child psychiatrist predict that we'd grow up to be serial killers or the like. We decided to leave the remaining frogs in the garden, and then I went back to the home, wearing dry clothes and polished shoes. None of the staff was any the wiser, thank God.

The next day couldn't come quickly enough. I dashed round to Barry's house, went into the garden, put my bag of frogs in my brown leather satchel and knocked on his back door. We had some breakfast, and then waited for the school bus, which soon arrived. When we got on the bus, Barry and I tantalisingly eyed up and analysed our frogs. Laughter from other boys our age and the older boys and girls filled the bus, as they shared jokes and the like. All the boys and girls that were going to the high school got off, including my two big brothers.

'See you later, Lug,' John, my older brother, chirped.

'Aye, see you,' I acknowledged.

'See you tonight, Jimmy,' Bert said.

'OK, Bert, see you tonight.'

By this time, John and Bert had earned themselves a bit of a reputation for fighting at school with the other hard boys. I don't know what it was about people, but they seemed to think that, if you were from the home, then you must be bad and hard. It turned out that my oldest brother John had battered an older boy on the Friday before. This incident was revisited on me when, on the Monday morning after, his younger brother came up to me on the bus and smashed my head against the floor. My face was covered in blood. He kept kicking and punching me. My head was swollen where he'd kicked me, but I never cried because that would have made it worse and I'd have taken a few doings off my own brothers. So I got up and carried on, trying with little success to wipe the blood off my face and jumper.

Once at school, the head asked me for my side of the story. I told her I'd fallen on the bus and banged my head. Of course, she called me a liar.

'Tell the truth!' she kept screaming into my face with her eyes bulging at me like Medusa.

'I fell, Miss. I fell,' I kept repeating, as I avoided her evil gaze for fear of turning into stone!

'OK, young Holland, have it your own way, if he hits you on the way home, then it's your fault,' she finished, glancing once more at me, trying to catch my eyes.

When I got back to class, I sat across from Barry. The desks were the type you could lift the top up and put any manner of schoolboy paraphernalia inside. On lifting up my desk lid, I saw my frogs wildly jumping about inside. I slammed the lid shut and threw a knowing glance across in the direction of Barry. He was sitting there all innocent, with a big grin on his face that broke into a smile from ear to ear. He soon caved in and rolled about with laughter.

I don't know what made me do it, but I lifted up the top of the desk, grabbed a frog in each hand and flung them at the teacher. I must have been a sight for sore eyes, with lumps and bumps on my head and dried blood on my jumper, but I didn't care. As the frogs hit their target, the teacher started screaming. I then flung the rest of the frogs at the girls and boys in the class. All hell broke loose.

The teacher, the girls and also some boys were screaming hysterically and running blindly out of the classroom. I started throwing some of the frogs down on to the children that were doing PT in the playground; they all gave an ear-piercing scream and ran uncontrollably in all directions. Pandemonium had broken out!

I loved it. This was my payback for getting battered on the bus. I got up on the window ledge of the classroom, and opened the window right up. I put one leg out of the window, then the other. I was standing on the window ledge, without a care in the world.

Barry's plea of 'Come back in' fell on deaf ears.

I told him, 'I'm OK.'

By this time, about five or six teachers were stirred by the commotion and came storming into the classroom and demanded that I come back in.

I told them to 'fuck off' or I'd jump. That got their attention.

'Don't be silly,' my teacher implored.

I'll call her Mrs Gallagher. She turned out to be a nice woman, but at that moment, I hated everyone. They waited for an hour, and then rang for Anne, the lady from my home, who pleaded and begged for me to come back in from the window ledge. I came back in and Anne took me by the hand out of the school and into her car and drove me back to the home.

I was dragged into Mrs Brown's office for one of the worst bollockings of my young life. I was then sent to my room until she decided what to do with me. The police came to see me and told me, if I kept behaving like that, I'd get put in jail.

'You don't want that, James, do you?' the policeman said.

'No, sir,' I sheepishly replied. 'No, sir.'

The next day, I returned to school with Mrs Brown to see the headteacher, where I was summarily dispatched with a suspension from school for a week. My first suspension at eight years old! That figure ballooned over the next two years up to fifteen suspensions.

I didn't know what the big deal was; it was only a bit of fun in my eyes, and the more fun I had, the more other boys and girls wanted to play with me, so I kept it up. Smashing windows, hitting teachers with rubbers and taking the belt in front of other children didn't bother me, but just made me more determined to show all the boys and girls that I could take six of the best and not cry or budge an inch.

I had a lot of pals in the playground. Barry was still my best pal, but other children wanted to play with us as well. Unfortunately, there were also school bullies, and I always received a doing off them. I just couldn't fight back. My two big brothers would hit me even harder when I went home with yet another black eye from school.

'Lug, hit them back,' John would bark at me.

'Fucking hit them back,' Bert supplemented, 'we can't fight all your battles for you.'

But I would have none of it. I didn't know how to hit them back, and the once or twice that I had lashed out in anger, I got battered. I used to just curl up in a foetal ball and take everything that was flung at me from the bullies and my brothers and anyone else that felt like having a go at me. I never cried, but I did feel a lot of fucking pain.

It wasn't all bad, though, as there were some good times too. One year, the whole of the children's home went on a trip to Butlins for the summer holidays, at the scenic location at the Heads of Ayr. I can remember that we were all over the moon, and were running around packing the little drop of clothes we had into suitcases. Mine, Bert's and John's clothes could all fit in the one case.

When we ran down the stairs to the bus that was going to take us, I was stopped in my tracks by what greeted my eyes. I stood still in disbelief. In front of me was a Strathclyde council bus with a lift on the back of it. None of this luxury coach stuff for us, oh no. The bus was the same colour as a tin of Germoline, and was especially designed for the disabled. Now I'm not a bigot, but at the time all our hearts sank. We all hummed and hahed, but, begrudgingly, got on it all the same. Every set of traffic lights the bus stopped at, we would look out of our windows at people in their cars and we'd stick our tongues out, slap one hand off the other and cross our eyes with slavers dribbling off our chins. If they were going to treat us like handicapped children, we thought that we might as well act like them.

In the meantime, I had discovered glue. I had two tubes of glue stashed in my pocket that I took from the puncture-repair kit that was in the bike shed. Once we got to Butlins, two other boys and I ran down to the beach away from all the other holidaymakers and started buzzing this glue. Nothing could beat the buzz the glue gave me. This was the best feeling in the world. I loved the way it made my ears go all warm and the good feelings I got from it. And then there were the weird things I could see.

We all finished our glue and made our way back to the chalets we were staying in, utterly out of our heads. The first couple of days were great, but we needed more glue to satisfy our needs. We couldn't get any of it at Butlins, so we came up with the idea of going to Ayr town itself, which was about fifteen to twenty miles from Butlins, where we planned to steal some. We got a bus from Butlins car park. Off we went, three ten-year-old boys into Ayr town centre to beg, borrow or steal some glue. Our hearts were thumping in our chests like drums, but it was an exhilarating buzz. Once in Ayr, we set about looking for a bike shop. Forty minutes later, we found one.

In we went, past all the many different bikes: Grifters, Choppers, racers and brand new BMXs. One of the other boys quickly spotted the glue sitting on the counter next to the till. The problem was in getting the young man at the counter away from it. But that was easy enough: I bumped into a row of Choppers and racers, causing them to fall over like a row of dominoes. I quickly apologised, and the man came over and helped me and one of the other boys from the home to pick them up. The other boy took the full box of repair kits and rather hastily left the shop. We made some more small talk with the man, then left the shop. Once outside, we ran as fast as our legs would carry us. We got around the back of some shops and split the glue into tubes, five or six apiece.

We all hugged each other in camaraderie, then went and got some crisps, which we hungrily ate, before using the bags for the glue. Oh, it was the fucking business! That same old feeling came back: the hot ears and hot head, and the pure light. We did a tube each, then made our way back to the bus. We jumped on and got off at the car park at Butlins where three Red Coats met us.

'Are you three here with Carluke Children's Home?' one of them asked.

'Yes,' we said.

They then took us to an office where Anne and another member of staff from the home were sat waiting.

'Where have you been?' Anne snapped. 'We've been looking all over Butlins for you with the Red Coats.'

'Oh, we were up in the woods looking for birds' eggs,' I nonchalantly replied.

'Don't tell me any more lies, James Holland,' Anne thundered, with a face that would melt ice. 'Now where have you lot been?'

'Ayr town centre,' one of the other boys blurted.

'How did you get there?' Anne asked.

We told her about the arcade and the bus, but we never told her about the glue.

'I've had enough of you little shits,' Anne seethed. 'I'm phoning Mrs Brown, you lot are going home, you just can't do anything right.'

'Aw, please, please, Anne, don't send us home,' we all begged.

She was a hard woman at times, but we won her heart over. We were told that we couldn't go anywhere without her for the next nine days of our holiday. But, only two days later, the three of us were done bang to rights, when we were caught buzzing glue in the bedroom of our chalet. We were sent straight back to the home, where we were put into our pyjamas and made to stay in our rooms for the next two weeks.

Some months after the Butlins trip, I heard a loud voice from the car park of the home. 'Where are my fucking sons?' the voice called out.

I looked out, but I didn't really know who it was, and just thought that it was some drunken tramp. John gawped and then blurted out, 'Oh, fuck, that's Dad. Look at the state of him!'

I didn't know what all the fuss was about because I never really knew him. John ran down and gave him a cuddle. One of the staff was out talking to them; a lot of shouting was going on.

'Fuck off, you cow,' I heard Bert shout.

John shouted up to the window, 'Get Lug and come down, we're going up the town with Dad.'

So off we went. This man was so drunk. He slurred out, 'Oh, son, I love you,' and grabbed Bert and me. His red face was covered in little short hairs that jagged at my face when he tried to kiss me.

'I love the three of you,' he drunkenly garbled. 'Come on, I'm taking you off home.'

He was taking us towards the train station. We didn't know it, but the staff had phoned the police and soon enough, a cop van turned up. My father was flung into the back of the van, and we were taken back to the home again. I never even got any money off him for glue, as I thought I might. I was upset, but not at him getting lifted, just at not getting money for glue.

It wasn't long after this that I was put up for fostering again. I didn't really want to leave, but my two brothers said to give it a go, so I agreed to live with a couple who I shall call the McAllisters. Things went pretty fast after that and I moved, lock, stock and barrel to their new house in Cumbernauld. The father figure of the house was a prison warden called Robert. He worked at Longrigend. His wife, Mary, was a head nurse who worked in a hospital in Glesga. I kissed and hugged my two brothers and all the other children in the home as I said goodbye, then got in the McAllisters' motor and never looked back.

CHAPTER THREE

Look Back in Anger

FOSTERED AGAIN IN CUMBERNAULD, 1982

The house was nothing like I'd ever seen before. It was a five-bedroomed joint, and was pure and utter class. That's the only way I can describe it. Within the first couple of days of staying there, I knew Robert and Mary loved the good life. I discovered that they had three children of their own, two of whom had grown up and flown the family nest, who I'll call Wonda and Mandy. Their youngest child, who I'll call Ben, still lived at home. Ben was a year older than me, but I didn't have much in common with him. After all, he'd had a far different upbringing, and had enjoyed the best things in life, whereas I, if you excuse the expression, was as common as muck.

On 27 September 1982, Robert and Mary enrolled me at the Abronhill High School. If any of you readers have seen the Scottish blockbuster movie *Gregory's Girl*, with John Gordon Sinclair and Dee Hepburn, you'll know what kind of place this was. I wasn't jumping for joy when they sent me there, as I had always really hated school, pure and simple, from my first days at Carstairs Primary. I still couldn't read or write and I had even less time to sit and listen to some snobby, stuck-up teacher telling me what to do. I enjoyed very little there, apart from the PT, football and my remedial teacher, who I shall call Mr Dingwall, who had time for me. Apart from that, I fucking hated it, true to form.

I only lasted three weeks before Robert and Mary were asked to come to school to have a first-time meeting with the headmaster. Forewarned is forearmed, and I think they were told even before they fostered me that I'd be a right handful at school. Back at home, they sat me down and told me that I didn't need to go back to that school. I jumped up and flung my hands in the air.

'No more school. Yee, ha!' I shouted in jubilation.

'James, you are going to go to another school,' came the thunderbolt of a reply, which shot me back down to earth with a thud.

'No, no,' I cried in protest, 'I hate school.'

'We know, but this place is different, James. We've seen it, and you will like it there. There are only fifteen children that go there with you, plus you get your own taxi every day, there and back,' I was informed.

There was no point in arguing my position any longer. What Mary said, she meant, and, in my opinion, she wore the trousers in that household. Even though Robert was a prison officer, he let Mary do the talking. At work, though, things were different, as he was making decisions that affected thousands of young lives.

The first day I went to my new school, I detested it. It was called Middlemuir in Lenzie, and was hidden behind a church. It isn't there now. The taxi driver that took me there was called Danny from Moodiesburn. If you're reading this book, Danny, I salute you, mate, and your lovely mum, who used to chaperone the little handicapped girl that we'd pick up along the way home. I'll call her Fifee; she was a little princess and had the heart of a lion. The illness Fifee had was life threatening, but she still struggled on every day of her painful life. God bless you, Fifee.

After a couple of weeks at this new school, I started to like it. I was buzzing as much glue as I wanted outside the art class with Archy and Fred from Dumbarton. The other children came from all over the West of Scotland: Dumbarton, Clydebank, Glesga, Motherwell and Greenock. They didn't like schooling either, so I had something in common with them.

Back in Cumbernauld, I had a number of pals who I would hang out with at night: Loussy, Gommo, Chris, Grimmy, Hands Greg, Little Andy, Simmy and a few others. We did everything together. It was about this time that I experimented with my first bit of hash and speed, with a boy called Kelly that used to jump about with us Hazel boys. We would all go up to the backfields on motorbikes. One night, when we were up there, I saw my first dead body. Unknown to Greg, his young brother had followed him, but had been hit head-on by a lorry when trying to cross the dual carriageway. He was only seven years old. My heart goes out to you and your family, Greg. You've shown to me over the last few years that you're my closest pal. God bless you.

A few months later, I was more friendly with a guy called Chris than with anyone else. Chris was the young up-and-coming Ned (Non-Educated Delinquent – Scottish definition), who could fight for Scotland. He was taking on boys of eighteen or nineteen when he was only thirteen. He could fight for fun! If you're reading this, Chris, mate, I've still got fond memories of you and your girlfriend, Alexis.

I usually have a disliking or liking for someone, with no halfway measures, but Gommo was different, as he was a boy that I could both like and dislike. He was a very brainy boy, with seven O-levels. The worse of it was that his family never had two pennies to rub together, so I would have thought I'd get on better with him because we were two birds of a feather. I used to steal food for him out of the kitchen to feed him when we all went down fishing to Banknock. He used to give me a battering once or twice a month, as I wasn't even capable of fighting sleep. It was a sign of things to come, as he eventually took a job as a prison warden in Longrigend – bastard. I once spotted him at a distance in the corridor of Longrigend. We exchanged glances, but no words were said. I know now he's out of the job, as he left once Longrigend shut its doors for the last time. Gommo, let me tell you, that was the best thing you could have done, because, if I'd ever seen you in the cons' jails, I would have cut your throat, you slug. But, as for the others I left behind in Cumbernauld, such as Grimmy, Simmy, Andy and all the rest of you, I wish you all the best in whatever you're doing.

Lastly, I have to mention my old friend Joe Hanlon. Joe went on to be one of the most feared, up-and-coming hard men in Glesga. He was Paul Ferris's best pal. In September 1991, he was murdered along with Bobby Glover. They had been set up and lured to their deaths. Their bodies were found slumped in a motor outside the cottage bar in the East End of Glesga. No one has stood trial or been found guilty for the murders. Strong rumour has it, though, that the Glasgow Godfather of crime, Arthur Thompson, since deceased, had shot the two underworld faces, as he blamed them for the gangland hit on his son, Arthur Thompson Junior. R.I.P, Joe, you were a friend.

Things for me weren't going too smoothly. I had progressed on to drinking vodka and whisky, smoking hash and snorting speed. Although I'd stopped wetting the bed, there were a few times when Mary had to change the sheets when I was so drunk that I not only pissed myself, but shit myself too. Mary would try and keep me in, but I'd have none of it, so she asked Robert, the father figure, to have a word in my ear. I'd give him a mouthful of abuse and run out of the house and go around to Morag's.

Morag was the wife of Brian Kennan, who at the time was doing twelve years in Perth Prison for shooting a policeman. The life and soul of any party, Morag was a good buzz, who liked a drink. Most of the time, Morag's house was full of young people on my wavelength, so I fitted in better there than round the road with the McAllisters. It wasn't long, however, before they sent the police round to get me lifted. The McAllisters couldn't cope with me, so I ended up getting sent back to the children's home. Fuck 'em, I wasn't bothered. I couldn't live my life the way they lived theirs.

I was then parcelled off to Flemington House Children's Home, the same Godforsaken place I was in between the ages of two and five. But it was now a new state-of-the-art home, and had been relocated to behind the post office, in Uddington.

FLEMINGTON HOUSE, SECOND TIME, 1985

The first person to say hello to me on arrival was Scott, the boy from all those years ago. He'd grown up to be a fit and strong fifteen-year-old boy. Helping me in with my belongings, Scott then showed me his room. The place was a real bachelor's pad. He had his own cooker and fridge. They were getting him domesticated so that he'd be independent when he left the home in nine months' time. Once his door was shut to prying eyes, he asked if I smoked hash. I burst out laughing.

'Yes,' I gladly replied, 'who doesn't?'

'Thank fuck you're here, Jimmy,' Scott let out. 'It's all mad young boys and girls of eleven and twelve that's in the home. I've just been sitting in here for the last year smoking hash,' he revealed.

On my way out from Scott's room, I bumped into another old friend: Bunty. On seeing me, she burst out crying. 'Oh, James, James,' she cried, running into my arms. 'I never thought I'd have seen you again.'

I gave her a kiss; after all, this was the woman that used to change my nappies and bedding years earlier when I was just two years old. I love this woman and, in my eyes, Bunty was my real mother and I would do anything she asked of me. I was always on my best behaviour in front of her. Sadly, Bunty is now dead; she lived until she was seventy-eight years old. God bless you, Bunty, you were a fine, fine woman. I still think about you some nights when I can't sleep. Rest in Peace.

I was still going to Middlemuir School. A new boy called Jimbo Hughes had just started the school, who I soon got on well with. He was a very smart dresser, with all the up-to-the-minute casual wear of the day. His family was respected in the criminal underworld. His dad, Ted, was doing a ten-stretch in Perth Prison for drugs. Back then, Jimbo and I did everything together at school: we'd go swimming, and then ice-skating down at the Magnum, it was just a laugh at the end of the day. Fuck the McAllisters, who needs to be a stuck-up, snobby cunt like them? Not me.

I met a few of the local Neds that were also into hash and drink. However, two of them, John from Bothwell and Jim from

Viewpark, were also into more hardcore stuff like screwing shops, houses, cars and factories. I loved breaking into things, and took to it like a duck to water. One time we did over a chip shop and took all the tobacco and fags. I felt invincible. The rush was better than that from glue, drink or hash. We went on to bigger and better things, and started screwing shops and rich people's houses for money and jewellery. We would also do over chemists. It was so simple back then: just smash the window on the door with a brick, then jump in. John would do the shelves behind the counter, Jim and I would do the perfume and aftershave displays, cramming as much as we could stuff into our bags, then we would bolt out the door – simple and effective. Once back at John's, in his bedroom, we'd eye up our loot.

Things were going great, as I always had money and drugs and my life was sorted. I felt like the bee's knees. John got a car and we'd jump about in this old jalopy of a Ford Cortina, going to Hamilton or Motherwell or Wishaw, trawling for more chemists to break into.

Then, one night, we were done when robbing a jeweller's shop in the South of Lanarkshire. I was held overnight in Lanark cop shop and then marched up in front of the judge. I was put back into the hands of the social work, because I still wasn't sixteen. I was put into Newfield Assessment Centre, in Johnston, whereas John and Jim were sent to Longrigend.

NEWFIELD UNIT, JOHNSTON, RENFREWSHIRE, 1986

Surprisingly, there wasn't any fence or wall around the place, which is the first thing I noticed on arrival. That would come in handy over the next couple of months. When I reached the reception and office block of Newfield Assessment Centre, the first person I met was Nick Kyle. He ran the place, and looked a right handful. He was barrel-chested, and I knew straight away he'd been about a bit just by his mannerisms.

'Hello, son,' he said in an almost inaudible whisper, 'you must be young master Holland.'

The way he said it chilled me to the bone. His eyes were black, with no blue or brown in them. He kept staring me out.

'Yes, sir,' I replied, half-shitting myself.

'So you think you're a wee hard man, do you, Holland?'

'No, sir,' I croaked.

'What did you say? I can't hear you,' he said, as he cupped his hand to his ear.

'No, sir,' I said in a raised voice.

'Good, young Holland. Your first lesson: it is *Sir* at all times in here. Do you understand?'

'Yes, sir,' I shouted, as if I were in the army.

'Do you want to fight me, Holland?' he asked in a deep growl.

'No, sir,' I barely gasped.

'What? *No, sir.* Good, because I would break your back,' he pronounced. 'I run this place. You do as you are told, when you are told, there's no soft option here for you, Holland. You're going into Gleniffer Unit, where all the others like you are ... smart arse punks,' he growled.

Another man walked into the office, who stood over 6ft 2in tall and must have weighed over sixteen stone. I later learned that his name was Jim Arbuckle. He was also a very intimidating character.

'Right, Holland. Follow me, no talking, do you hear me?'

'Yes, sir,' I shouted out.

We reached Gleniffer Unit in double-quick time.

'OK, listen up, this is James Holland,' this giant announced to the rest of the boys in this unit.

I was totally shitting myself. There were young boys with mars bars on their faces and others with skinhead haircuts. Their deadpan eyes never had any hint of life in them. A boy came up to me and said, 'I'm Davie Baxter, come on, I'll show you your room. Never mind that prick, Arbuckle; he's a big bum. I take it you've met nasty Nick?'

'Who?' I asked.

'Nick Kyle,' Davie said. 'Did he try all that hard-man piss on you, Jim, or do you prefer Jimmy?'

'Jimmy,' I replied

'Jimmy, OK, mate,' Davie said and went on to ask, 'Where are you from?'

Well, I hadn't really thought about that one because I didn't really have any real home.

I told him, 'Carluke.'

He asked me if I knew anyone in that home.

I said, 'Yes, my two brothers.' In fact, my two brothers had moved on, but we were in it for a year.

Davie told me he was in it as well, for six months, a few years earlier. I asked Davie where he was from.

'Brighton, Jimmy,' he replied and then asked, 'Do you smoke?'

'Yes,' I told him.

He got me a fag and we sat on a bed in the dorm of the Gleniffer Unit to have a chat. I met all the other boys who were all brand new. Davie seemed to be well respected by the other boys in the dorm. He was training with St Mirren Boys Football Club, and was going to go on a YTS (Youth Training Scheme) with St Mirren in a few months' time. Now that boy could play football, but his promise was cut short when, ten to twelve years down the line, Davie was brutally murdered in a gang hit. He was taken to a house, tied up, tortured and taken over to the river Clyde that runs through Glesga. He was told to get in the river with his hands still tied behind his back, while a gun was pointing at his head. He was told to keep walking until he disappeared under the water. Davie's body wasn't found for six weeks, poor bastard. R.I.P., my friend.

There were another three units in Newfield: Lomond, Campsie and Short Stay. Campsie was for children under twelve years old, Lomond was for the girls and Short Stay was for the boys and girls that were on their way out of the place.

I met a few girls and boys from the other units: Susan, Kate, Sharon, Kenny, Davie and Samantha. One of them, Samantha, was in for trying to kill another girl by hitting her over the head with a concrete slab. At that time, Samantha was only fourteen years old. She got two years for it. One of the other girls, Katie, was from Paisley. In later years, I'd become good friends with her brothers Paul, Bobby and Pondy. Paul, however, was stabbed to death not long ago. He had settled down after prison with his new girlfriend, and one night the girl's ex-boyfriend jumped in through the window and stabbed him. Pondy is currently in this segregation unit with me up here in Perth. Just now, he's being labelled one of the ringleaders of the latest Shotts Prison riot that cost the prison service over £1 million worth of damage, where a few screws were seriously injured.

I settled into the daily routine of Newfield for six mundane weeks or so, before a couple of boys asked me if I wanted to do a runner with them. I agreed right away, as I was pissed off with the staff telling me what to do, so off we went. But we never got far before the cops captured us and escorted us back to Newfield. We were put into our pyjamas and kept in the units that you're not allowed out of for anything. Daily, Nasty Nick would come around and try to bait us into a fight, the horrible little bastard that he was.

The rest of my time in Newfield was spent in one classroom or another or in the PT hall, playing football. I got called into Nasty Nick's office one day and was told I would be going to a place in Govan called the Blue Triangle. Now that sounded like a place you'd go into but would never come out of! It was for sixteen-to eighteen-year-olds that were homeless.

CHAPTER FOUR

Off to Sunny Govan and Then the Big Hoose

BLUE TRIANGLE, FEBRUARY 1987

Iovan is on the south side of Glesga. It's a hard-working, hard-drinking, hard-living and hard-fighting place. It's dog-eat-dog, and only the toughest survive and prosper, while the weak curl up and die. The whole of Glesga was like this; it's akinto some areas in English cities, like Scotswood in Newcastle, Dovecot in Liverpool and Aston in Birmingham. Govan used to be at the heart of the shipping world and has seen some of the best ships to sail the high seas coming and going from the magnificent river Clyde. But, nowadays, the place is a cesspit of poverty and crime, and is overrun with crack and smack addicts. It is infested with terminally poor, drug-crazed urchins.

This was my first time in Govan. You could smell and taste the thick smog in the air. The Blue Triangle was a new high-tech building, and it didn't look right standing there in front of older and more historical buildings. The Blue Triangle may have looked great from the outside, but once inside, to my horror, it was full of young teenage boys and girls full of deep and dark depression. It would be here that I first tried heroin, the drug that was to play havoc with the rest of my life. The boy who initiated me into smack, who I will call Tim, was at that time eighteen years old, and came from Castlemilk. His life was a helter-skelter ride of drug-fuelled binges.

I was introduced by Tim to some of his pals from Govan, a bright bunch of boys with an eye for making money, especially if it involved crime. They would break into houses and shops, and make snatches from night safes. They'd ambush cars at traffic lights, and rob the drivers at knifepoint. Most of the boys stayed in Crossland Road, so they were known locally as the Crossy Posse. I'll name a few: Doc, John K, Ally, Malkie, Minger, Righty, Ian, Bobby and Keltie.

We would meet-up in the morning, then split up into gangs of two or three, then go our different ways to see what money we could get our hands on. I was a dab hand at breaking into motors and swishing the radios, especially the new jazzy digital ones that had just hit the scene. If all else failed, I'd do three or four cars in one day and take the cassette players and whatever else was worth nicking, like leather jackets, briefcases, anything. Sometimes, the gang would have £2,000 if a snatch went well.

One night, I went on a lone mission to snatch the bag of a female shop assistant, as we knew she had the night's takings from the shop with her. My heart was pounding in my ears, my mouth was dry and I had a noticeably nervous laugh: this was my first solo and I didn't want to let the gang down. With my heart beating like a drum, I ran over, snatched the bag and made off into the darkness of the night. Once I was clear, I went back to the gang with the bag. As I turned the bag out, I anticipated the wad of money that would tumble from it. But it was empty! I couldn't believe it, and I immediately knew what the others would think.

'Right, come on, where's the money?' the older boys blitzed. 'What've you done with it?'

I protested, 'I've done nothing. I never even looked in the bag, I promise.'

'Where's the fucking money, Jimmy?' they spat venomously.

'I haven't got it,' I pleaded.

The gang turned on me like wolves and gave me the worst doing I'd ever taken up to then. A couple of days later, it was reported in the local newspaper that the robber that snatched the bag had got away empty-handed, as it was the guy from the shop who had the takings. Soon enough, every member of the gang apologised to me one by one. I was over the moon, because I loved that gang and I was loyal to them.

During this time, some 250 miles away, in the north-east of Scotland, at Peterhead Prison, the worst jail riot ever to take place had started to kick off. I would grow close to the ringleaders of the infamous Peterhead Prison riot years later. The two ringleaders, Malkie Leggot and Sammo 'The Bear' Ralston, I can safely say, are now my good friends. Malkie and Sammo took the prison warden hostage, put a dog chain round his neck and dragged him on to the roof of the prison. Once ensconced there, they made demands about the way the prisoners were being mishandled from the screws and about how far away the jail was for their visitors to travel to from their homes.

Peterhead was no stranger to violence; after all, the hardest and most violent men to ever live in Scotland have been there. I'll name but a few: Jimmy Boyle, Bobby Bennett, Kenny Kelly, T C Campbell, Johnny Boy Steele, Frank McPhee. So the jail wasn't any stranger to sheer, raw, cruel and brutal violence. Sammo and Malkie had had a sit-down and a heated debate amongst themselves to draw up their battle plans, and decided to grab and stab as many screws they could possibly get their hands on. The plan was crude, but was effective.

A few days later, a couple of cons lured a screw into a small room with a cooker in it. They hurled boiling water over him, causing the screw to be scalded so badly that his body sustained 70 per cent burns. Once he was cooked, they ran out into the middle of the hall with homemade daggers in their hands and murder on their minds. The rest of the group joined in the attacks on the screws. The screws tried to flee out of the hall like startled wildebeest, but some of them never made it. They were rounded up and taken hostage. Over the next four hours or so, the hall was totally busted up and set on fire.

The prisoners had managed to smash their way through the Scottish granite-lined roofs of the cells on the top floor of the hall, and successfully gained access to the roof of the prison. Over the next five or six days, Malkie and Sammo would parade and display the screw they had taken to the police down below, while taunting them with what they could do to the screw and making their demands.

The Prison Service couldn't cope with this bloodthirsty mob, so they asked for help from the SAS – the best fighting machine in the world was needed to help bring this siege to a halt. Malkie, Sammo and many others only heard the roar of the helicopters' rotors before they saw them. Under the cover of darkness, the SAS landed on the red-ash football field of the prison.

'Right, that's it! Bring the screw back up on to the roof,' Malkie and Sammo ordered. 'Fuck 'em, we'll just kill the bastard.'

The screw was led out on to the roof like a dog, wrapped around his neck was his own key chain. Malkie was armed with a hammer and Sammo had a truncheon, which he used to batter the screw over the head and body.

'Right, let's fling this fucker off the roof,' they roared.

By this time, they'd totally lost the plot. If it weren't for other cons pleading with them, they would have murdered the screw. In the meantime, the SAS entered the hall with stun grenades. They didn't take any prisoners. The screw held hostage was freed, and was put on TV to tell his side of the story. During the course of the siege, he'd shit and pissed himself with fear at the hands of Malkie and Sammo and their gang. At the court hearing, they would go on to get sentenced to forty years between them for their parts in the notorious Peterhead riots. It was the first time the SAS would be sent into a British jail, but not the last.

About three months after, I left Govan, and was living back at Carluke with my eldest brother, John.

CARLUKE, SECOND TIME, 1987

There I was, sleeping on my oldest brother's threadbare couch, in a pokey, one-bedroom flat. Things were uncomfortable for both of us, but I didn't have anywhere else to go. At least I had a refuge in the opposite sex.

I'd been with the odd girl on one-night stands. I soon met a girl called Lisa, who was two years younger than me. She stood at 5ft 2in tall, had long blonde, curly hair and the deepest blue eyes I'd ever seen. I had to work at winning her over, as at first she didn't like me. I would spend all my money on buying her flowers, cards, drinks, perfume, trainers but, more often than not, she wouldn't take them from me. I soon gave up on her and started sniffing around older women.

There was one older woman in particular, called Linda, who had a name for flinging about. She ran about with my oldest brother's wife. She may have had more pricks than a used dartboard, but I was attracted to her like a child to sweets in a confectionery shop. I built up the courage and asked her out, but she told me I was still just a young boy and she'd burn me out. This only fuelled my passions even more. I knew Linda was a bit of a drinker, so I got her a bottle of vodka. Bingo, it unlocked her chastity belt. She done things to me and got me to do things to her that I never knew existed, but I loved it. Whenever Linda's boyfriend was at work, I was around her house in a flash.

As well as becoming more and more initiated into the world of women, I was strengthening my links to the world of crime. I met a guy called little Wax who was into stealing motors and going for joyrides. I didn't see the point in just taking a car for the sake of it, so I persuaded Wax around to the idea of using the cars to make money. We started driving all over Scotland, with our minds brewing up new ideas for making thousands of pounds. We went to a place I'll call Smithtown, where I plundered the display window of the jeweller's and took £6,500 worth of jewellery. I wasn't satisfied, so Wax drove me to the next town on our way home and I did a newsagent's shop over, taking all the fags from the shelves. Man, was I happy. Our total came to over three grand, and I felt like a millionaire. I sure had a spring in my step.

It's important however, not to brag about having money, as you just attract other people who want to have a part of it. Other boys were asking me where I was getting that kind of money, but I just told them lie after lie. You couldn't trust even the ones closest to you, as, one day or another, they'd tell someone else and, before you knew it, everyone would know. Wax and I swore an oath of secrecy to each other never to tell another living soul about how we came by the money.

Over the next three months, things were going great guns, and we were making silly money. All in, we must have made about twelve to fifteen grand, but it went like water through our hands. As fast as we made it, we were spending it hand-over-fist on hash, drink and clothes. We were living a lottery winner's life.

One night, Wax asked me if I wanted to go to a party. I didn't really want to because I was smashed out of my head on a combination of Valium and hash, but to make him happy I went along. Once at the party, I remember downing a half-bottle of Vodka, and then crashing out. I woke up the next morning in this strange house, with Lisa on the bed with me, along with a couple of other, equally blathered boys and girls. I had been so wasted on drink and drugs that I didn't even know if Lisa and I had got up to anything that night. I wasted no time getting ready, as everyone was sleeping their heads off from the high spirits of the night before. I spotted the video recorder under the TV, unplugged it, wrapped the wires and the plug around the video, and set it by the door. I opened the different bags scattered around the floor, and took the three purses from inside them. On that delightful note, I bid them farewell. I never felt any pangs of guilt. I was out of the door as fast as Linford Christie with my booty from this Aladdin's Cave.

Later that day, I heard some chap's voice at my big brother's door. 'Jimmy, open up, I know you're in there.'

There was also a girl's voice accompanying the male voice that was less than friendly. 'Open this fucking door!'

It was Lisa. I opened the door and put on a poker face.

'Right, Jimmy, where's the money, jewellery and video?' Lisa demanded with a face like a bulldog chewing a wasp.

'What are you talking about, Lisa?' I replied nonchalantly.

'Jimmy,' she fumed, 'I know what you get up to at nights with that little bastard Wax.'

'Lisa, don't be silly,' I bounced back.

Without warning, she punched and kicked at me like a wild cat.

'Right, calm down,' I implored, as I grabbed hold of her.

But Lisa was nuts. For a bird of 5ft 2in tall, she could fight like a fucking lion.

'Calm down,' I shouted. 'I don't know what you're talking about,' I said, posing as a model of virtue.

'OK,' she demanded, 'let me search the house.'

'Oh, carry on,' I invited.

So she did. She pulled the cushions from the settee, practically swung cabinet doors off their hinges, pulled the corners of the carpet up and looked in every other bolt-hole and nook and cranny she could find. But she found nothing. I'd been fortuitous in stashing the stuff in the garden shed until I could sell it later that day.

'Whose money's this?' she demanded to know, as she held aloft a neat bundle.

'Oh, that,' I quipped as I looked her in the eyes. 'It's my brother's rent money.'

Showing her softer side, she put the money back. I knew I had her fooled, but she didn't give up easily.

'Jimmy,' she seethed, as she threw me a slow, quizzing gaze, 'someone stole Susan's video, jewellery and a load of purses from her house.'

'No. You're kidding on,' I said with a straight face, returning her gaze with a long, hard stare.

'No, I'm fucking not,' she shrieked back at me.

I asked her what she meant that she knew what Wax and I got up to. The stupid fucker had told her everything when wasted on drink.

'And don't think I agree with what you do,' Lisa continued screeching at me.

'Don't you listen to him,' I said, 'he's talking shit.'

'No he isn't, Jimmy,' she fumed at me with a face like thunder, 'and what about last night? You can't even remember, can you?'

'Remember what?' I replied innocently.

'We spent the night together in the bedroom. You were sick a couple of times and then you tried to kiss me.'

'No, I never,' I replied incredulously.

'You did,' she said, breaking into a half-smile. Now that was a sign. She said, 'I need to go.'

But I never wasted any time. I took her in my arms and gave her a big, juicy kiss. 'I'll see you later, then,' I cheerfully said.

'OK,' Lisa said, her demeanour now one of calmness, as she started walking away. In the doorway she asked me if I was going to the Crown on Friday night.

I said, 'Yeah, sure.'

Now here was a chance. The Crown was the local dance. It was also a villains' paradise. Later that day, I sold the stuff I had stashed, taking £100 for the lot, plus the £70 cash I got out of the purses from the bags.

Friday couldn't come fast enough. I got a bottle of Buckfast and swigged it down in three mouthfuls and then I swallowed the last three Valium pills I had. I headed down to the town centre, where I bumped into a life long pal, Wullie Robb. He was also out of his skull on booze. He gave me a big hug.

'Jimmyboy, Jimmyboy, where the fuck did you come from?' he asked.

'My brother's,' I replied

'What the fuck are you up to?'

'Fuck all,' I said, adding that I was going to the Crown.

'I'll come as well,' he said.

We made our way to the Crown Hotel.

'All right,' one of the bouncers said, 'How's your big brother, John?'

'Oh, he's OK,' I said.

My oldest brother would do the odd bit of bouncing work on the doors at the Crown.

'Mind, don't cause any trouble in here,' another bouncer advised Wullie.

'Oh, don't worry, there'll be no trouble from either of us two,' I said calmly, as I walked past him and into the razzle-dazzle of the nightclub.

Once the doors opened, the dance-floor noise hit us like a wall of bricks. Wullie ran straight on to the dance-floor, and started swinging his arms and legs all over the place like a demented windmill. Now our Wullie was barmy and could put on a spectacular display of violence, so I knew I had someone to help fight my corner if any trouble started in the barren yard.

I spotted Lisa through the blue clouds of neon-lit cigarette smoke. Although she had also seen me, she never made any move to come over and say hello. I also spotted the bird whose video I had stolen, but she just stared right through me.

I forgot about them and started dancing. Just as I was starting to enjoy myself, BANG! I felt a thud on the back of my head. I turned around, and saw this guy, a game fucker of about twenty years old, standing there with a Bud bottle in his hand. I think he was just as shocked as me. I hadn't fallen, as the Valium and drink I had taken was in full effect by now.

I ran at the lad, and punched him. We both fell on the floor like a couple of wobbly dummies. We scrapped for a while, then, the next thing I knew, Wullie had come over and started jumping on the guy's head. He was kicking him in the face. It was like a Quentin Tarantino movie. I got to my feet and allowed Wullie to put on a show for the watching crowd.

The lad turned out to be the boyfriend of the girl whose house I had done over. The bouncers let it go once it had finished, but they flung us out anyhow. We didn't even get the chance to look over our shoulders before the police lifted us, as a couple of birds had run out and grassed us to the police outside. We were taken to Lanark cop shop, and charged with assault. We were locked up all weekend, before being taken to court where we got a five-week remand in Longrigend Young Offenders Institute.

Now I was shitting myself, but Wullie was easy come, easy go. We were off to adult jail for the very first time. Destination: Barlinnie Prison, the biggest prison in Scotland, otherwise known as 'the Big Hoose'.

CHAPTER FIVE

The Road to Hell

BARLINNIE PRISON ON THE WAY TO LONGRIGEND, 1987

On the prison bus heading towards Glesga, I was lost in worrying thoughts. All sorts of bits and pieces about prison were running about in my head. Would I be battered by a gang of boys like in the 1983 movie *Scum*, or the way Sid Vicious was gang raped while imprisoned in the USA? I looked at the other prisoners on the bus in microscopic detail. They were all tied up in their own thoughts, even my pal, Wullie. That was the first time I'd seen him lost for words.

We drew up outside the gates of the infamous Barlinnie Prison; the grim stone walls had witnessed escapes, mortal combats, vicious tyrants, last-minute reprieves and a myriad of other dramatic and pathetic minutiae of prison life.

'OK, listen up you lot,' the policeman hollered, 'the reception is full just now, so you will need to stay seated in the bus.' This was about twenty minutes to five, on a Monday night. The sun had been blasting its fierce rays on to the roof of the van all day; it was sweltering hot inside this infernal contraption that seemed to be designed for transporting animals. We made small talk amongst ourselves and I listened to all the older boys' and men's stories and jokes.

I gazed at Wullie; he too was looking the worse for wear. The veneer of Civvy Street had melted away in the heat of the day.

'OK, you lot, two at a time,' the copper blasted.

'Here, you, fucking stop,' he screamed at a couple of young boys. 'Any more fucking about and you two little pricks will be sitting in the dog boxes all night.'

I didn't have a clue what a dog box was, but it did the trick, as the two young boys instantly settled down.

'Hello, Tam,' this big gruesome, oaf of a prison warden said to the copper. 'How many have you got for us?'

'Fourteen,' the copper replied.

We were brusquely put into these cupboard-sized rooms, four at a time, squashed like sardines – so that's what the copper meant by *dog boxes*! The door swung open.

'Do you want something to eat?' the new voice invitingly asked.

'Yes,' we all said together, as thoughts of cordon bleu cooking sprang to mind.

The trustee prisoner held out four plastic begging-type bowls of what I can only describe as pigswill. Once the door slammed shut behind us, one of the older boys pressed up against me chirped up, 'Here, little man, is this your first time inside?'

'Yes,' I nervously replied, not wanting to offend him for fear of being kneed in the goolies.

'What you're holding in your hand, little man, is called a

mystery bowl,' the con revealed to me, going on to give me further pearls of prison wisdom. 'You better eat it, as you'll not be getting anything else until the morning.'

I stood with my mouth hanging wide open in disbelief, watching these three other boys shovelling this prison muck down their necks as if it was the food of the gods. I was dumbfounded but necessity can be an overpowering thing; it wasn't long before I was doing the same as them.

As the stinking gruel hit my tongue, I retched ... I was nearly sick! Two of the boys burst out laughing at my total disgust. 'Don't worry, little man, you'll not kick the bucket,' one of the two laughing boys chortled.

I couldn't finish this slop. I didn't know it then, but now know that the mystery-bowl concoction was made up of cabbage, spuds, mince and chicken in gravy all mashed up together. This mish-mash, prison cuisine looked like a Glasgow night special that had been spewed up.

'Let Holland out,' I heard a man's voice calling.

The door deftly swung open. A face appeared and the trustee prisoner uttered the instruction 'Follow me.'

Not wanting to miss out on something, I duly followed the trustee down to the bottom of the corridor where a screw wearing a sparkling white ice-cream-man's coat was standing.

'Are you Holland?' the screw enquired.

'Yes, sir,' I replied smartly.

'How old are you, Holland?'

'Sixteen-and-a-half, sir,' I proudly boasted, putting an emphasis on the 'half', as if it would have been some sort of added benefit to me.

'Date of birth?'

'10 December 1970.'

'Religion?'

'Catholic.'

'Been inside before?'

'No, sir.'

After a barrage of further insignificant questions, the screw then shouted, 'LRU,' which meant: Longrigend Remand Unit.

'Right, Holland, go with him,' he instructed, as he pointed to another screw.

I was shepherded into a down-at-heel room by a voice shouting instructions. 'In here, son, the surgery doctor will see you in due course.'

About fifteen minutes later, Wullie was sitting next to me waiting to see the doctor.

'Holland, come in here,' the doctor in the room hollered.

Once inside the office, this fat, old, decrepit-looking woman with grey-white hair told me to drop my trousers and underpants. Now, when someone usually asks me to do this, I know some sort of sexual act is about to follow. With the precision of a theatre light technician, she deftly stuck what I can only describe as a car lamp to my private parts. No, that didn't arouse an orgasm in me, but she did do some dirty talk and asked me if I had any sexually transmitted diseases that I knew of. She also asked me if I wet the bed.

I answered, 'Yes.'

Her eyebrows rose quizzically. 'What! You wet the bed?'

'No, no,' I quickly corrected her, 'I stopped when I was eleven years old.'

'That's OK, but you don't wet it now, right?'

'No, miss.'

'Good. Now, have you suffered any mental illness before?'

'No, not that I know of.'

'OK, son, pull your pants up, that's you done. Is this your first time inside?' she casually asked me.

'Yes, miss.' And that was the end of the ordeal.

Leaving the office, she followed me and told the screw I was finished, and he took me back to the dog box area. 'OK, son, sit inside,' he said in a monotone, work-weary voice. I went into the cramped dog-box where the other boys were. I didn't know it, but, as far as I was concerned, I thought this would be where we'd spend the night. I had visions of us sleeping standing up! When I asked the other boys if we slept there, they all burst out sniggering at my expense.

'No, we're going over to the halls once everyone's seen the doctor. Did you have to drop them in front of Agnes?' one of the other boys asked me.

'Yes,' I innocently replied.

As if I was the comedian's stooge, more laughing came from the group of boys.

'She's seen more pricks than a hedgehog,' one of them quipped.

Another boy chipped in, 'Way, more cock-ends than weekends.'

We all rolled about laughing.

'Fucking shut up,' one of the screws shouted through the door, 'what's so funny, you're all happy. This is Barlinnie, you're not supposed to be happy.'

At this, in the dog box, one of the boys was gesticulating with his hand, up and down in a wanking motion. We heard other boys kicking the doors of their dog boxes in stark resentment at the screw. One of the impatient boys shouted, 'Come on, boss, what's taking so fucking long?'

'Shut up,' the harassed screw screamed down the corridor to the boys, 'you'll go when I'm good and fucking ready, and not before!'

To our chagrin, the screws kept us sitting there while we

twiddled our thumbs for another fifty minutes or so. Then, without any warning, the doors to the dog boxes were opened, one after the other. As each door opened, the upsurge of clattering and chattering in the passage rose to a crescendo, as cons talked nineteen to the dozen. The noise subsided equally as fast as it had risen, and stopped completely when a screw bellowed, 'Right, follow me.'

We all followed him like lost sheep. I couldn't believe the size of the place. The halls stood like giant edifices. I turned to Wullie and gasped, 'What's this place?'

'I know,' Wullie said back, 'it's fucking massive.'

We stopped outside D-hall, long enough for the screw to open the door. Once inside the hall, the stench hit me like a brick in the face: it reeked like the urinals at a football match ... a sickly odour of tobacco smoke and disinfectant.

'Right,' the screw at the desk pronounced, 'once you hear your name, I'll tell you what number and flat you're going on to.' There were over 200 cells with three to five prisoners accommodated in each cell, so you can imagine the amount of people that were in this one hall. As luck would have it, Wullie, two other boys and I were called out and told we would all be going into cell number nineteen, on the third flat. As we made our way up to the third flat, we ran a gauntlet of brutal, cold-looking men with ghastly scars and the look of murder in their eyes. We could feel their evil eyes following us all, accompanied by cat-calling and wolf-whistling at us, as if we were some sexy bird walking by a building site. I couldn't wait to reach our cell.

I didn't know it then, but everyone that came into the hall went through the same rites of passage from the cons that were congregated in the hall. Once in the sanctuary of the cell, the four of us let out a stifled sigh of relief and the tension in our faces visibly cleared. Brusquely, the cell door slammed shut behind us. We looked around this eight-foot by twelve-foot cell; there were two beds and two ominously stained mattresses on the floor. What stood in one corner of the cell was disgusting: two empty disinfectant canisters and one well-used and well-stained piss pot, the sort of chamber pot that people potty train their babies on before they learn to use the toilet.

The scenery was breathtaking. What looked to be yellow paint was flaking off the walls like old man's dandruff and, by the looks of things, alopecia had set in on some parts of the wall. This was the sort of place you wouldn't keep pigs or chickens in for fear of the cruelty inspector condemning the place, never mind people. If the health inspectors had seen the place, they would have shut it down.

About a month earlier, Bar L, as it's known locally, had experienced a major riot and hostage-taking incident because of the treatment of Sammo 'The Bear' Ralston after the Peterhead saga. The screws, in general, were under pressure, but most wanted an easy time, and eight out of ten cons were on some drug or other. The cons were adult prisoners, whereas we were classified as YOs (young offenders). The pecking order meant that the cons would shout at the screws to open the door of our cells.

'Boss, open this fucking door until I see my little cousin or brother,' they'd shout.

Once the cons were in the cell, they'd pull out razors or homemade daggers and rob the YOs of their trainers, leather jackets or jewellery. You couldn't placate them; it would be akinto expecting not to be bitten by a Rhodesian Ridgeback while petting it! Bar L was full of rough, colourful and out-of-control junkies who wouldn't think twice about stabbing you or slashing you just to get what you had on your feet to pay for their next hit of smack. I can't condemn most of these people that perpetrated these things against the YOs because some of them have helped me out and been loyal to me over the years, but I do think, looking back, that it was a nasty thing to do to vulnerable, young boys.

Just after the Peterhead riot, a couple of life pals of mine got ten-year bongos for the Easterhouse carry-on. The screw was lucky to live. I'll call him Spud, he knows who he is. He was held for three-and-a-half days before he managed to escape from the clutches of this mad pack of junkies. When the screw was dropped feet first from the third flat, his leg was smashed in two places, but he managed to crawl and pull himself to safety. At the same time, slabs of slate weighing a hundred pounds each were being flung down on top of the MUFTI squad (Minimum Use of Force & Tactical Intervention). They were squashed like worker ants with only their stupid little plastic shields for protection.

My first night in the big house was spent restlessly, as I lay uncomfortably on a lumpy mattress that had eaten away at 5,000 lost and pickled souls before me. At 6.15 the next morning the screw opened the door. 'OK, you lot, slop out.' I didn't know what 'slop out' meant. I just followed suit with the rest of the boys. There were between thirty and fifty boys fighting, jostling and scurrying about in the sluice recess like ragamuffins, jockeying for places to wash themselves at the twelve sinks.

Once I managed to get to a sink, to my empty-stomached disgust, it was covered with a collection of facial hair, discarded razor blades, plasters, snot and phlegm, all fused together into one stomach-churning mass. I retched, but nothing came up. My eyes watered at the festering sight, and my stomach was in knots as I ran my hand over the surface of the water. It was freezing cold. I flung the cruel liquid over my hair, then, as if straight from *Oliver Twist*, I asked one of the two screws that were standing over us like bouncers, 'Is there any toothpaste, sir?'

'Toothpaste?' they exclaimed with wide-open Dickensian eyes. 'Are you mad, little man. This is fucking Bar L, not your granny's yacht; if you want toothpaste, don't get sent to the jail! Now hurry up, there are another seventy or eighty cons to slop out after you, so stop fannying about. You lot will be going to Longrigend within the next hour and a half, so, once you get back to your cell, strip your bed sheet down.'

'What bed sheet?' I said in defiant disbelief.

None of us in that cell had a bed sheet between us. All we had was an itchy, semen-stained, stinking army blanket, with no pillow. Because this was all new to me, I didn't know any better, and neither did Wullie. We put on a brave face with one another, each not wanting to show our vulnerability to the other because some of the other harder young offenders were full of giggles and saying, 'Thank fuck they're going to Longrigend.' Some of these guys had done more bird than Bill Oddie!

Our time had come to be shipped out. We got into what was called 'a big green' bus with blackened windows. We were heading for Airedale, in the heart of Lanarkshire ... I wasn't looking forward to it.

CHAPTER SIX

Goodbye to the Bar L
(The Hate Factory)

Once we reached Longrigend, we were let off the green maggot two at a time. My former foster dad, Robert, was taking the handcuffs off the boys in front of me. Once he reached me, I involuntarily went bright red. He looked at me with disgust in his eyes; he leaned forward to my ear and menacingly whispered to me that he knew I would end up in here.

'You little prick,' he spat through his clenched teeth.

I thought to myself, Fuck you!

I wasn't going to let any of the other boys know I was once fostered to this cunt, as that would be like signing my own death warrant. I was cuffed to Mully, from Maryhill, who had sensed something and asked me what the screw had said. I told him he was just trying to be a wide boy. We couldn't know then but, within two years, Mully would be murdered in prison, stabbed through the back with a 22in kitchen knife by a poof called 'Dundee Fag'.

The same routine as Bar L was duplicated here: into see the doctor for a medical, pants down, given the all clear and put in a dog box and left to wait. I was put into the same one as Mully. Let me tell you, for a lad of seventeen years old, Mully was a big lad. He was in Long for being part of a street gang that had a bloody running battle with a gang called the 'Young Posse Fleets' – they were from the other part of the north side of the city. A boy caught up in the argy-bargy was critically ill with multiple stab wounds to his chest, neck and back.

Although Mully tried to escape the violence, he had a stark memento of that occasion in the form of a red, deep, angry-looking slash wound down his back, with twenty–seven stitches struggling to hold it shut. Anyone on the bus going to Long knew of Mully's capability and that he was game, but he didn't play up on that fact.

'OK, you two,' the screw ordered Mully and me, 'follow me. What size shoes do you take, Holland?'

'Eight, sir,' I said.

'And you, sonny?' the screw asked, looking at Mully.

'Nine, sir.'

'What size waist are you?' the screw asked me.

'Thirty-two, sir,' I said.

'Thirty-four, sir,' Mully replied to the same question.

The screw kicked a battered box towards us, and said, 'You'll find a pair that fit you in there.'

This box contained black hairy trousers, and black beetles were crawling out of it. Knowledgeably, Mully informed me that the trousers were known as BDs. My foster dad stuck his head into the room and asked to see me in his office. I obligingly followed him. 'Look, son,' he warmly said, 'I can make your time easy or hard in this place. Do you want to go on protection because, if the rest of the prisoners knew you were fostered to me, you'll get a hard time.'

I resented his intervention and said, 'Fuck off.'

I would take my chances in the lion's den. After all, I'd been living on the edge all of my life, so what would another doing be to a guy that had taken over sixty or so doings up to that point in his life?

'OK, you arseholes, listen up,' the screw shouted, 'the first five I shout out are going to A-hall: Smith, Carr, Allan, Holland and Robb.'

I was gutted because, Mully, who I saw as someone I could look up to, wasn't coming to the same hall as me.

'The next eight of you are going to C-hall ...' I heard all the names, one of which was Mully's. The screw continued, 'And the rest of you twelve are going to D-hall. Do you little pricks hear me?'

All in the one voice, we shouted out, 'YES, SIR.'

'OK, no talking, single file and follow the officer that will take you to your halls.'

Once out of reception, we must have looked some state, with our ill-fitting shoes, black hairy BD trousers and a blue and white striped shirt with two buttons barely holding it together. Wullie was with me; I don't know if it was fate, but we were put together everywhere we went.

'Right, this is the dog leg,' the screw barked with a grin on his face, as if it was his pet project. 'There are ten cells,' he pointed out, as if giving an impromptu tour, 'in there for any of you little fucks that think you're tough.'

I didn't know how I knew it, but I knew that, over the two years or so, the dog leg punishment block would be like my second home every time I was back in that shit hole of Longrigend.

'Holland, Smith, you're in number five. Well, what are you waiting for, someone to take your hand?'

'No, sir,' I barely whispered.

'Good. Well, fucking move it, then.'

Can I just say now, for the record, if other humans treat someone like that, don't expect him to grow up to be a nice person. You may be paranoid at first from the screws, but you soon grow to hate them and want to lash out and cause as much damage as possible against them or their jails. That's just my thought on the matter, but what am I? A half-illiterate convict that only learned to read and just about spell. That's all one institution after another has ever done for me.

I was in with this boy for the five weeks I was there; I'll call him Tam. He was in for robbing a newsagent's shop. Religiously, every day, Tam used to get visits from his girlfriend, mum and dad. I felt a bit gutted because I knew no one was coming to see me, but, to Tam's credit, he would share any sweets, drugs or tobacco he had with me. I couldn't really read back then, but Tam used to read books and he kept asking me to read a few lines out of the book *Cane and Abel*. I struggled, but, a year or so later, I didn't put that book down, having completed my first read.

Now I can read perfectly. I've read *War and Peace* by Tolstoy and *Les Miserables* by Victor Hugo. I love reading now, but, if it wasn't for that boy Tam from Hamilton, I don't think I would have picked up a book. To this day, I still struggle with my spelling, but if I can write a book, anyone can. So, never say *never*. You can do almost anything if you put your mind to it. Be it the perfect murder, robbing a bank or owning your own company. I don't go along with Prince Charles's maxim that everyone should know their place and limitations.

At that time, the other three boys told me I was on the heavies.

Now that means carrying the steel food trays, and everybody that was seen carrying them was classed as the bam of the table from the older boys. This I didn't mind, but, after four days of being the bam, other boys started taking the piss out of me saying, 'Eeh aw,' like a donkey, so I confronted Butler that teatime. I wished I never had, because I got four steel trays off my head, bursting it wide open! Fair dos, he done me over belter, but I was still learning my trade. I would come back in later years fitter, stronger and give as good as I got, but not at this point in my fucked-up life.

Anyway, Wullie and I survived our five weeks and appeared in front of the judge at Lanark Sheriffs' Court. He was a nasty old cunt, and saw me off with three months, while Wullie got six months for the assault in the Crown. So it was back to the big house, Bar L, then on to Polmont, in the jolly green prison van again. Polmont is in the middle of a housing scheme around Falkirk, and used to be a borstal where some nasty, young, bitter men were put. When I first set eyes on the place, it was a couple of big wooden, churchlike structures; it didn't look much like a prison. For a start, there wasn't a fence or a wall around the place.

A boy's voice boomed over the rest, as he pointed to a multitude of places, 'That's the north wing,' 'That's the north wing, up there's the east and west wings.' Inside, the place had the fragrance of spring flowers, not like Longrigend or Bar L. The reception was freshly painted in light, gentle shades as well. Poor Wullie was sent to the detention centre in Glenochil. Now I had heard horror stories about that place from some tough, young teens that had spent time in the place.

'OK, here's your two kits,' a young boy with a spotty complexion and dirty greasy, mousy hair said. 'The BDs are for recreation, visits, church or chapel. The denims and dungarees are for the worksheds and the shorts are for through the day.'

The training shoes they dished out to you were like something you would write to Jimmy Savile to fix, but hey ... I thought to myself, I'm here to be punished. After a couple of weeks in Polmont, I started to become more assertive and began arguing with older, bigger boys. I loved it. This is where my ugly side would make some scary and unpredictable appearances. Even to this day, I can go from a happy-go-lucky cunt to the devil on acid.

I can be as bad if not worse than the worst of them. I'll show every cunt that I'm not just that little boy that's taken all those doings in my life. Don't get me wrong, I've still come off second best in roll-abouts or stabbings, but I've stood up for myself enough times.

In Polmont, everyone was acting the hard man and giving it the large. I had to fight or cosh or do something to be accepted. I can tell you, it was better to be in a gang than be on your own, and I'd do anything in Polmont, no questions asked! Some said I was as mad as a Muller, some said I was a bam rocket. These pricks are dirty shit-bags. My time in this fucking place was one mad, non-stop, roller-coaster ride of turbulent trouble with other boys and screws.

One day a screw asked me to get a bucket, a nailbrush and cloth and told me to scrub the full Allycally floor. Well, this was like a red rag to a bull! I angrily grasped the handle of the metal pail, hoisted it up, and duly flung the contents – including the bar of carbolic soap – at the screw, and then I took to my heels with one angry, wet screw and two other dry screws in hot pursuit.

When they eventually cornered me, the ruthless bunch gave me a cracking doing: I suffered a black eye, bloody nose, lumps on my face and head. There was no getting away from prison life in the eighties. It was a hate factory, where I was the apprentice, learning the hard way. I was the same as a couple of thousand other boys, but I didn't want to just lie down and take the shit off them. I would still take some shit from some older boys because they were in gangs, but screws were a different matter, because everyone hates the screws in prison, not so much in this day and age because they've come up with the good old-fashioned idea of giving the cons a carrot: TV, Gameboys, drug-free halls, wearing your own clothes, and all that shit.

I had two weeks left until I got out of Polmont: Yeehaaaaa! I didn't really know where I was going to go after. The day came faster than I could have imagined, and I decided to head to Carluke to my brother John's. But he told me I could only stay a couple of days because his wife, Linda, didn't want me around the house.

I went to see Lisa, my old girlfriend. We had sex, then I got thirty quid off her, got on a train and headed off to my brother Bert's in the Westend of Glesga. The Westend of Glesga was like Las Vegas. All the bright lights amounted to a few million watts or so; plenty of pubs, clubs and the like. It was easy to make a living as a petty criminal.

CHAPTER SEVEN

Westend Ned With No Bed

NOVEMBER 1987

My brother Bert's flat wasn't what you could really call a flat; it was more of a down-at-heel bedsit, with one bed and an old, sexually war-torn, rotten settee that had seen better days. I found Bert fixed up with his new girlfriend, Irene, who was already staying with him. From the minute I set eyes on Irene, I didn't like her. She was a little bit too cocksure of herself for her own good and she was more than eight years older than Bert.

I turned up at Bert's front door out of the blue with all my worldly possessions in a plastic carrier bag: two pairs of boxer shorts, one pair of denims and a T-shirt. Not much for a boy at seventeen-and-a-bit years old.

Bert shouted through his door, 'Who is it?'

'Me, bro, Jimmy,' I hollered and insisted, 'Come on, open up.'

'Fuck me, Jimmy, I thought you were someone else,' Bert blasted in relief.

I later learned, within two hours, that Irene, his bird, had pulled a fast one on some local drug dealers. She and my brother were hooked on smack. It was her that got him into it. She was sticking needles into her legs and arms as though she was a pincushion, and so was he. Hell, I even tried it as well, not jacking up with any needles, but with the foil the way I did in the Blue Triangle, but this time I got a better buzz from it.

Before long, I'd turned my attentions to crime. I excelled in house-breaking, I quickly advanced up the proverbial criminal ladder and carried out street muggings on men. I soon became a dab hand at using a blade and used my knifepoint talents to relieve nervous men of their fat wallets. At cash machines, I was a menace. When I heard the machine whirring, I knew it was counting some punter's money and was about to cough it out; I was at it in a flash! I would unleash a barbaric-looking attack on the unsuspecting victims for the £100 and then, rather sharpish, I'd make my swift getaway on foot.

I had to live and keep my brother and his girlfriend happy for the privilege of me staying there because they didn't work. The Westend covered a big area: Great Western Road, Byers Road, Partick Gorges, Kelvinhead, Hillhead up to Annesland and the beginning of Maryhill. So you can imagine, I had a field day, as money was so easy to come by through what I did on a night. I was in the car park of the Governor Hotel when I spotted a car full of cigar boxes, spread tantalisingly over the back seat. I smashed the window and took the lot. Unfortunately I didn't know then that the cigars were out of date by over two years!

I raced with excitement all the way back to my brother's bedsit with them... three full bags. The three of us sat up all night, putting them into bundles of £20-worth so that we could get half the marked retail price of £10 from the local off-licence shop for them.

The following morning, I swaggered around to the shop like a man on a mission with a holdall full of cigars. I'll call the shop Ali's.

'You come into my back shop,' Ali told me.

Once in the back, we did the business. When I opened up my holdall, Ali's eyes lit up like Blackpool illuminations as he feasted them on the contents.

'Oh, nice,' he said then he delivered the bombshell news that they were out of date.

After haggling, he said he'd give me £150 for the lot. Although there was over three grand's worth of cigars, I begrudgingly agreed. That day, the three of us were sorted, so I was happy but sad at the same time about being ripped off by Ali. I now know, cigars can last up to three or four years before they become unsmokable, but I didn't care. Once back at the flat, Irene got her shoes and jacket on and then headed out of the door to score some smack. While Irene was away on that errand, my brother was in his bed with the Possil flu. To those of who are uninitiated in the art of drug taking, that means he was rattling off his head for smack. Just for the record, I wasn't using needles.

No sooner had she left, Irene was back in double-quick time. She put a bit on my foil and then cooked up the brown powder on a metal spoon for her and my brother. What a state they were in, it was tragically funny to watch, but I knew smack was heavy-duty shit to fuck with. I've seen Meany, a good pal of mine, overdose on the smack or other drugs. Once they get out of prison, they all think they can handle the same amount of stuff that they were used to before they came into prison.

I'd like to take the opportunity to give some of my dead pals a mention that overdosed: Sid, Slonny, Robbie, Eddie and many more. There was Jack as well, who was a pure character from Castlemilk.

I was having a field day down the Westend; my deep pockets were jingling and full of money nearly every day of the week. My brother's bird, Irene, wanted a fur coat, so I got her one by throwing a brick through the shop window and grabbing the coat off the shop dummy. Once I got to the bedsit, I put the jacket on and waltzed into the flat looking like Liberace, the two of them burst out laughing. Irene was like a tramp eating chips.

'Let's try it on, Jimmy, please?'

As she swooned around like Joan Collins with the fur coat on, she had the air of a council-estate beauty queen about her.

'Do you want it?' I teased Irene. 'It's yours. I done the window down on the Great Western Road and just took it, simple as that,' I bragged.

I loved the summer months when I was on the run from one place or another because the Westend was the place to be, with all the Chinese tourists going to the Botanic Gardens. I snatched a few cameras from their hands. I also pulled knives out on them and took their wallets and money and travellers cheques. By now, so long as I was pleasing my brother and his bird, I just didn't give a fuck for anyone. I wanted to show them that I was a good earner and a go-getter. I think they were more relying on me to make the money for their drugs than doing any graft for themselves. I didn't mind, after all, I would have been on the streets if they never let me camp down on their rotten settee, and what a sleep I got on that flea-ridden thing.

Irene never had the fur coat off. The saying 'all fur coat and no knickers' certainly applied to her. At nights, she would waltz up to the red-light district like Marlene Dietrich and work the seedy area with it on. I don't know if it helped pull more punters for her but, some nights, she'd come home with £200 and an eighth of an ounce of smack stuffed into the pockets of the fur.

I started to develop a penchant for the odd hot foil of smack. After all those years of calling junkies 'the scum of the earth', I had now fallen by the wayside and had become a junkie myself! The preacher falls! I also got up to a lot of naughty business down the Westend: snatches, creeping in the back door of pubs, clubs and hotels, stealing whatever I could lay my thieving hands on. I remember once, I went to rob these two poofs down the walkway. What a mistake that was! They gave me some doing over. I was more gutted getting done in off a couple of poofs than not taking any money home that night.

While I was letting myself into the bed-sit, I saw a beautiful bird talking on the payphone. I asked my brother who this nice bird was.

'What colour hair has she got?' he asked.

'Blonde,' I eagerly replied in the hope that he would know her.

As quickly as he'd asked what colour hair she had, he burst out laughing and told me it was a guy, a transvestite called Marilyn!

'She stays in number two, down the corridor from us,' he told me.

If you didn't know the difference, I swear, you hot-blooded males would have loved to get into her pants. I'm not a poof, never have been, never will be, but, if she asked me out, I would have been right there, until I put my hand down her pants and then I would have run a mile. Ha, ha! Now, Bert and Irene were friendly with this transvestite, Marilyn, so they asked her – or him? – to come in for a cup of tea. Crikey, she even talked like a bird. To my utter embarrassment, Bert told Marilyn that I thought she was a pure darling.

'W-e-l-l, thank you,' Marilyn schmoozed to me in a deep husky voice.

I started blushing, as if I was done having a wank or something. I was startled to have been told from a transvestite that she thought I was a little cheeky charmer. I couldn't wait to leave the flat to prove my male prowess round the Westend.

I must have done about twenty-five housebreakings while the occupants were tucked up safe and sound in their beds. That didn't bother me one bit because I was always tooled up; I always carried a hammer and screwdriver on me. I wasn't taking any chances, because, if the man woke up, I'd have rattled the hammer off his head. Mind you, with all this emphasis on the householder now being able to use 'reasonable force' to protect their home, I wouldn't even consider it. I mean, look what that Farmer Tony Martin did to those creepers!

I took rings and chains off sleeping birds. I emptied purses and wallets out of bags and trousers hanging over chairs in the bedrooms. On every turn, I was getting braver, I thought I was invisible, or so it seemed. I would always carry these creeps out alone, that way you were double alert for trouble if things were coming on top. I recall, I did over one shop, where I took six electric guitars worth more than £10,000. I was over the moon with my latest adventure, but it didn't last too much longer because every copper had my description by now, so I had to pick and choose the turns I would do.

I went back to basics. I was stealing digital car radio cassette players, the well-known brands like Clarion, Blaupunkt, Kenwood and Pioneer. I picked the right motors: Saabs, Audis and Porsches, stuff like that. Nowadays, you could only get between £10 and £15 for them because they're that inexpensive to buy and easy to get. I remember the Ford cars that had a digital radio cassette in them called a 752. It was one of the early ones where you had to punch a code into restart them if they were removed from the car. There was a lot of palaver involved, you had to scrape the code number off it and put it in a polythene bag and freeze it to death so as to fuck the coding elements in the radio cassette, and then, once it had thawed out, it worked without you having to punch the manufacturer's code into it. These days, you can obtain all of the radio unlocking codes you desire via the Internet by logging on to the right website and paying a fee for the unlocking code ... simple as that! You can even obtain cracker computer software programs for the lesser-known makes of radio cassettes.

I met a lovely mixed-race girl who, for legal reasons, I'll call Nonian. With her being homeless, I saw her about the Westend nearly every day. Before long, we were hard at it with great sex and even greater drugs. I loved shoplifting with this sexy girl. Nonian also knew how to do credit-card fraud, and she got me some very nice stuff with stolen cards.

A few weeks later I got a pull by a beat copper. I was in my thuggery clothes, old tracky bottoms and trainers.

'Where are you off to, young man?' he said with a stiff upper lip while in the middle of Byers Road.

'I'm just heading home from work,' I replied innocently.

'What kind of work do you do?' he probed.

'Painter and decorator,' I retorted, quick as a flash.

This silly copper asked me my name, so I gave him my brother Bert's, plus his date of birth: 22/11/67.

The muggy copper put an APB over the airwaves. 'OK, Albert, sorry for taking your time up,' he replied.

I knew my brother didn't have a criminal record.

'Oh,' the copper added, 'and one more thing, Mr Holland, do you know where your little brother is staying, because we need to have a word with him?'

I told him that I hadn't seen Jimmy for months.

'OK, son, have a nice day,' he finished.

It wouldn't be too much longer before Nonian and I would get done red-handed while doing the rooms at the world-famous Grosvenor Hotel. I had Rolex watches, rings and chains. Accompanying me, Nonian had more jewellery, perfumes and money. On the way out, we got a pull from a security guard, so I hit him with the best punch that I could muster up. It did the trick and allowed the two of us to put the boot down, but we never got far! We were bundled into the local cop shop.

'Look, young Holland, you've been a one-man crime wave! In two months, crime in this whole area has gone up by thirty per cent,' the copper raged.

'What's that got to do with me?' I replied smugly, 'I've only moved through here with my bird Nonian. We've been living in bed & breakfast. Is this some dig out?'

SLAP! I saw a bright flash in front of my eyes.

'Don't you try and be a fucking smartarse in here, Holland, this is Partick cop shop you're in,' the irate copper retorted.

'So fuck,' I snapped.

Once again, off this skinny prick of a copper went. BANG! SLAP! PUNCH! It was more like a *Batman* movie! He could hit me all night, but it wouldn't make any difference. Unbeknown to me, Nonian had broken down under the pressure that this rotten mob had put her under, poor cow. My faith in Nonian keeping schtum had been worthless.

I got done with creeping the hotel, six house-breaks and assaulting a copper. Nonian walked out of the cop shop. I've never seen her since, but I wish her all the best because I know she was just a young, homeless, drug addict, not a serious criminal.

The same old routine followed: spend the night in the coppers' cells, court in the morning, back to the big house, Bar L, and then up to Longrigend for a three-month period to await trial. After three-and-a-half months, I went to court, and got sentenced to three years imprisonment. I took it all in my stride. I was like an old hand; I knew what was to come. I was a right jack-the-lad, always trying to score brownie points with the young hard boys like Dada, Wullie McPhee, Aldo and the like.

One day, I was told to do twenty-five press-ups. I'd just done thirty, but this little prick of a PTI screw said I was cheating by not doing them right. I was in a snarling mood and lost the plot, got up and walked over to him and planted a belter of a right hook on his rotten dial. He stumbled backwards. I chased him round the PT hall before I was held back by the other YOs. Some bright spark had pressed the riot bell, whereupon about twenty screws came charging in. I was restrained even more by the screws and put in the usual arm locks that even a grade-one yoga student wouldn't be able to get free from! All the way down to the digger, my feet never touched the ground.

Later that day, the PTI that I'd attacked that morning came in.

'Right, you little prick, get on your feet, we'll sort this out like men,' he insisted.

You've got to take into account that he was a man in his mid-twenties who was fit as a fiddle. I knew I was going to come off second best, but up I got. No sooner had I stood up from being seated on my bed than he kicked me in the chest, which took the wind out of my sails. I mean, this prick had a lot of support from his fellow screws but, give him credit, he could bounce on the doors of Mothercare for a living if he wasn't a screw. I think he was trying to kick me in the face, but he missed and, before I knew what was happening, he was sitting on top of me punching lumps out of my face, head and body. I started laughing at him.

He was just trying to win some respect back by giving me a doing. I got a doing, plus I was put on what's called a 'Rule 34' for a month in the segregation cells. This is when a prisoner can be confined in a special cell for the maintenance of good order and discipline. The screws banged me up every day of that month's rule down that scabby, four-cell seg unit known as a digger.

Sometimes, I'd only see the screws twice a day. Often, they wouldn't even open my door for exercise that, by law, every prisoner on a rule was entitled to. This was still the Eighties and there was a little band of screws that thought they were the mafia godfathers.

But there was one screw that was brand new with me, Mr Dickson. Even to this day, I still get on with him, he isn't any bam; he's a very hard and fair man. He was the Scottish power-lifting champion back then, but he had a bit of time for me and I had, and still have, respect for him. I don't hate every screw. I do like some, the way some like me, but most can't stand me because I don't back down from them or take any of their shit. My motto is: hit first, ask questions later.

I got off the Rule 34 one month to the day after the palaver in the gym hall with the PTI. I got moved into A-hall, which is the biggest hall in the jail. It was similar to Bar L, except it was clean and smelled fresh. I had a friendly face to talk to, as Raymie was in this hall with me by now as well. Mully was also in the hall; he was super-fit by this point and was looking good for it. He helped me out with a couple of T-shirts and football shorts. I was grateful because I wasn't getting any visits at the time.

I've seen people go totally mental because their loved ones

didn't turn up, or never got into see them because they missed their visit session. So, in some respects, I didn't have that burden on my shoulders to carry like a cross. Don't get me wrong, I would have loved to have visits, who wouldn't, after all, we're only human.

I started work in the top joiners shed. I didn't know one person in the place, it was like going to a new school, having to wear a mask and kid on you're this or that just to be accepted by your peers. Anyway, it didn't take me too long to make friends, as I'm a bit of a comedian when I want to be. Before I knew it, some of the top boys would shout me over to sit at their camp. Once I had a couple of draws of the marijuana joints that got passed round, I'd take centre stage like my favourite comedian, Billy Connolly. I got put on report a few times for not doing any work because I was so fucked with the hash.

About two months or so after being in this jail, something happened that shocked and sickened me to the pit of my stomach. My pal that I met in Longrigend, Mully, was brutally murdered in this jail. It all came about through drugs. A boy called Jackie Stevens from Edinburgh brought thirty tems in, and when he came off the visits, he went to the Dundee puff's cell to divvy up the drugs. They opened the parcel on his bed, and Mully was in the cell.

They counted the tems; there were only twenty-eight, so two were missing. The four of them hunted the cell high and low, but still never came up with them. The puff and his pal turned to Mully and asked him to give back the two tems. Mully never had them, as he didn't take drugs, but the poof had to blame someone. A fight broke out. Mully was super-fit, and he could bang like a shithouse door in a gale, so he had no trouble in battering the three of them that were in the cell. Mully left the cell to wash the blood off his hands, face and T-shirt. This all happened at ten minutes to nine on a Friday night, so there was no time or point in trying to get it sorted out, as bang-up was at nine o'clock.

The poof was one of the early-morning cooks. He'd be in the jail kitchen cooking breakfast with five other cons from 5.30am until 7.15am, then the poof would get a rubdown search, but he'd planted the biggest knife in the kitchen under the bottom of the food barrow that had the breakfasts in it. Once safely out of the kitchen and back in the hall, the poof took the knife from under the barrow and wrapped it in a towel.

As he was making his way back to his cell, the hall was just getting opened up for showers and slop-outs. The poof went to his pal's door and told him what his plan was. His pal didn't really want to take anything further because he and Mully came from the same area, Maryhill. The poof persisted, 'He's not getting away with battering me,' he fumed. So off they went in pursuit of Mully.

At this particular time, Mully was standing with his head facing into a cell talking to his pal. When the poof thrust the 22in knife at Mully, it went straight through his back up to the hilt.

The destructive path of the knife had mangled Mully's inner organs. The poof tried to pull the knife back out, but it was stuck fast! Leaving the knife sticking in Mully, the poof and his pal bolted from the scene.

Staggering to the screws' office, Mully was morgue material, but, still, he managed to tell them he'd been stabbed.

'Can you make it down the stairs?' the incredulous screw asked.

'Yes, I think so, boss,' muttered Mully.

These were the last words Mully would utter; he staggered for two steps and fell with a thud, before rolling down a flight of stairs to his death.

The blood that gushed out of Mully didn't seem real; it was as if someone had painted the prison landing crimson. At that time, most of the prisoners were making their way to the dining hall for their breakfasts that the poof and five other cons had made a couple of hours earlier. We were all kept in the dining hall for over two hours; the cops and forensic mobs were taking samples and sealing off that part of the stairs. Afterwards, we all got interviewed and taken back to our cells, two at a time, up the back staircase.

There was all sorts of chitchat at the windows about what had happened to Mully and then it came on the radio that he died at the scene of the crime. Some sick fucks were banging on their doors, cheering at my pal Mully's death. Another couple of hours later, I got taken to the cellblock and got told I was a suspect in the murder of Mully. I couldn't believe it! I thought this was some sort of sick joke, but it wasn't. A cop came in and apologetically said, 'Sorry, son, you're the wrong Holland, it's the other one, you can go back to your cell.'

I felt like hugging this copper for giving me my life back, yet all prisoners hate them. The poof's pal was taken down in my place and the two of them were grassed by more than 60 per cent of the hall. Even though I saw it and Mully was my pal, I told them I never saw anything. I said, 'I was in the shower.'

They said, 'For fuck's sake, it must have been a very busy shower today, son.'

'I don't know, boss,' I said to this copper.

The thing is, the guy that brought the drugs in was the one who had stolen the two tems, but it's funny, he was the main witness against the poof and his pal, getting them life sentences.

Fate works in strange ways, because Jackie Stevens was found dead of a drugs overdose some four years later in a block of flats in Edinburgh. The poof is still doing his life sentence and his pal got out of his life sentence after doing fourteen years for keeping his mouth shut. Rather ironically, he's got a death sentence of HIV to live with now as well, but, mate, you know I love you like a brother. But I hate that Dundee poof with a passion – in my eyes, he's worse than a grassing rapist.

I stayed in the jail another seven months, and then I was moved to Polmont Young Offenders Institute to a hall called Eastwing that was just opened for long-term prisoners.

CHAPTER EIGHT

The Sullen Majesty of a Young Offenders Institution

POLLMONT YOUNG OFFENDERS, FEBRUARY 1989

I'd already been in this prison, so I knew what sort of Godforsaken, unforgivable behaviour to expect from the screws. They were mean bastards, the lot of them, not just to me but also to every last young offender that had the miserable misfortune to be incarcerated in this house of horrors.

It was just before dinner when Dessy, Tam, Bobby and I arrived in Eastwing.

'Right, OK,' the self-important, officious screw barked, 'there are no gangsters in this hall,' *I* am the only gangster. My name is Mr Johnson. If you want to act like a hard man, well ... you'll have me to deal with.'

We just stood there, staring straight in front of us. This mean bastard was marching up and down like an agitated windmill in front of our eyes. I had the measure of him all right; this cunt took to his job like an onion takes to soup!

'OK, drop your stuff here and join the food queue, no talking,' was the blunt instruction. Off we went with a firm warning ringing in our ears. I knew then that it would only be a matter of time before something would happen with the screw that thought he was the bee's knees. I don't know why these sick fuck sons of bitches think they're better than us, when really they're not.

About two months after we came to Eastwing, there was a lot of tension brewing between the Glesga and Lanarkshire boys in the hall against the Ayrshire boys; you could cut the atmosphere with a knife. The tension came to a head in the dining hall, when my pal, Paul from Paisley, ran over and coshed the biggest boy in the Ayrshire gang with a PP9 battery in a sock. That was it. Chairs, fists, feet and pool cues were flying everywhere! Someone had kicked the big bucket of custard all over the floor next to the door that we would usually go out. When the twenty unsuspecting screws ran into the dining hall, they slipped on the custard and landed on their arses.

Miraculously, at the sight of this theatrical farce, all the young offenders stopped boxing with each other, and we turned on the screws in a rampage of wanton destruction. Suddenly, the cocksure Johnson and his hit men didn't know what had hit them; they fell apart like toy soldiers! We took on every last screw that ran into the dining hall, and were over them like a rash and annihilated the place. After we finished, it looked like the scene of a road accident!

In order to stop it, they took some serious damage – burst heads, broken arms, black eyes. I can safely say that we gave as good as we got. To this day, I don't know why we all joined forces to fight against the screws, but I do know one thing: every cunt was pissed off with the way the screw Johnson behaved towards us. Once the screws manhandled us down to the seg block, we made a pact to give the enemy a sore head. Every day, a different person would assault a screw that opened their door or we'd fling our excrement over them. They daren't let us out as a group for fear of what we'd do!

Mind you, these animals would be just as vicious back to us by charging in the cell at us five-handed, and proceeded to remove the excrement from us by methodically battering us with their riot batons, giving it big licks! I've still got a belter of a scar on my head as a memento from where a screw coshed me full force over the head. I was seeing more stars than Patrick Moore; he didn't half give me a sore fucking whack on the nut. The bastards are all cowards and that's why I hate them.

I was lying naked in the silent cell, covered in bruises from head to foot from the beatings I was receiving. I used to have to stick my toes in my mash spuds or piss on them to keep them warm, anything to heat myself up. I believe the most degrading thing in the world is to be treated worse than a starving dog by five growling, muscle-bound thugs, better known as screws! I never had a bed; they'd throw me a blanket in at eight o'clock every night and I'd sit there with it on looking like Big Chief Sitting-bull. This throwing in the blanket and taking it away at 6.45am every morning and leaving me naked for the rest of the day went on for a week.

I was starting to crack up at what this mob was getting away with. I'd had a bellyful of this and I got my lawyer to visit me in the jail. He couldn't believe the bruising over my body, so he pulled the governor and asked why I was covered in marks. The governor said to my lawyer that it was 'self-inflicted' and was caused by my 'running into walls'. That part was disproved because walls don't leave footprints all over your body.

I don't know what happened with all the lawyers kicking up a ruckus, but we were taken off the rules we were being held under in the seg block and returned to the hall. Johnson was there to meet us with a couple of his henchmen. He seethed, 'OK, you little bastards! I'm coming after you, you might have pulled the wool over your lawyers' eyes, but, no, siree, are you getting it easy in this hall, now fuck off out of my sight.'

This man had a big problem … me!

'Get them out of my way,' he stormed againto the screws that were standing there. Tam McCall from Hamilton and I were sniggering like a couple of school kids at Johnson's expense. Tam called him a bam and I was intotal agreement with my young pal.

A couple of weeks later, I was told to stay off recreation and to clean up my cell, but it was already spic and span, so I knew it was a wind-up from Johnson and his bully boys. I told my friend, Spike from Fife, that I was going to sneak in and set their office on fire, which would teach them to stop fucking all of us about. The plan was simple; I ran into the screws' unattended office with my lighter at the ready in my hand, I set the bin on fire and all the wall charts that were pinned to the poster board. Flames licked around the place like a prairie dog at a waterhole, and the thing was on fire within seconds! I merrily skipped back to my cell with glee, like a child that had just stolen some apples out of an orchard – guilty as sin, but blissfully without a spark of remorse.

I told Spike that he'd hear the screws. Sure as fuck, a couple of minutes later, we heard the screws in uproar, screaming for a fire hose! They would know it was Spike or me that was responsible for this mayhem, because we were the only two off recreation. I told him we should jump into our cells and smash them up, so off we went to demolish the cells. The screws were standing outside my door telling me they were going to batter the living daylights out of me.

As the flames began to engulf my cell, before too long, I couldn't see my cell door for the dense black smoke. The last thing I can remember was holding a wet towel over my face and lying on the ground. When I realised what was going on, it was too late to struggle, they had me in the dreaded locks and were hastily dragging me down the corridor towards the seg unit again.

'That's it, Holland, you'll not see the light of day in this prison again,' the screw shrieked at me through the Judas flap of the cell door. The next day, two CID from Falkirk came and charged me with fire raising and putting the safety of others at risk, but none of the screws was ever charged with being a pure animal towards me. They get off scot-free as per usual. I lay languishing in the forgotten world of the seg block on the rule for four-and-a-half months before I was told the news I'd been waiting for since I first went down the seg block.

'Holland,' the screw said gleefully, 'you're going down to Dumfries where all the little hard men are, that will sober you up.'

Little did the screw suspect, but this news was like music to my ears. Dumfries was where most of my pals were. At least you were treated like an adult, not like this Polmont pitch. I can tell you, I more than resented Polmont. This was a stomach-turning place, not because I couldn't cope with it, oh no! It was because the way the screws treated the boys that were sent to it like dirt. They should have blown the fucking pitch off the face of the earth. I don't know how the young boys get treated nowadays, but I hope it's better than the way they treated all of us then. I would just like to say to all of you rotten screws that punched and kicked me and the hundreds of other young boys, I hope you all rot in hell, you're worse than the worst animals I've ever met, and that includes us prisoners.

DUMFRIES YOUNG OFFENDERS, SEPTEMBER 1989

Her Majesty's Young Offenders Institution Jessiefield (HMYOI Dumfries), as it's locally known, is in Dumfries, down at the borders. I'd never felt so far down in myself before, to be truthful. At first, I thought Dumfries was in England. The jail is the third oldest in Scotland, after Perth and Peterhead. Driving in through the main gate of the prison was like taking a step back in time to the 1920s.

There it was, in all its sullen majesty. I winced at what lay ahead, as the place seemed to glower at me from behind incongruous flowerbeds. The halls were decorated with pigeons' nests on every available window ledge. The windows were old Victorian ones and the walls had green slime and moss oozing out of them like some big abscess ready to burst. From the road, we drove over the cobbles and up to the reception.

'Oh, here we are,' the driver of the mini van said, 'Dumfries Young Offenders.'

Two starched-collar screws came out from an old green door to meet us.

'Listen up,' one of the two voiced, 'when I call your name out, shout out your reg number. Holland!'

'14806, sir,' I swiftly replied.

This cacophony between screw and YO went on until the last of the other three boys had shouted their names out. The screw enquired, 'Have any of you been here before?'

We all answered 'no' by shaking our heads from side to side.

'OK, follow me,' he ordered.

We got off like the animals from Noah's Ark, two by two. The reception had a strong aroma of industrial disinfectant.

'How long are you doing, son?' the screw asked me.

'Four years,' I replied.

'What about you?' the screw asked one of the others.

'Seven years.'

'And you, little man?' he said, pointing at the smallest of our group.

'Five years, sir,' the boy said back.

'Here, son, how long are you doing?' he asked the last boy.

'Twelve years, boss,' the boy shouted back.

'It's, *Sir*,' the screw yelled back.

'No,' the boy retorted, 'it's boss of fuck all.'

'Oh, Tony,' the screw warned his colleague, 'we've got a right, little, hard man here! OK, sonny.'

The screw named Tony started walking menacingly towards the boy and seethed, 'Do as you're told in here; do you hear me, boy?'

'Do I look like a fucking prick to you?' the boy responded fearlessly.

To my surprise, and instant gratification, the screw stopped dead on the spot as if an invisible wall was in place between him and the boy.

'OK, boy, have it your own way,' he spat dejectedly.

I'd seen, for the first time, another young offender sticking up for himself. From that day onwards, I had respect for that boy who went on to prove himself through his late teens, his twenties and early thirties. The boy in question is now a top businessman; I'll call him Johnny. Anyway back to the story, Johnny, the two other boys and I left the reception.

'OK, stop here,' the reception screw ordered. The sign on the wall, just above the door read, *Welcome to B-hall*. We could all hear a barrage of noise coming from the other side of this big, thick, wooden door. Without warning, the door swung open. All I could see was a horde of young boys and young men running about like a colony of ants. They'd invaded the place and were over us like a spring shower. It didn't take them long to ask us where we came from, how old we were and whether we smoked.

'Oi, here, you. Ya bam,' a big boy of over 6ft 3in screamed down to one of our group, 'I'm going to fucking slash you, ya grass.'

I turned round to see who the unlucky bastard was that this monster of a boy was shouting at. It was one of the other boys who was doing seven years.

Spontaneously, all the young prisoners started chanting: 'GRASS! GRASS! GRASS!'

The reverberating noise booming around the hall was deafening.

As fast as lightning, the boy being chanted at ran into the screws' office screaming, 'Get me out of here, get me out.'

'OK, boys, you've had your fun for one day, back to your cells,' the screw ordered us. We were shown to our cells. I was put into cell number eight, which was on the second flat. Someone was tapping on my wall and then someone called out for me to put my head down to the pipe that ran through all of the cells to keep the place warm. The boy's name was Paul Ness and he was from Edinburgh. I called him Nessy.

'What's your name?' he asked.

'Jimmyboy, pal,' I shouted back through.

'What jail did you come from?' Nessy asked.

'Polmont,' I shouted back, best as I could.

One question led to another and we were getting on like a house on fire after I managed to pull off some of the cladding around the hole in the wall where the pipe went through. I asked him who the big boy was that was calling the new boy a grass.

'That's Pat Crawford,' Nessy told me.

I didn't know it at that time, but I'd soon be one of Pat's pals. A few mates that I met in Greenock Young Offenders were down here, so I knew a couple of boys like Raymie Dalgarno from Aberdeen, Little PK from Paisley, Mouse Egan, Aldo Aitkenhead and Fat Mick, so it wasn't as if I never knew anyone.

Nessy told me how the place was run. 'We go back to the sheds after dinner until 4.30pm, then back here for tea, then we're banged up until 6.15pm, then down to recreation or PT until 8.30pm, then back to our cells to slop out. Then at 8.55pm, it's bang-up for the night. Monday to Friday, Saturday and Sunday, we're banged up at 4.45pm until the next morning.'

On the way to the worksheds, I stood there hoping to catch a glimpse of my pals. Five minutes after, I was standing at the window and I spotted Mouse.

'MOUSE! MOUSE!' I screamed at the top of my voice.

'Aye, hello, who's that?' he shouted in reply.

'Jimmyboy,' I replied.

'What, Jimmy Holland! How are you doing, Jimmyboy?' he asked in disbelief at hearing me.

'Brand new,' I shouted back.

'I'll have a chat with you tonight at recreation, Mouse,' I said.

'OK, mate,' he replied hurriedly, as he strode off to the sheds.

'I'll see you tonight,' I finished.

I stood and watched the rest of the young offenders walking to their worksheds. The sun was splitting the trees outside. I felt red hot and was starting to spit feathers. I took my prison shirt off to cool down, when suddenly the door sprang open.

'Are you, 14806, J Holland?' the screw asked me.

'Yes, sir,' I bounced back.

'Get your shirt on and follow me,' he instructed.

I did as I was told; I met Johnny and one of the other boys that I came down with.

'OK, listen up, you're going to the surgery, so the doctor can see you,' the screw informed us.

On the way to the surgery, Johnny informed me that the cunt we came down with had stuck Big Pat in at the High Court some two years earlier, so Big Pat had all the rights to threaten the little grass. Just a point worth mentioning here, grassing and beasting are not tolerated. They would be slashed, stabbed or have the face burned off them with a kettle for breaking the prison code of conduct.

Well, in my opinion, Pat was right in what he done. Even at first, when he was screaming down, he couldn't have been doing it all for nothing, but I felt better after I knew the score because I was taken aback at first. One by one, the doctor saw us, gave us the all-clear and then we headed back towards the hall.

'No, no! Where are you going, this way,' the vexed screw demanded. 'I'm going to take you round the sheds.'

I was nervous and excited at the same time. We went into the joiners shop. I saw my pal, Mouse, who came over and we shook hands. Mouse told me that the jail was brand new. 'The screws on the whole don't bother you unless you bother them,' he told me.

'Holland, come on,' the screw that was showing us around shouted.

'Coming, sir,' I said.

Mouse burst out laughing. 'Don't call them *sir*, Jimmy, call them *boss*, everyone calls them boss.'

'I will then,' I said to my friend Mouse 'I'll call them *boss*.'

We went through a door into a different workshed; this

one was the textile shop where my pal Raymie Dalgarno from Aberdeen was.

'Jimmyboy,' he shouted from amidst the crowd of boys that were sitting, 'how are you doing, little man?'

I repeated what I'd told someone else earlier, 'Brand new.'

'What floor are you on?' he asked me.

'Second floor, where are you?' I asked back.

'I'm on the top floor. You're going to the recreation tonight, mate?' he asked. I replied that I was.

'I'll bring you a couple of joints down and a ¼ oz of Golden Virginia.'

'Cheers, Raymie boy,' I gratefully replied.

'OK, let's go,' the impatient screw said.

We went through another door into the painters. There, stood in front of me was a midget; he wasn't any taller than four-and-a-half feet with his shoes on. I burst out laughing ... sorry, I couldn't help myself and I should have known better. I could find a fault in someone in less than a split second, which wasn't hard to do on this occasion.

He tottered up to me and said, 'Do you find something funny, boy?'

I didn't know he was the head of this shed.

'No, sir, no, I don't find anything funny,' I said, as I stifled any thoughts of more laughing. I mean; this was like meeting wee Jimmy Krankie ... fandabidozi! No one knew it then, but he would go on to be found guilty of flashing and tampering with young children. These were not the sorts of people that we wanted to look after us. Anyway, Johnny, the other boy and I made it back to the hall. That night, we had a great time at recreation. I was out of my face on hash, telling jokes and meeting new people from different parts of Scotland.

I've got a few good memories of my time in Dumfries. I remember one time, I was working in the cookhouse with a bunch of other boys: Tam McC, Kev L, Scott McK and a few others. We were all smoking hash when I came up with an idea to give them a laugh – as I've already said, I'm a bit of a comedian when I want to be. I got up, took a couple more deep draws on the joint. As I made my way into the giant walk-in fridge, I said to Tam, 'You and the others, open the door in a minute.' I fired straight in and pulled the door shut behind me. It was freezing and dark. I fumbled my way over to where all the raw chickens were. Once I got one, I pulled down my pants and stuck my private parts in the neck of it for a buzz.

The fridge door flew open. I was standing there with my privates in this chicken. When I saw who it was that opened the door, the air of expectancy on my face disappeared faster than a line of cocaine in a low-rent Govan bedsit! It wasn't my pals that opened the door ... it was the flaming cook himself! They had turned the tables on me and had told him, for a laugh, that I was hiding in the fridge, so you can imagine my face and his when he clapped eyes on me like that. I started stuttering, saying that it was only a joke. He was purple in the face with rage. Up until that time in my life, I had never been more embarrassed.

All my prison pals were standing behind the cook, pissing themselves laughing. I can see the funny side of it now, but not at the time. I was put on what's called governor's report. The next day, in the orderly room, when the governor asked me what was hiding in the evidence bag, I told him it was a chicken. He said he knew that and not to be smart.

'I'm not being smart, sir,' I pleaded.

'OK, Holland,' the governor said as he looked at the rap sheet, 'you are charged with exposing yourself and breaking health and hygiene codes. I have no option but to sack you from the cookhouse and give you fourteen days' punishment in the digger without a bed through the day.'

I was kind of used to that way of life already from being in the Polmont digger. Another time, I was in the workshed when the bell went off for all of us to go back to the halls early. No one knew what for, but we soon found out. My pal Mouse and his pal, Kenny Platt, had dug a hole in the roof of the PT building and climbed up on to the roof of the jail. As the rain belted down, Mouse and Kenny were only wearing PT shorts and a vest, but that didn't put them off. The speed at which the two of them ripped slate after slate off the roof, and the way they were throwing them down into the car park to smash car windows, you'd have thought the local roofing contractor and Auto Windscreens were paying them.

Then a team of riot screws came running out of a door, whereupon Mouse and Kenny started throwing well-aimed slates at them. They were holding big plastic riot shields up to protect themselves from the onslaught ... they were like ants in a hailstorm! A man's voice boomed out over a loudspeaker, 'Can we not talk about this, lads?'

'Fuck you,' I heard Mouse shout. '*Anti-screw crew*, if you want us, you'll need to fucking come up here and get us, you dirty pricks!'

At that, every boy on that side of the hall let out a big cheer for the two of them. This went on for about three or four hours before the cold had got the better of the two of them. Without breaking any rooftop-siege records, the bedraggled and wet pair came down into the arms of the awaiting riot screws. And, surprisingly, for a change, they never suffered any beatings; they got taken to the digger and put on a rule, pending police investigation. Some nine months later, the two kings of the roof stood trial and received eighteen months apiece on top of their sentence ... oh, and the roofing contractor was ecstatically happy.

Another time, a few of the boys, Pud Jefferies and a couple of others, and I had a bucket of home brew that was just about coming to maturity. Our brew would have been ready to drink within the week. None of us had an inkling about the screw spying on us as we secreted this bucket of nectar back into the hideout we had made for it.

The next day, when we went to add more sugar to our illicit brew, it wasn't there! We were all gutted because we'd gone out of our way to keep it a secret so no one would find it, but some lucky bastard had. As we searched for answers, a screw swaggered into the hall like a dog with two tails; he was swinging the previously full bucket around his arm by the handle, like a hoopla-hoop. He asked us if we'd lost something. Pud just blew his top and blindly bolted towards the screw. As the screw's nose burst open from the impact of Pud's granite head, the screw was thrown backwards to the ground faster than a priest out of a brothel window during a police raid! For Pud's sake, we had to pull him off the scumbag screw.

At that exact time, another screw on the second flat spotted what happened so he hit the riot bell for backup. We never had much time, so we opened up the fire hoses in readiness for when the screws ran into the hall. We blasted the unsuspecting screws from our makeshift water cannon, then we all rolled about on the wet floor – it was magic to have a running battle with the enemy. We all ended up in the digger, again, for three months, but we were young and doing things like that was just part of our rites of passage, as we travelled through this human zoo.

Around about September or October, I was sitting in the joinery shed when, out of the blue, a guy punched me in the mouth and told me he wanted a ¼ oz of Golden Virginia from me every week. He was trying to bully me. I'll not put his name down because I'm embarrassed to say who it was, but he's a well-known pure prison bam ... as thick as two building bricks! Anyway, I told my pal Big Pat what happened, and he wasn't too happy; he wanted to smash fuck out of this prick. I told Pat to leave it. 'I'll do it,' I said.

'That's it, little man,' Pat applauded, 'stick up for yourself.'

Let me just tell you, there was a lot of bullying going on in the young offenders that the screws turned a blind eye to. I picked up a wooden chisel and, once the boy sat down, I stuck the wooden chisel through his ribs and leg. The cowardly cunt started screaming, 'You've stabbed me, you've stabbed me.'

I said through clenched teeth, 'The next time you try and bully any cunt, I'll fucking murder you!'

Pat was so proud of me. 'That's it, little man, don't take any more shit from any boy in here.'

And, from that day on, there would be no more bam-ups or getting battered from my fellow cons. I'd already put a stop to screws trying to be wide, because I'd just attack them, now I was doing it to other boys that a couple of months beforehand I was scared of.

I also met a young boy called John Simpson; he'd just turned sixteen years old. For his age, he was a giant – 6ft 1in tall and nearly fifteen stone of pure muscle. Now, John could handle himself all right, but no one could have predicted that, nine years after meeting him, he'd be brutally and fatally shot four times in the chest. That was after surviving an earlier attempt on his life, when he was shot in the head at point-blank range.

Well, it was this boy John who told me to stab, slash, cosh, bite, kick or punch anyone that wants to fight, as that's what he'd done while growing up. Even though this boy was younger than me, I took his advice. I got put on a rule, even though the screws couldn't prove it was me that stabbed the boy, but they had an idea that it was me. I was kept on the rule from October until the beginning of January the following year.

Then I was ghosted to Glenochil Prison, which was a cons' jail for people aged twenty-one years and over. I'd turned twenty-one in the December and was now officially classified as an adult. What a way to celebrate a birthday, Christmas and New Year, lying ruled up in a punishment block. It was my first one spent in solitary, but certainly not the last. I promised myself that I wouldn't get into any trouble in Glenochil Prison.

CHAPTER NINE

This is a Man's World

GLENOCHIL, JANUARY 1992

On the way up to Glenochil Prison from Dumfries, the roads were coated in silver ... with a thick layer of ice on them. The gritters were out battling against what Mother Nature threw at them. I was freezing my balls off in this brass-monkey weather while huddled in the back of the blue jail van. I was handcuffed to one of my pals, Joe, who was being shipped on an inter-prison visit to Perth Prison to see his brother, Rab.

My fellow prisoner was a couple of months younger than me; he was from Parkhead, in the Eastend of Glesga. We had a right good snigger, catching up with all the jail politics that were happening in the hall, as I didn't know what was happening from being on the rule. The two hours in transit flew by and, before I knew it, we were just outside Glenochil Prison. The place was impressive, to say the least. The van didn't stop until we were on the secure side of the prison gates. This was my stop, and Joe would be travelling onwards.

'Right, Joe, I'll catch you later, mate,' I said warmly, as I shook his hand, 'mind, tell all the troops back down the road I send them my regards.'

'Aye, don't worry, mucker,' Joe consoled, 'I'll drop you a line at the weekend.'

'Joe, that would be brand new,' I gushed.

I hate saying cheerios to the people you grow close to in the jail. One minute, you're all pally and hang out with the guy for years, then bang! One of you gets moved or one of you gets outlived. Being sure to conceal any emotion, I cast an eye to the now moving prison van; it was taking Joe and the three screws that brought me to this jail swiftly out of the heavily fortified main gate. The reception screw's voice dispersed my lingering moment of sadness, 'Right, James.'

I was taken aback at the screw's politeness; I'd never been called 'James' by a screw before. There was also a prisoner by the name of Feg that worked with the screw in reception. Over the next few years, I got to know Feg. I knew straight away that he was no mug: he stood 6ft 2in tall, and his long hair was in a bandana. He had a big, Mexican-style moustache and his arms were rippling with muscles.

'James,' the screw's last word rang in my ear.

I politely mustered up, 'My name's Jimmy.'

'OK, Jimmy,' the screw said, 'what size shoe do you take and what waist size are you?'

I told him what he wanted to know and Big Feg went into a side room and came out with the garments in his hands.

'There you go, little man,' he flashed. 'I keep a stash of good clobber for the Westcoast troops, know what I mean?' He gave me a friendly wink.

Another screw came into the reception area. 'Hello, Bertie,' he said cheerfully to the other screw, 'is the boy ready?'

I was standing in the dog box putting on my jail shirt; the adrenalin was surging through my veins. I wasn't scared, I was excited at finally being in a cons' jail – a man's jail! But I wasn't blindly entering the lion's den; this place was a war zone of drugs and poison that went with the territory. I reached the hall and, once inside, a bunch of hard and tricky-looking, heavily tattooed bastards were huddled in a crowd on the stairs; they were waiting to rob the nurse of her medical bag. I didn't know this at the time or any of the boys involved, but I now know them all, and I'm pally with a couple of them. You know who you are, eh, troops?

I made it on to the flat where I met another screw. I'll not mention his name, but he's a total animal, a real hothead! Even to this very day, he kicks about. I will call him Joe Bloggs. Not knowing his background and accepting him as a dummy, I reached out and shook his snakelike hand. This screw told me he'd received a phone call from a screw in Dumfries telling him all about me, which was really a euphemism for telling me my card was marked and I'd be on his hit list.

The first thing they did to intimidate me was to put me next door to a man that I can only define as being totally mad, his name's Stevie Mc from Edinburgh. Stevie had been up in Carstairs five times. The reputation this man had amongst the other cons in the hall was fearsomely gruesome. I didn't know it then, but the screws had set Stevie up to try and give me a fright. I don't care what any other person says about Stevie, as he was a brilliant cunt to me. I used to get some buzz with him. The screw's game had backfired on him when Stevie told me Joe Bloggs had pulled him in and asked if Stevie would bash me up a bit because I was a bit of a 'smart arse'.

The idea of being told what to do by a screw repulsed Stevie.

Don't get me wrong, back then I would have rolled about with Stevie, but I knew, within my heart of hearts, that he would have given me it tight, but, thankfully, not one blow was struck towards me. My pal Macky from Royston was on this flat and no sooner had he found out I was in the hall than he came down to see me. I couldn't hold having a big nose like Barry Manilow against Macky, as he was a spot-on guy and the patter that came out of his mouth was top dollar. Macky knew how to make people burst out laughing. Everyone in the jail loved the bald Macky boy. Within two years of coming to this jail, Macky and thirteen other cons would develop HIV, three of them have now since died. God bless them.

'Have you had a charge yet?' Macky quizzed me.

'No, not yet,' I quickly replied.

'Come on, leave your stuff,' Macky enthused.

I followed my pal up to the section he was in.

'This is my little mate, Jimmy,' Macky said to all of his pals and fellow cons that were in his section.

The introductions out of the way, we went into his cell where he told me to close the door over. No sooner had I done this and turned back around than Macky had a set of 2mm needles in his hand and a £20 bag of heroin.

'On you go,' I gushed to my pal.

'I knew you'd like it. Keep your foot at the door, Jimmy, don't let any cunt in at all,' he said quietly, as he cooked the heroin up on a spoon. 'Right, little man, you can go first,' he invited.

Without further ado, I rolled up my sleeve and Macky gave me a hit. Once it hit me, I felt on top of the world! He let the blood run back into the tools and then pushed it back into my arm. This technique is called flushing, the more you did this, the quicker the heroin surges around your body. The hairs on the back of my neck felt tingly. He pulled the needle out of my arm and washed it out, then he made himself up a hit.

'Fuck, Macky,' I asked excitedly, 'is it like this all the time?'

'Most of the time, Jimmyboy,' he answered with a smile across his face as big as the noonday sun.

A desperate voice sounded from behind the partially closed door that I still had my foot against. 'Macky, Macky, let me in, it's Meechy.'

'Let him in, Jimmy,' Macky chortled.

Meechy was Macky's pal from the Eastend of Glesga. I knew him in the young offenders, but didn't sit with him. On recognising me, Meechy asked, 'How are you doing, Jimmy?'

'Brand new, pal,' I replied.

'When did you come up, little man?' he asked.

'About an hour ago. Here, it's some place this, Meechy, eh, mate?' I cooed. 'Aye, Jimmy, this mob let us away with murder,' Macky said, as he burst into laughter.

'When's little Gordieboy due up?' Macky asked me.

'Eh! Oh, I think it's another couple of months,' I responded.

'Little Gordie's brand new,' Macky praised.

'I know, brother, he's a wee diamond,' I confirmed, as I went on to tell him how he had helped me out. 'I was shouting on him from the digger every night, he'd send me down some snout and a little charge nearly every night. I hope he gets this jail.'

'What jail's he put in for?' Macky asked.

'Here and Shotts,' I told him.

Meechy said, 'This flat's spot on, there's only a couple of guys older than forty-five, all the rest are young guys. You'll know a power of them, ' he proffered, and he rattled off a boatload of names. 'Geo Stillie, Johnny Huton, Wullie McCausland, Fats, Carrotts, Jimmy Graham, Bilko B, Tommy Gordon, Stevie McNair, Livi, Farkie, Gogs F, Cha G and many more.'

The couple of old guys were Kenny Kelly and Sammy Martin. The rest of that day was spent making new friends and having a gas with everyone. I started work in the textile shop with Macky, Bilko, Johnny and Wullie. We all sat at the one table having a great time. The old-time gangster Walter Scott Ellis from the late fifties used to sit in front. He was the last man in Scotland to miss the hangman's rope. His book's called *The Arch Criminal of Glasgow*, but I think it might be out of print now. This man was a real character from days gone by.

I remember this particular incident one day when a boy called Tiny was getting married, four days after he bumped Wattie for his stuff. The old yin waited until the time Tiny was walking towards his sewing machine with a batch box in his hands that was full of material. Old Wattie stopped in front of him and flung a belter of a right-hander into Tiny's face, blacking his eye in the process.

'That'll teach you, you young yin, to fuck me about,' he quipped.

Tiny got married with a black eye. When he got his wedding photos back, in every one of them, he had a belter of a black eye. Old Wattie got a good laugh at it. Another time, one of his own old pals was sitting at Wattie's machine when he spat on the ground in front of him; Wattie stuck a stitch pick through his arm and called him a dirty animal. What a man our Wattie is.

Some months after I came here, Macky and I were plotting and planning how to raise the money for a tenner bag of smack, so we ended up going through the screws' jackets that they had hanging behind the door of their office. I kept the screw talking about a lot of shit, while Macky rummaged through their jacket pockets. Once Macky had safely walked out of the office, I fannied the screw up and made my way to Macky's cell. Once safely inside, he opened a little plastic green wallet thing. We couldn't believe our eyes! We'd got £18 out of it and a photo of what must have been his bird or wife. Macky gave me a big hug and we started dancing and flinging high fives.

'Come on,' I said, 'we should get two bags for it,' and off we went to see the con that was punting the happy bags.

'Look, mate, we've got £18, will you give us two bags?' we asked the dealer.

The prick refused, so we had to threaten him at knifepoint and he ended up giving us the two bags.

'What was so hard about that?' I demanded of the dealer.

'Nothing,' the boy told us, 'but it's not mine. I'm only doing it for someone else.'

Macky retorted, 'Are you trying to scare us by saying that it's some cunt else's, now!'

'Macky, no mate, I'm just telling you,' he replied feverishly.

Macky fumed, 'Tell the boy that he's lucky he's not getting it taken off him. Come on, Jimmyboy, let's go.'

We left the boy's cell at a brisk pace and with an air of anticipation, and eagerly made our way back down to Macky's, where we got our hits made up and took them. I love sticking the needle in a couple of different veins – on my neck, arm, hands or legs. Once we took a couple of flushes, we were gouching – an appearance of nodding off to sleep – for fifteen or so minutes.

Macky remembered he had to see old Sammy about the jewellery box he was making for Macky's mam. Old Sammy was and still is the best at making stuff out of wood in the jail; he had a little cottage industry set up making anything up to £300 a week. I followed Macky into old Sammy's cell, and what we saw sent shivers of revulsion through our veins. Macky walked in first, with me directly following behind. I wasn't watching where

I was going, so, when Macky stopped suddenly, BANG! I crashed my head into his back and burst my lip open!

Getting a shag in these places was as likely as being hit on the back of the head with a snowball in hell ... our cocks were starting to look like pistol grips, so, when I looked up and saw old Sammy having full anal intercourse with someone I called the Dundee poof, this was unreal! The poof turned his head towards Macky and me. He told us he would stab us if we said anything to anyone, and I don't think he meant that he would stab us up the arse with his dick. As fast as we had gone into his cell, we were out of there as fast as a bullet. We hadn't left sharpish for fear of what the poof had said he'd do to us, but more out of being gobsmacked at what we'd just witnessed. As soon as we got outside, we burst out laughing.

We made it back to Macky's cell where we couldn't stop sniggering. After a while, Meechy, Dougie McKenzie, God bless him, and a couple of others came into the cell.

'What are you two sniggering at?' Meechy asked.

Macky told them what we'd just seen.

'What did the Dundee poof say?' Meechy enquired.

'He would stab us if we told anyone, but fuck him,' Macky insisted.

'By the way,' one of the others in the group said, 'because he's murdered a guy in jail, he thinks no cunt's going to stand up to him, that'll be right.'

That was it, war was declared on him.

A couple of days had gone by when I was told, 'The poof wants to see you.'

I went up and saw him, with a dagger concealed up my sleeve. The poof was sitting in my pal's cell. When I went in, Johnny was shouting at him, but, when he saw it was me, he turned his anger in my direction.

'Here, Jimmy, have you told anyone about me and old Sammy?' he demanded.

I glibly replied, 'Yes, everyone.'

'What did you do that for?' he growled.

'Because I did,' I replied, 'and it's the truth ...' but before I finished the sentence, I pulled my dagger out and stabbed him five times in the chest and stomach.

'Jimmy, what are you doing?' he screamed as he fell to the floor.

I told him to shut up, and then I stabbed him twice more. I think he was more shocked that someone would even try and stab him because he'd just killed a prisoner and got a lifer for it.

'Don't think you're going to walk about like Lord of the Manor when you're just a fucking poof,' I fumed.

I got off him and left the cell to get rid of the dagger. Johnny darted after me and said he thought the poof was dead on the cell floor.

'Fuck him,' I raged to Johnny.

In a state of panic, Johnny told the screws that, when he walked into his cell, he'd found the poof on his floor stabbed to fuck.

'LOCK UP! LOCK UP!' the screws started shouting.

CHAPTER TEN

Smacked Up

Amidst the pandemonium, the riot bell was pressed and about another twenty screws came running on to the flat. We all got pushed and shoved into all sorts of different cells. Once in the cell, Carrotts, Fats, Jimmy G and Geo S told me to strip and clean my nails in the sink. I hastily did as I was instructed, changed into clean clothes that were lying about in the cell and washed myself down. My old bloodstained clothes were set on fire and were sent flying out of the window in a blazing fury.

We heard the paramedics whizzing by our cell door with a trolley. I asked Carrotts if he thought the poof was dead.

Carrots speculated, 'Well, he might be dead. You didn't miss him!'

' Too fucking right,' I glowed, 'it was either him or me.'

Fats and Jimmy G agreed, 'You did the right thing, fuck him.'

Our cell door opened up and we were taken to our respective cells for a strip search and cell search. Once they had done this, my door was opened again. This time there were seven screws.

'Look, Holland,' the most senior of them announced, 'we're taking you to the digger.'

I was led away and put in the digger. Once the screws went away, I heard a bang on my wall followed by a voice calling out. 'Who's that?' the voice in the cell next door asked.

'Jimmy Holland,' I shouted back, hoping my voice could be heard through the thick cell walls.

'All right, Jimmy, it's Taggs here,' came the muffled reply.

'Is that you, Beufford?' I yelled.

'Yes, little man,' Beufford hollered back.

To most people, Beufford was called Taggs, so I'll just call him Taggs from now on.

'What you down for?' he asked.

'Fuck knows,' I innocently replied, 'this rotten mob said I stabbed the Dundee poof.'

'Do you want a smoke sent in?' Taggs offered.

'Yes, big chap, how long have you been down here for now, Taggs?' I enquired.

'Oh, Wullie and me have been down here for three months for fuck all, I kid you not, little man, it's a fucking dig out,' he professed.

'Holland,' a screw called through the Judas flap on my cell door, 'get yourself ready, the CID are here to see you.'

All sorts started running through my head, *he must be dead, that's it!* I said to myself, *I'm done for!* Looking me straight in the eyes, one of the two coppers barely whispered, 'Hello, Mr Holland, is it James, Jim or Jimmy? OK, son, you know why we're here.'

'No,' I replied cantankerously, 'I have not got a clue.'

The copper pointed his finger at me and, in mock certainty, coughed up, 'Come off it! You know why we're here, you stabbed a boy, who's now critically ill in hospital.'

'No, mister,' I angrily replied, as I pointed my finger at him, 'you've got the wrong guy,' I declared in mock anger.

'Oh, have we indeed?' the copper said scornfully, with his face screwed up.

'Yes,' I retorted, as I withstood the onslaught of his unremitting questioning and wrestled with what would come next.

'Well, who's responsible?' they invited me to answer.

'I don't know,all I know is, it wasn't me,' I insisted, as I pointed my finger at myself.

The younger of the two coppers pulled a couple of bits and bobs out of his war-torn case. 'OK, Jimmy, we're going to take a hair fibre, your prints and a scrape from under your nails, OK, son?'

'No problem,' I replied, still feigning innocence.

'Do you know that the boy's got a punctured lung and his liver's been cut open, he might not pull through the night,' the copper with the case sighed, as he shook his head from side to side.

I told them that I hoped the poof would make a speedy recovery because I liked him. I don't know if any of them picked up on my lie.

'Right, you'll be hearing from us soon, Jimmy,' one of the coppers finished.

'No, bother, I'll be here and I'll also be glad to help you track down the boy that done this,' I ended. I never heard from them again.

Don't get me wrong, I'll give the poof his dues, he never opened his mouth, as he's old school, just like the rest of us. Even though he's a poof, he's not a grass. As I've told you earlier, he murdered a fellow con, and half the treacherous cunts in the hall in Greenock YOI shattered the golden rule of keeping schtum and dropped him and his co-accused in it for murdering another prisoner. With this in mind, he had no reason to remain loyal when it came to him keeping schtum over what I'd done to him.

For the first and last time, I'll thank him for not grassing on me because it would have been so easy to do it. On the way back to the digger, I passed by Taggs, Wullie and Jim Irvine in the corridor; they were having exercise indoors because it was raining outside.

'How did it go, little man?' the three of them were keen to know.

'Brand new, the CID took hair samples, prints and the stuff under my nails. I've already told them, I've fuck all to do with what happened,' I announced, as I was led away.

Once in my cell, I heard Macky and Meechy shout across from B-hall, 'Jimmyboy, Jimmy.'

'Oh, hello, Macky,' I responded.

'Are you OK, mate?' they asked.

'I'm spot on,' I continued. 'I had the CID up seeing me there and, up 'til now, everything went well.'

They told me that the poof was in a critical condition in Stirling Royal. Later that night, when the screws had fucked off and left the all-night watchman on, Big Taggs asked if I took smack.

'Does a bear shit in the woods,' I said and continued, 'I'm rattling right now, man.'

'Give me a minute, little man,' he said.

A couple of minutes later, he flung me a line, which I got by reaching out of my cell window.

'Right, Jimmyboy, take the bag and joint out,' he instructed.

I desperately grabbed at the little bag that was tied to the line, pulled it in and ripped at it like a tramp raking through a five star hotel bin because my body was all sore from the lack of smack.

Heroin is a very ruinous drug to have a habit on. I was shaking and shivering. I was rattling that much that even my fingers were shivering. My hand was like an agitated tarantula. I couldn't keep my hand steady to empty the powder on to my spoon. I had two ml plugged up my arse; it's the safest stash in the jail. I got them out and fumbled to make up my hit, and, once I'd injected myself with the dark, honey brown liquid, I felt 1,000 times better. All caution was flung to the wind; I didn't have a care in the world, because I'd spent my whole life in one institution or another. Jail didn't and still doesn't bother me. I was lying in a bundle on my bed, out of my head when I heard someone up the stairs on the second flat of A-hall shouting at me.

'Jimmyboy!'

'Yes, who's that?' I nonchalantly asked.

'It's me – Joe,' came the reply.

'Joe who?' I asked.

'Joe Boyle.'

'All right, Joe? How are you doing, pal?'

'I am OK, little man,' he told me.

'When did you come down from Perth, Joe?' I asked

'This afternoon. Some cunt told me you were done with stabbing the poof,' he spilled out.

'Yes, but I'm OK,' I said to my friend who I hadn't seen since the Blue Triangle, in Govan.

'Danny's asking for you,' Joe said.

'Where's he, Joe?'

'He's up in Polmont, on a rule.'

Danny was doing ten years; his life sentence was dropped to a ten for murdering a gangster in Govan. He was doing six years for robbery, and he could go for Scotland. He was mixing it with gangsters ... he was off his head and battered every one of them;

he's now doing a life sentence after he got out from his six years.

Currently, Joe's up in Carstairs Mental Hospital, but I'm glad to say my friend has got his head sorted and is due for release soon. Good on him, I still stay in touch with Joe.

'Jimmy,' Taggs shouted through, 'how are you feeling now?'

'Spot on, pal,' I told him.

Wylie shouted, 'Little man, do you want to do a crossword down at the doors with us?'

'Yes, fuck it, I will, mate. Give me a minute,' I said.

We lay down at our respective cell doors 'til about 2.30 in the morning doing crosswords and swapping stories. I couldn't remember falling asleep; I came to the next morning with the sound of seagulls screaming out their ear-piercing shrills. Every morning's the same. They fly down and rummage around for scraps of food the cons fling out of their windows. I felt like shit because I was starting to rattle like a baby's toy for smack again. Twenty minutes later, the screws told me that I was up in front of the governor and to get myself ready. Once in at the governor's, he told me I was to be placed on a rule, out of circulation for the good order and safety of other prisoners and staff.

'Have a nice day,' I wished him.

I got taken back to the cellblock and apart from being fed and watered, I lay down there for seven weeks. Then the door of opportunity opened.

'Right, Holland, that's you going back to the hall,' the screw informed me.

I told them, in no uncertain terms, that I didn't want to go back to the hall: 'So, fuck off!'

They went out and slammed the door shut. They came back a couple of hours later with the PO (principal officer) leading the way.

'Look, young Holland,' he implored, 'you can't stay down here.'

'All right,' I begrudgingly said with a hint of sarcasm, 'get me up the hall then.'

I went back to the hall; I was put on the same flat as Big Taggs and Wylie. I made my way down to their cells.

'All right, little man,' Taggs greeted, as he put his hand out in a gesture of accomplishment.

I shook his hand and Wylie's.

'Come in and close the door.'

I didn't recognise Gordie at first because there were a few people in the cell.

'Hi, Jimmyboy,' my little friend said.

'All right, Gordie boy, I didn't see you there,' I said cheerfully, as I gave my pal a cuddle. 'On you go, little mate, it's great to see you.'

'And you,' Gordie boy said. 'What section are you in?'

'Section one,' I replied.

'So am I,' Gordie affirmed.

'Thank fuck,' I said in relief, 'at least we can talk to each other at nights.'

'Yes, I know, Jimmy,' Gordie replied cheerfully.

I was handed a freshly made joint that Taggs had very kindly constructed for me, and it was fucking colossal. The name given to such a joint is a 'cone'. After taking no more than four or five deep, lung-filling draws off this thing, my head was spinning, then I burst out laughing and started cracking jokes.

A couple of weeks later, my little pal from Edinburgh came to the jail. I was camped up with Scott in Dumfries, and it wasn't long before he had settled in. We were at the canteen one morning when the riot bell went off. Scott and another guy called Jim Sinclair and I were looking at each other in a knowing way, as the screw had to leave the canteen to help his pals out with the riot bell going off. All that was separating us from gaining entry to the goodies in the canteen was a small snib lock!

The screw hurriedly pitched, 'Look, I know it's only the three of you here, if anything happens to the canteen, I'm coming for you.' Then he bolted to the unseen riot that was taking place. Well, it turns out it wasn't really a riot; Joe Boyle was battering a con and two screws in the section.

I was asked by Scott if I could boot the door in because it was only the snib lock on. I told him that I thought the two of us could if we charged it at the same time. While Scott and I proceeded to demolish the flimsy door in half, Jim kept a lookout. When we kicked the part-smashed door out of the way and went in, the sight that filled our eyes caused them to wobble and dart about as though they were fixed on springs, as we tried to take everything in. We were like junkies in a Guatemalan smack factory!

We grabbed all the phone cards, the moneybox and snout that we could stuff down our shirts, and made a quick exit back to the flat. We quickly divvied the stuff up amongst the boys in the section. We weren't giving our fellow cons the stuff; they were only giving it a safe harbour, helping to counteract detection. The head drug dealer in the hall was approached by Jim and was asked if he wanted the nuggets – £1 coins – and the phone cards. He took the lot. We had over £200 in cash and seventy phone cards. Inevitably, Scott and I knew we were going to be flung back down the digger, but we weren't giving a fuck because we had eight £10 bags each stuffed up our arses. They could throw away the key, as far as I was concerned.

The third in the trio of canteen breakers, Jim, had a heart condition. So, when the shit hit the fan, Scott and I took the rap to save Jim getting put on a rule. Once they took us down to the cell block, again, it was starting to be a home from home for my pal and I. My pal from Perth, Joe, was already there. He had taken a benny – Benzedrine – and went mental in the hall, punching two screws on to their arses and breaking another con's nose and jaw. The guy was badmouthing Joe to other guys. When the screws tried to break it up, Joe went crazy. That'll teach those meddling fools that they should leave the cons to it.

A boy called Gogs Millan from Aberdeen and I were slopping out when we just lost the plot. I flung my piss pot full of piss round a screw's face and Gogs flung his shit-filled pot round another one. We ran at them like banshees, but, before long, we were lying on the floor with half a dozen burly screws sitting on us, punching our ribs and head to bits. After we were restrained, Gogs and I were taken into a couple of cells called 'silent cells', which is nothing to do with them being connected to a library. We were stripped naked and battered like fish. They left us like that for seven hours or so, and we were frozen to the bone.

After this punishment, we were given our clothes back and were put back into our original cells. We ended up going to court for it, and got six months consecutive added to our sentences, so I wasn't due out until March 1993. The rest of my time left in Glenochil, I was up and down from the digger. In fact, I got released from my sentence straight from the digger, which isn't supposed to happen. The prison service is supposed to get you ready to rejoin society, but they just count time and throw you back on to the scrap heap of life. Of course, HM Prison Service will deny this.

I was ruled up with Taggs, Bongo, Tessy, Duffy and Peter McGee. I told Taggs that, after my release, I'd be up in a couple of nights to do a parcel drop over the fence for them. Sure as fuck, two days after I got out, I was crawling through the woods like a seasoned commando with white tracksuit bottoms on! I might as well have had a flagpole stuck out from my arse 'Here I am' emblazoned on a flag, as I stood out like a sore thumb! I heard my pals talking at the windows on the bottom flat of A-hall. I gave them a little whistle so as they'd know I was there. Bongo whistled back, and hung a towel out of his window so I would know where to throw the tin.

I swung my arm back, brought it forward in an overhead throw like throwing a grenade and let it go. It smashed off the window on the second flat and fell down below Bongo's window! I bent down and hid in amongst all these bushes and marshland until I knew they'd fished the tin in and then I got a whistle of confirmation. I whistled back and made myself scarce.

A couple of weeks later when I was up seeing Taggs on a prison visit, the security principal officer, John, told me he knew it was me that was snooping about the woods a couple of weeks earlier. Some cons had stuck me in, bastards, but the screws couldn't prove fuck all, and I told them it had fuck all to do with me.

CHAPTER ELEVEN

Man in a Suitcase

EASTERHOUSE, DRUMMY, MARCH 1993

I can vividly recall the morning of my release from jail. I was full of myself. I jumped off the bus in the middle of Easterhouse; I was looking for the address where I was to meet up with Taggs's pal, Rusty. I found the address, no bother.

After I tapped on the shabby-looking door, a fit-looking female opened it and I asked her if Rusty was there. 'Yes, give me a minute,' she purred and pushed the door to.

The door opened, 'All right, Jimmyboy. Come on in,' Rusty invited.

'Jimmy, this is Alison,' Rusty introduced, 'and the little man's name is William.' He pointed to a sleeping baby. I asked Rusty if Taggs had phoned. 'Yes,' he said, 'he was just on the phone about forty minutes ago.'

'Do you want a cup of tea,' Alison offered me.

'No, I am OK,' I thanked her.

I was handed a small bit of hash by Rusty to roll a joint.

We sat there smoking joint after joint before he said, 'Fuck, come on, I've not shown you the house that you're going to be staying in.'

We headed round to the street.

'See that top-floor house up there, Jimmyboy,' Rusty pointed out, 'that's your house. Taggs's little brother, Phillip, stays with his bird, Sharon. Phil's still in the jail. Here are the keys to the house, go on, batter up and check it out,' he finished.

I went up. The place was brand new.

'OK, Jimmyboy?' Rusty asked.

'Yes, spot on, thanks, brother,' I replied.

'Come around every night to ours for your dinner,' Rusty invited.

'Spot on, Rusty,' I replied thankfully to his offer of kindness.

'Oh, before I forget, here's a little something to help you out,' Rusty said, as he held his hand out and thrust £200 in mixed notes at me. 'That should tide you over until you see the social security.'

I never had any plans to see the social, but Rusty didn't know that. Then, Rusty took me over to meet Sharon, Phil's bird. There were a couple of other boys I had never seen before in the house when Rusty and I went in. They all looked liked they were from the rogues gallery.

'All right, Rusty?' they all greeted in unison.

'Yes,' Rusty replied, 'this is Jimmy, he's one of Big Taggs's pals.'

'How are you doing?' the group of boys asked.

'I'm OK,' I returned casually.

'Do you smoke hash?' this boy of about sixteen asked me.

'Aye, little man,' I said, leaning over another boy, to get a joint.

'How do you know Big Taggs?' the same boy asked me.

'We were in the jail together,' I disclosed.

'My name's Muzz,' he said, 'Rusty's little cousin.'

'I am Sash, Muzz's big brother,' another one said.

The bird said, 'I'm Sharon,' putting an emphasis on, 'Phil's bird.'

'I know, Rusty was telling me,' I replied.

'Right, Jimmyboy, I need to get back round the road. You can stay here with them and I'll call back round tonight,' Rusty said.

'Yes, I'll be all right,' I replied reassuringly, as Rusty left.

'Jimmy, here's a space,' Muzz said, as he patted the settee and shifted along.

I sat down next to Muzz who had a little cheeky grin on his face. He had thc look of a Ned.

'Are you into jellies?' Sash asked.

'Yes, I love jellies, so long as they're not royal jellies,' I replied jokingly to Sash. He gave me seven 20ml jellies, which are sleeping tablets. I took them and before I knew it, I was buzzing off my nut. These tablets were also known as 'wobbly eggs', as they were shaped like eggs. I loved them. The hours flew by and, before I knew it, Rusty was back round to get me. We were going to the pub, then round a few doors to collect some money that people owed Rusty. One of the guys we called on was being lippy, not wanting to give Rusty his money. The boy never saw the punches coming. I smashed him on the chin at 60mph, four or five times, he stumbled backwards and into the corridor.

'That's enough,' Rusty said, 'leave him, Jimmy, he gets the message.'

Rusty told the boy he would be calling back to see him in a couple of days. We went back round to Sharon's house, where everyone was still bouncing all over the place. I took another five eggs to get into the swing of the party mood with the rest of the group.

My first two or three exploratory weeks in Easterhouse flew by, but I felt as if I wasn't pulling my weight, so I asked Rusty to get me a gun. He burst out laughing at me. No way was he giving me a gun. I had to ask Sash to get me one on the sly. At first, he was reluctant, but he eventually got me one, a nice, easy-to-handle .38 revolver. I felt like Dirty Harry, only my weapon wasn't as big as his! I don't know what it is with guns, but, once you've got your hand on one, you think you're one of the untouchables.

I was sitting in my house one day when Muzz came round to see what I was up to.

I told him, 'I'm skint, I'm going out to rob a post office or building society.'

I'll not say what I robbed; I'll just call them turns. Muzz didn't understand what I meant, so I told him that this was what I did for living, I robbed places. At this news, he was all excited and asked me if I could take him on a turn. I told him, 'Definitely not.'

He wasn't very happy with me, but I wasn't bothered, after all, he was just a kid. I told Muzz I'd meet him over at Sharon's, at nine or ten bells for a little party later that night, so long as he told Rusty and Sharon that he hadn't seen me all day.

'Is that a deal?' I offered in consolation to the little man.

'Yes, it's a deal, Jimmyboy,' Muzz said with a smile on his face.

Embarrassingly, I had to ask Muzz for the bus money down to the city centre. Here am I planning on doing a turn and I've not even got the bus money to get to it! Once I got off the bus in the town centre, my head was racing with mad thoughts. *What do I hold up, that place or that place or that place? Keep walking and walking*. I wasn't scared, I was excited, and the adrenalin was pumping through my veins and the feel-good endorphins were pummelling my brain! I ended up going into this turn, I couldn't believe it, there were eight or nine customers inside the place, but it was too late to turn back because I already had the gun on show in my hand!

'All right, listen up,' I barked. 'It's a fucking robbery, any cunt wants to be wide and I'll shoot them in the head.'

They all got the message quick. So did the guy and the girl behind the glass partition.

'Open that fucking door!' I screamed at the top of my voice.

The little bird opened it; I never even had a mask on. I was in there with my face up front and on show.

'Give me the fucking money, move it, move it,' I yelled menacingly at the guy and bird. 'Put the money into a plastic bag and give me it. OK, so far so good,' I said, backing out of the place, 'now just you all stay calm.'

Once outside, I put the boot leather down, and I ran round a few roads and through a few closes, changed my top, well ... I really just flung away the one I had on over my sweatshirt. I took a deep breath to get myself back to normal, then walked out of the front of this building, out to the main road and hailed a taxi over to Easterhouse.

'Pal,' I said to the driver, with an air of self-assurance about me, 'here we are, pal.'

The taxi driver said, 'That'll be £7.50.'

'Here's £10, keep the change,' I said.

I called in at the shop and got twenty fags and headed round to the house. Once safely inside, I stashed the gun under an old floorboard and counted the money. I had £1,300; I was pissing myself laughing at how easy it was to hold up certain places. I stuck £300 in my pocket and stashed the other £1,000 with the gun. Then I made my way over to Sharon's house where Muzz and Sash were lost to what was going on while playing on a Playstation. Sharon was busy in the kitchen.

'Hi, Jimmy, do you want a cup of tea?' Sharon offered.

'No, but I want twenty jellies,' I wisecracked.

'Oh, so do I,' she wished, 'but we've not got any money.'

I told her not to worry about the money. I asked Sash and Muzz if they wanted any, and they all did. I said to Muzz, 'Come on, little man, I'll come with you to score them.'

We bounced out of the close down to Provie, another scheme in Easterhouse, to buy seventy-five jellies.

'What did you do?' Muzz asked me.

'Fuck all that I'm telling you about,' I said, 'so don't ask me again, little chap. That way, everybody is safe if I ever get the jail. If you don't know anything, they can't try and turn you against me in the cop shop, plus it keeps you in the right.'

He was a brand new little guy, just your typical teenager from anywhere in Glesga. Eager to learn more, I discovered that Muzz and Sash came from a good parentage. Their mum and dad worked their hands to the bone to provide everything they needed. They were always telling their sons about the pitfalls of drugs. I never showed Muzz how to use or take drugs; by the stage I met them, they were into wobbly eggs, Valium, Es and hash, plus bottles of cheap wine and beer. I don't know too many boys at that age that aren't into one or all of the above.

I took a shine to Muzz straight away, and treated him like the little brother I never had. There was a six-and-a-half-year age gap between the two of us, so I think he looked up to me as well. We got sixty-five jellies, as the boy had run out of them. This certain boy, who I'll keep anonymous, was punting about 3,000 to 4,000 jellies a day to people on the other side of Glesga for £1 for every sleeper, so, you can imagine, there was a lot of money being made for the drug dealers.

I'm not going to be one of these people that say that these

dealers are scum, not at all, because, if it weren't that boy or this boy, then it would just be someone else. Let's face it, the cops couldn't control it and still can't. So it's down to the person that wants to buy it to stay away from them. No one has been threatened into swallowing jellies or to make them take a hit of smack the way the papers have made out over the years. The father grieving over his dead daughter blames the drug dealer for supplying her with dodgy ecstasy tablets, yet no one forced her to take them. It's a free country, or so they say.

We got back to the flat with our pockets jam-packed full of eggs and, to my surprise, Rusty was sitting in the house.

'Fuck,' he vexed, 'I was looking for you all day, Jimmy.'

I told him I was just out of my bed at twenty minutes past seven that night. 'How's everything, OK?' I sought reassuringly from my pal.

At seeing the mountain of jelly, he quickly settled from his irritable state. 'Yes, yes, brand new,' he chirped up, 'it was Alison, she'd made your dinner, and your denims and sweatshirt are washed and cleaned.'

'Thanks, pal,' I said to Rusty.

He asked me if I wanted any Es.

'Yes,' I said, 'what kind are they?'

'Barrels,' Rusty replied and then went on to extol their virtue, 'they're wicked, Jimmy. I was out of my box on them, last night.'

'Yes, Rusty,' I welcomed, 'give me a couple of them.'

From the five Rusty gave me, I swallowed two of them in a single gulp, gave Sash and Sharon one each and kept the other one. I held on to this E, as I was observing drug dealer's protocol by not giving Muzz his in front of Rusty. I was earlier told by Rusty that Muzz still owed him £15 for the two he got him the previous weekend. After a while, Sharon said that she was starving, so I said Muzz and I would go round the shop and get some munchies. Once I got out in the open and away from Rusty, I handed Muzz his E, and he was over the moon. We battered around to the shops and got all sorts of shit to eat and sixty smokes and a bottle of Buckfast, which Muzz and I drank between us in six gulps. This gave us some blow on top of jellies and Es, so you can picture the two of us; we were out of our boxes!

When we got back round to what we thought was *the* house, we found out that we'd only gone and walked into the wrong place. Luckily, Muzz knew the people and we all had a good snigger about it. By the time we got back, Rusty had left with his pal who had come round in a jazzy motor for him. I was glad he'd left because he didn't really like having Sash and Muzz around him, I don't know for what reason, because they were a great pair of boys. Maybe it was because he was their big cousin, I don't know.

This drugfest was like the bats coming out, and it turned into a daily occurrence. In order to fund them, I would go out and do a turn, then we'd get a party in Sharon's. Even if I had money stashed by, I'd still do turns. I was, by then, as addicted to the robberies as much as I was to the drugs. I was committed in body, soul, mind and spirit to all that was bad in life!

I got Muzz a leather jacket, at £300. I got it for myself then let Muzz jump about with it, as money wasn't any problem to me. I always had it and loved splashing it about. When I look back now, I'm a fucking idiot for not doing other things with it. I was popping jellies down my neck faster than a gambler feeding a slot machine, but I started jagging them with smack for an even more enhanced buzz, which is when my troubles started.

I soon met Rose and her family. Rose is my best pal Gordie's aunty, who stays in Easterhouse with her husband Macky and two girls, Lynn and Lizzy. I was asked by Gordie to look them up. Little Denny took me round to see them. I was going to get Gordie's uncle Macky to show me the whereabouts of the boy that got Gordie a life sentence. I was going to shoot him for what he did to Gordieboy, but Rose and Macky insisted, 'No, you're not, Jimmy. Thanks for the offer, but no.'

I found them to be a very caring family and they showed an interest in me, and Rose became like a mother and Macky a father figure to me. I loved it. I also had two girls I called my little sisters. Lizzy was the older; Lynn was only fourteen years old or so, but as bright as a button. Rose shook me when she asked, 'Do you take drugs?'

'No!' I lied.

As she looked at me, Rose opened up her heart, 'Look, Jimmy, I want to help you. I know you're on drugs, so this is the house rule: don't come around to our house on drugs or ever offer my daughters any drugs.'

I ended up telling Rose that I was mad with the jellies. I'll give that woman her dues, she tried and did help me stop jagging. She also put me wise to people that were just hanging on to me because I always had money and drugs. I couldn't see this because I was that out of my head. I was still going up every couple of weeks to see Big Taggs and, on these prison visits, he advised me I would need to stop robbing places at gunpoint and taking drugs. What I didn't tipple to was, he had it in mind to use me as a bit of hired muscle or to collect drug money or whatever. He was just using me. After a while, Rose, Macky and the girls finally put me wise to all the false generosity that Taggs and Rusty were showing me.

I was to be their enforcer, as Taggs had seen the potential of me in the jail and wanted to exploit that on the outside world as well. Once I told Rusty that I wasn't going to be any cunt's rocket, things started to go pear shaped, until one night it came to a head with eight or nine local Neds that hung about the shops. I was walking by them when two of them tried to stop me, so I stuck the nut on the one nearest to me, whereupon the other one bolted back over to the crowd. They all started talking, saying they were going to do this and do that. I was a bit paranoid because I didn't want to pull the gun out. I had no option; I'd started to walk the walk! I pulled the gun out from my waistband and pointed it at them. 'Do you want this?' I threatened, as I waved the handgun around and barked at them, 'The first cunt that comes near me is getting shot!'

That slowed them down. I then walked round to the house where I found Muzz slumped. He'd been stabbed through the left arm! I asked him what happened. He told me the gang at the shops had done it to him because he was running about with me.

After crazily searching for the knife attacker, Muzz's brother and I eventually got the boy in another part of Easterhouse. We did him over with a hammer and a pool cue; he looked like a piece of raw liver by the time we'd finished with him. I went round to Rusty's house to see if he knew anything, but his bird Alison lied to me when she said he wasn't in. I knew he was in, but I respected Alison, and I didn't want to call her a liar, as it had nothing to do with her.

'OK, I said, 'will you tell him I was round?'

'Yes, no problems,' Alison replied sheepishly.

I made my way round to Rose's where she already knew what had happened. She asked me if I was OK or hurt.

'No, I'm OK, Rose,' I said, as I saw the look of relief come to her eyes.

'Look,' Rose said, 'let that mob, Big Taggs and Rusty get on with things themselves.'

So I did, after all ... they were trying to use me. I was in a deadly game. One mistake or false move and I could have been next. I just carried on doing my turns, but this time I was keeping my money at Rose's. Even though I was out robbing, Rose helped me budget my money by taking me shopping for clothes, food and stuff. I respected her and still do, because she opened my eyes to some so-called pals.

Instead of visiting Big Taggs behind bars, I was up visiting Gordieboy a few times. Taggs didn't like it, but I wasn't giving a fuck because he was trying to use me. All the shit he told me about getting on my feet was pure piss, as he tried to get me working for him. Around about this time, Sash went out and tried to rob an all-night garage, but things went awfully wrong and he was done out the park. For his crime, Sash got five years in the young offenders because he was still only twenty-years old. I don't know why he tried to rob an all-night garage, as there's no point, because all the money gets flung down a tube into the ground. After that, Sash's mam and dad disowned him, they didn't visit and his bird flew the nest too.

Determined not to be seen to distance ourselves from Sash, Muzz, another lad called Copper, a girl called Theresa and I made our way to Longrigend to see Sash. Once in the visiting room, Sash got his bit of hash and twenty tems, but we didn't give him smack. I instructed Muzz, 'You can say you got Sash a parcel.' Muzz was in his glory and Sash was proud of him coming up with a parcel. I think he knew it was me that got him it, but he didn't say. Little did I know, but that would be the last time I would see Sash. Life pans out in the most peculiar of ways, as he hanged himself in jail, the poor cunt! I was gutted for him, and

Muzz and his family took it real bad. Then his mam took it a step further by saying it was because of me that Sash had robbed the garage. Well, to put the record straight, I had nothing to do with Sash robbing the garage. Later on, it came out that he was coming off smack and he couldn't handle the side-effects. R.I.P., my friend.

As for me, I scored another six years for robbery in June 1993. I was out of prison for a total of three months before I got done for the robbery. I've seen Muzz and phoned him on the odd occasion. While I was in Bar L, Rose and the two girls and Macky would visit me daily. I knew in my heart of hearts that I was getting another sentence, so what can you do except get your head down and get on with it? I stood in front of the judge, and he read me the riot act and sentenced me to six years, plus a further five years to run concurrent for the gun charge.

CHAPTER TWELVE

Hostage Takers Demand Rubber Dolls and Planes to Ibiza

BAR L (BARLINNIE PRISON), SEPTEMBER 1993

Barlinnie Prison stands on dark and bloody ground. It is a temple of lost souls, and a place of living nightmares. It's been the breaker of many a man's dreams for more than a century. This prison works to a model of penitence with no pretence of rehabilitation. The criminal population that society has forsaken has filled this once seemingly bottomless pit to overflowing with their despair and nightmares of pain. More specifically, it is the battleground of an undeclared war that still rages to this day between the screws and the cons. The screws, backed by their authority, would use violence, but in return the prisoners would have to resort to their cunning, guile, and the odd sudden act of violence.

Although I didn't get up to much in my time there, the place certainly made an impression on me. The hall was jet-black and smelled of rancid piss, and there were scurrying cockroaches in very cell. No one bothered about the hygiene. Instead, people were obsessed with drugs. Back then, the screws turned a blind eye to the drug culture, not like today where the screws are chasing you all about the hall to try and stop you from getting them or passing them on to your pals.

I had made good friends with a wee guy called Ronnie, who I knew from my shoplifting days. He was a little diamond. He had never had any sort of easy ride in his life, as his mam and dad were killed when he was a little boy, and his big sister booted him out of the house when he was fifteen years old when she caught him jagging tems in his bedroom. We continued to do drugs in prison. Ronnie would later be found dead after being stabbed through the heart in 1999. He had got into an argument with another boy over drugs when the other boy – who had been a life pal of Ronnie's – lifted up a kitchen knife and stuck it through his chest, puncturing his heart, poor cunt. The boy in question never got a sentence; he walked scot-free from court, but I don't think Ronnie would have wanted his pal to go down for a life sentence. God bless you, Ronnie, my friend. I hope you're taking it easy, little man, love and respect.

Bar L wasn't too bad in general, especially as you would get lots of visits due to it being slap bang in the middle of Glesga. I was getting my visits from Rose, Macky and the two girls, the first time in my life that I was to get visits. Anyone that's been behind bars will tell you it's good to have a visit from someone that loves you and wants to make the effort. No one can say that they don't like getting visits, as I would call them a liar.

BACK TO THE HILL, DECEMBER 1993

Very little passed by the Wallace Monument on the road to Glenochil. I was daydreaming, just staring out of the window of the bus. The rhythmical drumming of the diesel engine was playing havoc with my ears, especially every time the driver changed gear. I couldn't wait to get to the jail to get off the bus. Once at the jail, it was plain sailing ... the same routine as the last time. I got put on the bottom flat of A-hall beside some lads called Billyboy, Sean and Goofy. They came from all over Scotland: Billyboy came from Maryhill, Sean from Easterhouse and Goofy from Paisley. I started by getting out of my face on smack with Billyboy. Sean couldn't believe how fast I slipped into the jail routine. I settled in right away, like an asylum seeker takes to the back of a truck.

A couple of weeks went by when Big Taggs asked me to do a prison contract hit on a cunt called Tam. I asked him how much he was paying; he told me he would give me one-eighth of an ounce of smack. At the thought of this, my eyes lit up like an infrared beam. He just had to point me in the right direction and press the 'go' button!

I promptly said, 'Yes,' and asked him what he wanted done.

'Slash or stab him, whatever you prefer.' He was talking as if he were describing art or something.

This was another human who had never done anything to me, but I was so hooked on smack that I knew it would help me out, so I didn't think about anything else. I badly needed a fix, so I pushed Taggs on a time. 'When do you need it done?' I pressed.

'In the morning or the next day,' he replied nonchalantly.

Fucking hell, I needed a fix fast! I put it to him, 'What about if I done it right now, can you give me the smack?'

'Yes,' he responded.

My torment would be nearly over. Big Taggs went up the stairs to get me the eighth of smack. I called Sean and Billyboy over and informed them, 'I'm getting an eighth of kit down in a couple of minutes, off Taggs.'

Billyboy gave me a hug.

Sean said, 'Nice one, but how are you getting it?'

'Well, I've not told you this, but I'm going to see that guy that came up on the bus with me, Tam. Well, Taggs asked me to give him it and I said that I would. So he's giving me an eighth of kit down.'

'Why, what's this boy done?' Sean asked.

'Fuck knows, Sean,' I answered back, 'look, it's an eighth of kit and we're going to be strung out by tomorrow morning.'

'Yes, you're right,' Billyboy accepted.

Taggs came back and gave me a belter of an eighth of smack.

I made my way back to my cell with Sean and Billyboy, where we each made a hit and injected it. It was good shit.

'Right, so what's the plan?' Billyboy asked.

'I don't know. What about going down to his section and just stabbing him in the neck?' I suggested.

'No, no! Bad idea,' Sean spewed out, 'we're better off trying to get him up to our section.' This was by far the better idea.

A few minutes later I had secreted myself in the first cell on our section, looking out for Sean and the cunt I was going to slash. After fifteen minutes, they walked on by up towards Sean's cell. I stealthily walked up behind them with a lockback knife in my hand. Then, as quick as you like, I seized the boy and slashed his face off him. I quickly released my grip whereupon the boy turned around, with blood gushing from his face. I don't know why, but Sean, spurred on by some dormant pack instinct, stabbed at the torso of the fleeing victim, sticking it to him in his ribs.

After that, we gave the blood-spattered knives to Billyboy to get rid of. The screams of our victim alerted the screws to the fact that something had gone down. The screws came streaming up into the section as soon as they saw him running by their office back into his section with the face ripped off him.

'Right, everyone back to your cells,' the screws were running about shouting.

'What for?' we all cried out amidst the uproar.

'Because there was an attempt to take a boy's life that took place in here, amongst you animals,' one of the screws blasted.

'We don't know what you're talking about,' we answered back.

'Fuck you, none of us are going in,' Billyboy and Goofy vowed.

'No cunt was hurt in this section. I've been sitting here watching the TV all afternoon and I've not seen or heard any cunt screaming,' Goofy raged at the screws. 'So you'll have to come up with a better one than that before we go behind our doors.'

'Look, boys,' one of the screws pleaded, 'no one's trying to be smart. But we need you to go behind your doors.'

Eventually we headed to our cells. I was sniggering away, when BANG my cell door flew open.

'OK, Jimmy, we're taking you down the digger,' one of the screws shouted.

'How?' I asked. 'What have I done?'

'Come on, you know what you've done,' one of the screws said.

'No, I don't know what the fuck I've done,' I insisted one more time.

I needed to make it sound as realistic as possible. I was panicking because Sean had the smack and I didn't know if he was going to get pulled in as well. When I was being taken out of the section in the arm locks, I shouted to warn Sean, 'I'm getting taken to the digger.'

'What for?' he enquired innocently.

'Fuck knows, I'll see you later,' I yelled.

'You'll see him shortly, Holland,' one of the screws blasted to me, as he revealed, 'he's coming down with you as well.'

'You're trying to dig us out, you bastards,' I hollered.

I got put in the digger. Sean soon followed, and was thrown in the cell next door. Sean shouted, 'Jimmy, Jimmy, this mob have carted me in as well.'

'I know, Sean,' I yelled through the solid-steel cell door. 'The fuckers are trying to dig us out for that carry-on up the hall.'

'That'll be right,' Sean bellowed, 'we've got fuck all to do with that. We were sitting with everyone in the section watching the TV all day.'

'I know, mate,' I trailed off in confirmation of what our alibi would be.

The next day, we went up in front of the governor. To our surprise, he took our side of the story, and let us back up the hall. The screws in the hall weren't pleased when Sean and I walked back on to the flat. On seeing us, one of them gasped, and his jaw dropped so far down that it nearly touched the floor. 'How the fuck did you not get put on a rule, you pair of troublemaking bastards.'

I told him to fuck off. Sean told him to go and play with himself. For legal reasons I'll call the screw Sam. He was a fat arrogant bastard with an attitude problem. He told us he would make sure we got carted, as he didn't like the little gang of us that were in section three; in fact, he hated the lot of us. The rest of that day, you could cut the atmosphere with a knife.

Relations with the screws continued to get worse. By the third day, it came to a head. The day had started like any other day in prison, as we were all opened up as normal to have a shower or shave. But, just after breakfast, Andy ran into the office with a homemade dagger and threatened to stab the screws. They freaked out and hit the riot bell. Before anyone knew it, there were half a dozen screws on the flat shouting, 'Lockup. Boys, lockup.'

None of us was happy at the way the screws were acting towards us, but we went behind our doors, anyway. One hour led to three hours, and we started to get restless.

'Where the fuck's our exercise,' I heard a boy shouting in anger.

'You're getting opened up in ten minutes, so just settle down,' one of the faceless screws shouted up the corridor.

Ten minutes led to forty minutes. Finally, the doors got opened, but none of us was happy, to say the least. I sat down with some of the other lads on the floor outside our cells, properly pissed off.

'Right, fuck this,' one of the group coughed up. 'We aren't letting them get away with this fucking shit any longer, do you all agree?'

We all agreed.

'OK then, what about taking them hostage?'

My heart missed a beat and jumped up and hit my tonsils. 'What!' I nearly choked.

'A hostage!' the group exclaimed.

Not wanting to lose face, I stifled my reticence and boldly added, 'Yes, brand new.'

I didn't really believe that they'd carry it through, as a lot of people in prison talk hot air. Nevertheless, we plotted and planned the rest of that day around achieving our aim. It was decided that the best time to grab the screws would be at recreation later that night. Everyone was on edge. Nervous laughs were the order of the moment.

'OK, you lot,' ordered the screws walking into our section, 'that's bang-up.'

The screws were going for their tea before they opened us all up for recreation. On the dot, the doors opened at 6.30pm. We all made our way into the one cell and huddled together for one final confab.

'Are you still wanting to go through with this?' the gang asked one another.

We all answered that we were.

'OK then, let's fucking show this mob what trouble's all about,' came the order.

The boys started running back and forth in and out of the cells, trying on masks that were made out of the sleeves cut from their jumpers. You'd be amazed at the tools they had, from lockback knives and chair-leg ends to pool cues and Stanley blades. Now the only problem they had was cornering the screw or screws without them pressing the riot bell. They asked a boy to go into his cell and press his emergency button then to come out and shut his door over so the screws would think it was a con that hadn't been opened up for evening recreation. The screw would need to walk into the section to open the boy's cell door back up, and that's when he'd be nabbed.

Lo and behold, after the boy had pushed his emergency button, Sam, the fat arrogant screw, swaggered up the section, all on his ownsome. He thought he was King-fucking-Kong. Little did he know then that he wouldn't be walking back out. At least, not in one piece!

He opened the boy's door, but there wasn't anyone in the cell. He shouted the boy's name out in the section, pissed off at him for having to get off his fat, lazy arse. Then the surprise: a couple of masked boys came out of their cells, and stood to the front and the back of him. The fat cunt turned four shades of red.

'Boys, what are you doing?' he pleaded.

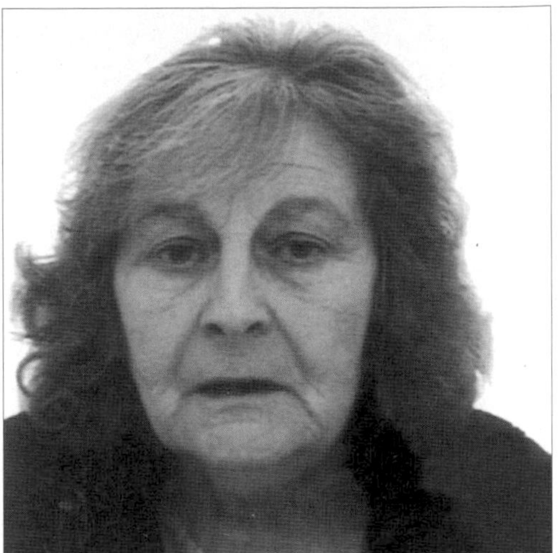

The Holland family – My eldest brother John, *top left*, my mother Lizzie, who I've never really known, *top right*, and my brother Bert serving in Bosnia, *below*.

Above, from left to right: Lynne, my Auntie Rose and my cousin Lizzy. Auntie Rose has been like a mother to me.

Below: My cousin Lizzy's lovely little son, Lee.

Close friends who have helped me through everything.

Above: Joey Boyle's family – Scott, Linda and wee Jay. They have been so kind and done so much for me.

Below: My uncle Mick and my half cousin Delia having a laugh together.

An overturned snooker table and broken ceiling tiles – the result of our riots at Shotts Prison.

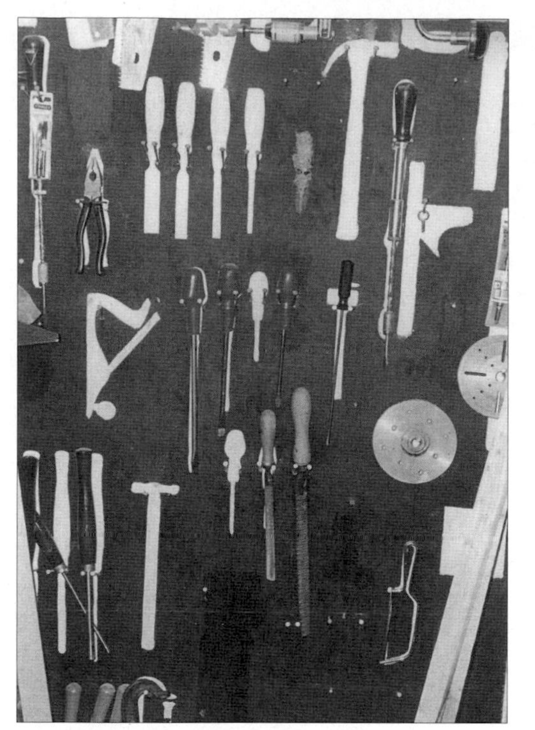

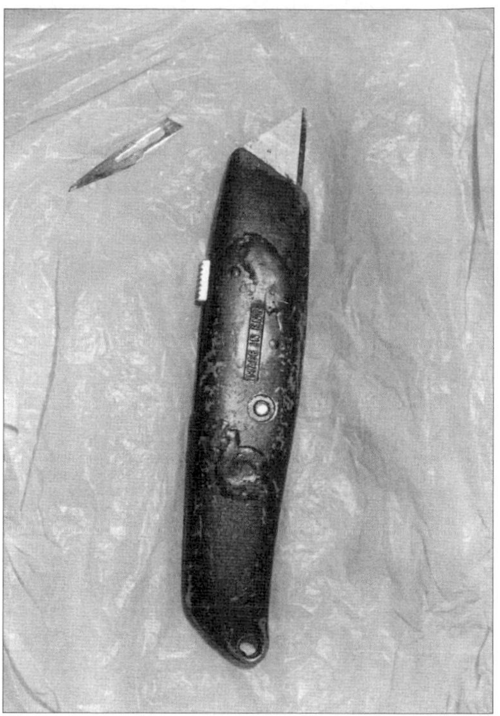

Above: These are the tools that the police claimed were evidence against us.

Below: Danny Boyle is my co-accused in the Shotts Unit case.

Above: Mine and Billy's co-accused in the Shotts Unit case.

Below: George, *left*, and Scobbie, *right* were both involved in the riots at Shotts. They both did me proud in the witness stand.

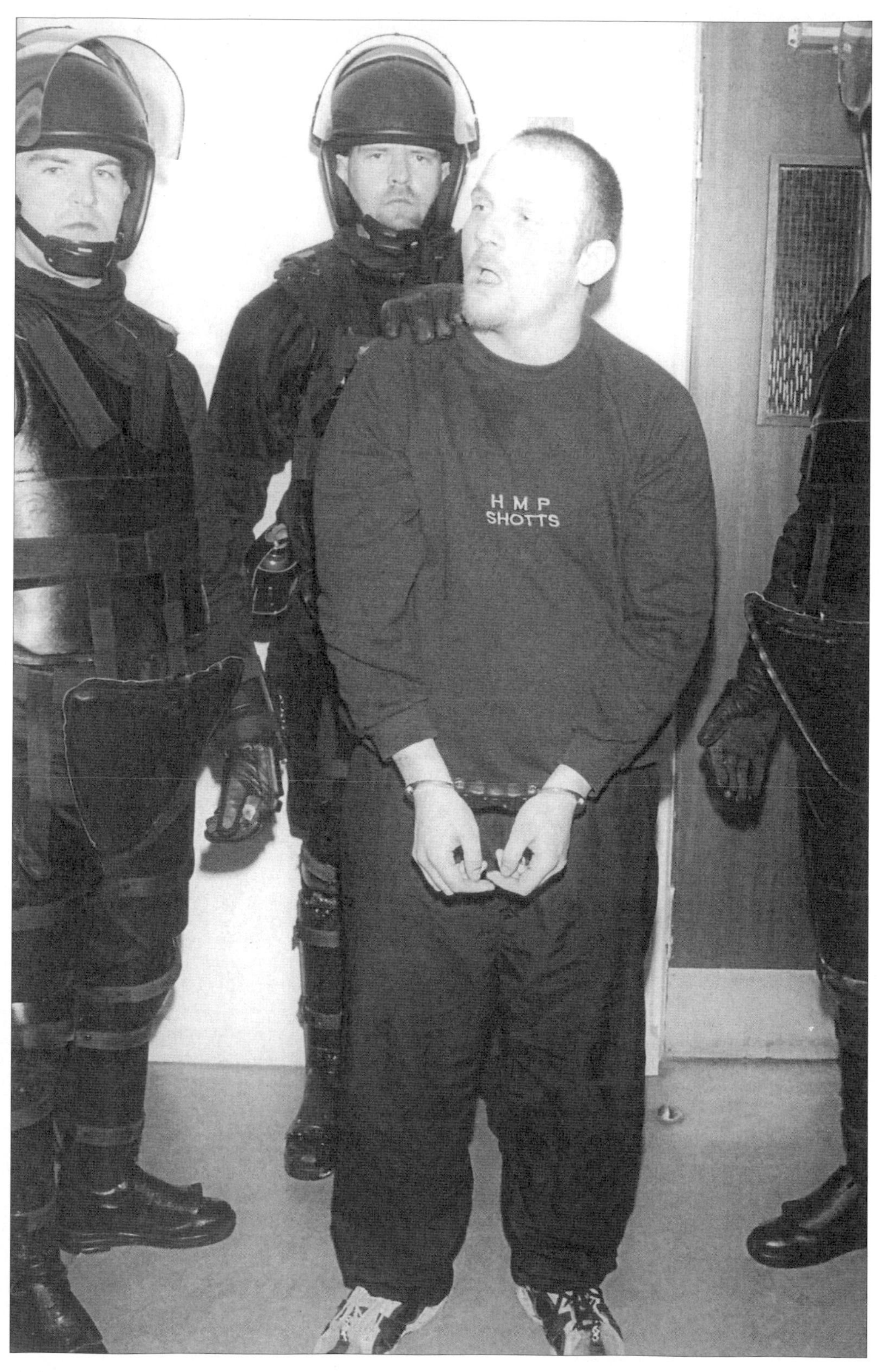

Shortly after the riot at Shotts HMP, this picture was taken of me.

THE SUN, Thursday, January 29, 2004 39

15

RIOT LIFER GETS LIFE

Trashed . . . Lewis and other inmates wrecked Shotts Prison's special unit

Murderer stabbed 3 jail guards

By DAVE FINLAY

A DOUBLE murderer was yesterday given a second life sentence for stabbing three prison officers during a riot.

William Lewis, 33, slashed one guard in the arm and back, another in the stomach and a third in the armpit as violence erupted at Shotts Prison in Lanarkshire.

He was convicted of attempting to murder officers George Brown and James Harrigan and also stabbing Kenneth Aitken.

Ordering Lewis to serve a minimum 12 years, judge Roderick MacDonald QC told him: "It is clear that you are an evil, violent and highly dangerous man.

"In my judgement the safety of the public would be in grave peril if you were at liberty."

Trouble flared at Shotts' special unit last January when Lewis' inmate pal Daniel Boyle was told he was being segregated. The jury at the High Court in Edinburgh saw CCTV footage of Lewis leaping a barrier and attacking staff.

Inmates were also seen using the snooker table to barricade the unit and chairs and tables were thrown at prison guards.

A tropical fish was even microwaved during the riot after Boyle smashed a tank with a table.

Boyle, 30, was jailed for two years for his role in the fracas.

Judge MacDonald told him and Lewis: "You both played your parts in an incident of disorder and violence. It is an outrage that prison officers, especially men clearly dedicated to helping you, should have been subjected to the kind of conduct in which each of you engaged."

A third inmate, James Holland, 30, was found not guilty of attacking a prison officer by chasing him with a screwdriver.

Lewis was jailed for life in 1992 for murdering two men in knife attacks in one night in his home town of Greenock.

He was sentenced to a further five years in 2000 for attempted murder while behind bars.

Chaos . . . smashed snooker table at unit where fish was microwaved

'Self-defence' claim

AN inmate accused of trying to murder FOUR prison officers claims he acted in self-defence.

William Lewis alleges that he and co-accused James Holland were under attack by the officers in the special unit at top-security Shotts jail in Lanarkshire.

In the special defence lodged by Lewis, he insists he and Holland were targeted by officer George Brown and three others.

The pair, both 33, and fellow prisoner Daniel Boyle, 30, all deny attempting to murder the four – and breach of the peace charges which include claims they threatened to set the officers on fire.

By DAVE FINLAY

One of the warders, Kenneth Aitken, 43, told the High Court in Edinburgh yesterday that a "stand-off" developed on January 7 last year after inmates were told they would be transferred as the unit was closing.

Agitated

Holland accepted the news but Boyle became agitated.

Mr Aitken said: "He just got angrier and angrier. He was very loud, swearing, making threats."

He added that Boyle had said: "If it was a fight we were looking for, we will take the roof off."

Officers tried to calm him down, but a heated argument developed and extra staff were called in. Mr Aitken said: "There was a stand-off and then the prisoners rushed forward to attack us."

He told the jury Lewis stabbed him in the arm and back, adding: "I'm sure it was a screwdriver. I didn't feel any immediate pain."

At one stage he thought a colleague, James Harrigan, had been punched, but he slumped back clutching his stomach and there was blood on his shirt.

Lewis's address was given as Edinburgh prison, Holland's as Perth prison, and Boyle's as Barlinnie jail in Glasgow.

The trial, before judge Roderick MacDonald, continues.

WARDER 'HELD CUE'

A PRISON officer denied yesterday that his boss "lost the plot" when he brandished a snooker cue during a prison riot.

Kenneth Aitken, 43, told a court that supervisor George Brown intended to protect an isolated officer at Shotts jail in Lanarkshire.

Mr Aitken told the High Court in Edinburgh that Mr Brown "went to the defence of his staff."

William Lewis, 33, James Holland, 33, and Daniel Boyle, 30, deny trying to murder four officers. The trial continues.

These are some of the articles that appeared in the press about my case.

BANG! He got smacked over the head with a broken chair leg. He fell to the floor in screaming agony – it wasn't a gentle hit. A dagger was put to his neck. He wasn't so tough now. Blood was dripping from his head wound, down his face and on to his starched shirt.

'Come on, boys,' he pleaded once again, 'enough is enough.'

'Shut it,' someone exploded, 'shut the fuck up or you'll be stabbed up, understand?'

He understood all right. He was marched to the end of the section so the other three screws in the office could see the sight: a bunch of masked men holding their blood-covered colleague at knifepoint.

I've seen people move fast, but nothing like this. They were up and off out of the flat faster than a speeding train. We took advantage of this by ripping and smashing the flat to bits, razing it to the ground. The boys from the other section who didn't know what was happening came out to help us obliterate the place. They also helped build barricades at the gates of the flat so none of the riot mob could get in.

I've never had a rush of pure adrenalin like it in my life, I was buzzing. We were all buzzing, screaming and singing to the rotten mob outside the gates of the flat. They were totally helpless, whereas we were in full control of the flat. Along with having the fat bastard as hostage, we held all the aces in this game.

'Come on, boys, let's talk about this,' one of the riot screws shouted through the front doors of the hall. 'What's caused you to do this bang?' he asked.

Before he could move from the doors, a Molotov cocktail was flung at him. WHOOSH! The flames danced like a flower in the wind, up the wooden doors. His plea had fallen on deaf ears.

'Jesus, fuck!' the screws shouted, recoiling back from the flame-licked doors with the grace of a drunken skunk.

'What the fuck are you doing?' one hateful screw spat at the mob.

One of the boys roared a threat at the top of his voice in a disguised Irish accent, 'Get to fuck, if you try and come in, the screw is getting murdered.'

We all retreated to the safety of our section where the screw was being held, tied and gagged like a prisoner of war. To see this fat horrible screw that thought he was Jack the lad cry and piss himself like a schoolboy made my day and night. The hours during the siege flew by and, before we knew it, it was three o'clock in the morning. Everyone was colder than a well digger's arse. We were tired and wet through. The exhaustion of smashing up the hall and the adrenalin that was once flowing through our veins like an engorged river had subsided, leaving us all exhausted. We were all lying on mattresses in the corridor, talking amongst ourselves when I heard my name shouted. 'Jimmy Holland, will you come out to the end of the section and talk to us?'

I never answered them. They proceeded to shout all of the other boys' names for someone to talk to. We eventually decided that Billyboy and me would go and talk to the negotiators to see what they had in mind.

'Hello, Jim,' the negotiator greeted. 'Is everyone OK, no one hurt?'

'No,' I disappointed him, 'we're all brand new.'

'What about Sam? Is he OK?' he asked.

'Yes,' we said.

'Can we see him?'

'I don't know,' I told this guy, 'as I've not got anything to do with this.'

'Well, who has then?' he enquired. 'What if we shouted for Sam, can he shout back and let us know if he's OK?'

'I'll ask the guys with the masks on if they'll let him shout back,' I replied.

Once I went back into the section, I told the boys what the cunning negotiator had said. They agreed for Sam to shout to his pals that he was OK, which he did, the fat fuck.

Everything fell silent. I was sitting with Billyboy playing bella, a card game that gets played in jail, also known as Klaberjass. Billy and I were on patrol shift, looking to see if there were any members of the hostage squad about. We needn't have bothered, as they weren't going to risk their screw pal's life in an attempt to get him out.

As dawn broke, the screws started banging their riot shields with their sticks. I didn't know it then, but that's part of the screws' psychology to demoralise and confuse you into thinking that they're coming in. All the boys on the flat flew up out of their crumpled heaps ready for a running battle with the riot screws, but they never entered the hall. It was a Zulu standoff. We decided to take the screw out in the arm locks to show these pack of wolves that we meant business. The trussed-up screw was dragged, squealing like a pig, to the opening so that the riot mob could see him. He was visibly broken – no more Mr Hard Man.

'Look,' the captive screw pleaded to his own people, 'give them what they want. Please, give them what they want.'

He was then dragged back into the section.

The negotiator shouted me back out, 'What is it that you want, Holland?' he asked.

'I don't know,' I said, picking my words carefully, 'I've already told you, I've got fuck all to do with this.'

Then a boy shouted in a funny voice from within the section,

'I want a rubber doll and a gram of kit.' Another boy shouted that he wanted a helicopter and a plane to take him to Ibiza. Everyone in the section burst out laughing.

'OK leave it with me,' the weary negotiator said, 'I'll get back to you with your demands.'

Once I walked back into the section, I burst into a giggling fit like a schoolboy. Here was this pack of riot screws, growling like fuck, wanting to rip our heads off and all we wanted was a rubber doll, helicopters and planes. What was even funnier was the fact that the negotiator thought that our outlandish demands were for real. He came back twenty minutes later and told us he couldn't possibly set up our demands.

But everyone was getting pissed off, and soon enough we wanted to get out. Everyone took off their masks, and walked out to where the screws were. We told them we wanted out.

'OK, but first you'll need to let Sam go,' one of the negotiators belted out.

A boy went into the cell where the screw was and cut the ties binding his hands and feet.

'OK,' he informed the fat cunt, 'you're free to go.'

The screw didn't need to be asked again, as he was off like a greyhound out of its trap. Once he was safely back with his own crowd, the negotiator told us how we should come out one at a time, where we'd get cuffed and escorted to the cell block. We'd be videoed, get a change of clothes and some food and also be seen by a doctor.

One by one, the screws shouted out our names. I was third out. When I left the safety of the flat, three of the riot mob snatched me by the hands and head.

'OK, you little bastard!' they raged.

At that point, I knew we had made a grave blunder. I got

videoed at the main entrance to the hall, where there were about forty riot screws and an independent witness to make sure we never had any marks on us. Once this was done, my feet hardly touched the ground all the way to the seg cells.

Once through the doors of the seg cells, and out of sight of the video camera, I got punched and kicked. But my attacker, aiming for my nether region, never quite got me in the cream crackers, and only caught me in the inner thigh, at the top of my legs. It was still very sore, but I never let out a scream. I started struggling; there wasn't much I could do, as my hands were tightly cuffed behind my back. They laid this shit on me for fifteen minutes, until I was deemed to have been done and then I was flung, unceremoniously, and balls over heels, into a cell and the door slammed shut behind me.

I still had the handcuffs on, so I felt very vulnerable, to say the least. Over the next two hours, I heard all the other boys coming down, who were all dished out the same treatment as I got. I must have fallen asleep for a couple of hours, as it was dark when I awoke on the cold cell floor.

My arms were numb. The jagged steel handcuffs had been biting into my wrists with unremitting cruelty when I was sleeping. I blindly shouted out in the cell and kicked wildly at the door, but no cunt came. Then, about five minutes later, the door swung open.

'OK,' the voice boomed from the silhouetted figure, 'you're moving, Holland.'

'Moving! Where to?' I moaned from my twilight state of pain.

'Peterhead seg block,' replied the shadowy voice.

The screw came back to put some pants on me, as I was still cuffed. I got taken up to the reception area of the jail. I was surrounded by about fifty riot screws.

'OK, what's this prick's name?' I heard a frosty-faced screw ask.

'This is one of the ringleaders, Holland,' came the steely reply from a surly-looking screw.

'Oh!' he exclaimed. 'So *this* is Holland!' He raised his eyebrows quizzically.

'Holland, listen up,' an anonymous voice behind me ordered, 'you're going on a lorry. Once in the back of it, lie still on the floor and don't lift your head, do you hear me?'

I never answered him, so I got punched to the back of my head, which made me stumble forward.

'Take this piece of shit out to the lorry,' the voice trailed off, as I was dragged away.

I was thrown in the lorry. It was pitch dark, but I could hear and sense that I was not alone. In a short while, another two boys came into the lorry, then it's engine kicked into life, and the lorry lurched forward and we were off.

I don't know how long we were on the move before the kicks, punches and riot sticks came smashing down on all of us. The screws didn't fuck about; they beat us black and blue. The beating was so intense that they punctured one of the boys' lungs through breaking his ribs.

We had thought we were going to Peterhead seg block, but in actual fact we were taken to the Wendy House of Barlinnie. Now, let me tell you, at this point, the Wendy in the Bar L was the worst seg block out. What's more, there was a reception committee of riot screws waiting to give us even more of a beating. Our hands remained restrained tightly behind our backs with cuffs, so we had no resistance. You can imagine what we got put through. When I look back, they beat us to within an inch of our lives, and that is no fucking kidding!

The boy who had the punctured lung was left overnight in a

cell before Dr Dansen did his round. On entering the boy's cell, his blood boiled at what he saw. 'This man needs to go to hospital straight away,' he demanded.

The screws said, 'He's going nowhere!'

Dr Dansen stood his ground, and the boy eventually got taken to hospital, where he spent nine days. The doctor resigned from his prison duties in protest at the way the screws barbarically treated us. A total of seven screws ended up charged and stood trial for seriously assaulting us, but the case collapsed four days into the trial. As for me, I got moved to Shotts four days after landing in Bar L, so never became fully acquainted with the famous Wendy House seg unit.

CHAPTER THIRTEEN

Man-eater Survival

HMP SHOTTS, JANUARY 1994

E-hall is the oldest part of Shotts Prison, and it was to be my destination. This spine-chilling, gruesome looking building stood on its own from the rest of the prison. E-hall had been built to cope with the overflowing number of prisoners. It had opened for business with a show of spin-doctor publicity in 1987. It didn't take long for the screws to christen the place and, by the time I arrived from the Bar L seg unit, the 'man-eater' had quickly gained a mythical reputation for breaking the minds and bodies of prisoners.

I waltzed into the hall with my escort of five screws like some rapper with his well-paid entourage. A fiendish-looking little bastard with blonde hair and a crooked nose came up to me and said, 'OK, Holland, welcome to Shotts. Welcome to the man-eater!'

I burst out laughing at his remarks and puckered my lips up to him. 'Whoop-de-do!' I squealed in ridicule.

'What's so funny?' he raged back at me.

'You and your *man-eater*,' I spat the words back at him.

'Oh! So we've got ourselves another wide boy here,' he called out to his pals.

He glared at me, and grimaced. He growled, 'It won't be long 'til you're like the rest of them, pleading to get out of here.'

'Not me, sir,' was my mocking salutation, 'not fucking me!'

'We'll fucking see,' he seethed.

His forehead frowned into a heavy collection of wrinkles worthy of a Japanese fighting dog. He spoke through teeth so clenched that they seemed to have been superglued together, 'Oh, by the way ... my name's Simmons.'

'Right, Holland, you're going on the second floor.'

The five screws manhandled me up the stairs on to the second flat, where there were another three screws, none of whom had riot gear on.

'OK, what's your name?' one of them said, as if they didn't know.

'Holland,' I shot back at him.

'No, what's your first name?'

'Jimmy,' I told him, a bit confused and taken aback at the regime.

'OK, Jimmy,' this screw quipped, 'you play the game with us and we'll play the game with you.'

I didn't know if this was a mind game or not, but I told them that I hadn't come here to cause trouble or get into trouble.

'OK, that's a good start,' they commended.

I was uncuffed, strip-searched for the third time that day and given some new jail clothes. Then all the screws fucked off from my new cell. I could hear the sound of banging on the wall, which was followed by a muffled voice frantically searching out for a reply: 'Who's that. Here, pal, who's that?'

'Jimmy Holland,' I coughed up, 'who's that?'

'Branny,' the boy in the next cell shouted back.

I had never heard of him.

'What jail did you come from?' Branny asked me.

'I've just come from the Wendy House at Bar L. I was only in it for four days. I was up Glenochil,' I shouted back

'Were you one of the hostage takers?' Branny asked.

'No,' I said, 'but this mob's saying I was. Who's in here from Glesga?'

'Fuck, nearly the full hall,' he sniggered.

'Branny, Branny,' another guy shouted on him.

'Yes, Dougie,' Branny replied.

'Who's that just come in?' asked Dougie

'Jimmy Holland.'

'What? Little Jimmy from Glenochil!' Dougie excitedly replied.

'Aye, Dougie,' Branny confirmed.

'Jimmyboy, Jimmyboy, hello! Are you all right, son?' Dougie's voice rang out.

'Yes, hello, I'm brand new,' I answered.

Dougie was in his late forties and had been in every jail in Scotland. I'd met him in Glenochil digger the year before.

'Are you OK, Jimmy?' he again asked me.

'Aye, Dougie, this mob won't break my spirits,' I told him.

'No fucking chance of them doing that,' Dougie agreed.

I soon found out that Taggs had been asking for me. I was baffled because Taggs hadn't been involved with the hostage riot in Glenochil. Why was he here?

'What flat's he on, Dougie?' I enquired.

'He's just down the stairs from you, Jimmy, give him a shout out of the window,' Dougie instructed.

'Taggs, Taggs, Taggs,' I shouted.

'Aye,' a familiar voice boomed out in reply. 'Hello, who's that?'

His easily recognisable voice was like music to my ears. 'It's Jimmyboy,' I gushed.

'Oh, for fuck's sake, little man, are you all right?' he anxiously called out to me.

'Aye, big chap, I'm OK,' I confirmed.

'Jimmy, it's been all over the papers, the doing you took on the way to Bar L. The Bar L mob are saying the Glenochil mob done it and that mob are saying the Bar L mob done it.'

'Taggs,' I yelled out, 'the fucking two mobs gave us it all, stinking, but we're still going strong. *Anti-Screw Crew*.'

At this, every boy on that side of the building started cheering and shouting Anti-Screw Crew. The screws came back into my cell while I was shouting out of the window. It was time for some exercise, so they led me out to the yard. The exercise pens were on the other side of the building from the side I was on, and consisted of four metal fencelike monkey huts. It all reminded me of being at the zoo.

'OK, Jimmy,' the screw said, 'you'll be out for forty minutes. Once you're out, you can't come back in until your time's up.'

'Yes, boss, brand new,' I acknowledged.

I immediately recognised another boy in the yard.

'All right, Billy,' I said to him.

His eyes lit up on seeing me. 'It's Jimmyboy. For fuck's sake, you've lost a bit of weight!'

'What are you locked up for, Billy?' I asked him.

He told me of his involvement with the riot that had taken place in May 1993 where a screw got stabbed and the cons smashed up A-hall. Billy told me that there were fifty prisoners in this hall, twenty-five from Shotts itself, and ten from Glenochil, with the other fifteen or so from Perth, Aberdeen and

Saughton Prisons. They had a troublemaker from every jail in Scotland banged up under the one roof – a lethal cocktail mix, sure to create trouble.

I settled down into the man-eater no bother. But trouble was always brewing. A couple of weeks went by before all the boys in the hall decided to smash their cells and windows to fuck in protest at the shite food we were being given. It's one thing eating jail food, as it's disgusting, but it's another thing to eat frozen cold or half-cooked jail food all the time. We were given frozen mince for four or five days on the bounce. I remember the incident as if it were yesterday. It was ten o'clock on a Friday. We wrecked and flooded the hall, with our sinks and toilets spewing hot and cold water like Niagara Falls from the severed plumbing pipes. The noise was deafening. We were all up at our windows, smashing up the light fittings on our ceilings and flinging them out like Frisbees. We set fire to sheets and quilts, then threw them out of our cell windows, sending showers of upwards spiralling starbursts. I pitied the boys like Taggs, Billy, Pat, Steph below us, because the bourgeoning flames were licking right up to their smashed windows. They must have been sweating like lobsters.

The next few hours flew by. At about one in the morning, we all heard the familiar drone from the jail vans' diesel engines. Or so we thought. It was actually the fire brigade out to dampen down the riotous flames. Then we heard the unmistakable and familiar sound of footsteps and riot shields coming into the hall. There must have been about fifty screws, suited and booted in their 'Ninja Turtle' suits. But it doesn't matter what they wear, as these cunts are amateurs, and they are always going to get hurt.

Our cell doors crashed in one at a time. The mob jumped in

and grabbed each prisoner, hitting everyone a couple of times before putting on the arm locks. Now, arm locks are fucking painful, and when I was younger I used to scream out in pain, but, over the years, I've mastered the way to stifle the pain. Soon enough I heard the door next to mine crash open. My heart was racing like a Formula One car engine, not with fright, as I've had it that many times, but at not knowing how to channel my adrenalin.

A screw's eye appeared at the spy hole in my cell door, 'OK,' he ordered, 'stand at the back wall with your hands on the bars of the window.'

'Fuck you, pricks,' I retorted. 'Come on in, you bastards.'

When the door flew open, I flung myself at them. This was all premeditated, as I knew that things would go faster if you got some adrenalin out of them. After the initial hit, I was put in arm locks, and led outside the cell while some screws cleaned it out of the smashed-up contents. Then they led me back into the cell, laid me on the floor and jumped back out of the cell, slamming the door shut behind them.

That was a fucking hard night. There I was, alone in my cell, lying soaked to the skin on an unwelcoming cell floor with no bed. The only company was the cold wind of January, tormenting me through the windowless prison cell. This had to be the coldest prison cell on the planet. I vowed to myself that I wouldn't pull this sort of stunt again in a hurry. I've never been so deathly cold to the bones in my life before, then or after. It was as though hell had frozen over. That night seemed to last an eternity, where minutes seemed like hours, until we heard the screws back in the hall the next morning. The cell walls had started to ice over, caused by the moist molecules of my damp breath that were clinging and cracking in the dense, cold atmosphere. But the cunts didn't even give us breakfast. When my door eventually opened, it was round about quarter to eleven in the morning.

'Right, Holland,' it was Simmons, the dirty cunt. 'You're on report for smashing your cell up and lighting fires. Have you anything to say?'

'Yes,' I chirped up, 'have a nice day.'

His face went bright red, which warmed the cockles of my heart, if not my frozen bones. I knew I had got the better of him, as he was expecting me to ask for a breakfast, a deluxe Slumberland mattress and a thick quilt. He walked out with his henchmen and slammed my cell door shut behind him, while I burst out laughing loud enough for him to hear me. I had got one over on this arrogant, diminutive fucker.

It wasn't long before Simmons came back into my cell and told me that half of the so-called hard men had revealed to him that it was Billy, Taggs, Steph and me that had instigated the kick-off the night before. He told me I was getting my bed back, but without a blanket to hang up at my window to keep me warm. I know he gave other prisoners a blanket to hang up over their windows to stop the elements from blowing in, but I still never lowered myself to beg him. Fuck it. I lay, like the rest of my pals, in a frozen cell for three weeks without windows.

After this carry-on, it wasn't long before we took our revenge on the screws by putting them up to their ankles in our shit and piss. The place was so bad that we had to tie our T-shirts round our own mouths as makeshift air purifiers to try and stifle the foul stench. It had all started over a minor matter, when they'd turned a boy's visitors away after his bird was two minutes late. The next morning, at slop out, we all showed our support for the boy and his family. We should have emptied our chamber pots into the sluice, but instead, one after another, we flung the shit and piss all over the walls and roof of the hall corridor.

I'll tell you, the screws' faces painted an even greater picture than my words can describe. We kept emptying our pots in the hall for two weeks before the screws started emptying our piss pots for us, but this didn't last too long after we started calling them *bellhops*.

After this, it wasn't too long before Simmons was on my case full-time. He'd been trying to get a reaction out of me ever since I landed in this shit hole, but little did he know he'd get a reaction out of me sooner than he thought! He came into my cell one morning with three of his henchmen and told me to get out of my bed. I didn't want to get out my bed so told him I was having none of it. Simmons and his three pals pulled the quilt off me, and jumped on me, put me in the arm locks and carted me, naked, into an empty cell. Once I was in this cell and they'd left the room, I went on my buzzer. A screw came to the door and looked through the spy hole, and I asked him why I got moved into this cell. He told me that Simmons was searching my cell.

A couple of hours had passed when my door sprung open. 'Oh, Holland,' Simmons buzzed, 'you're on report for having this in your cell.' He pulled a toothbrush out that had a razor melted on to one end of it. 'For making a makeshift knife.'

I told him he was a lying bastard.

'OK, fine, Holland, you're on report for threatening me as well,' he said.

I went up in front of the governor the next day. He took fourteen days' wages off me, put me on closed visits and barred me from using the phone. I was pure gutted inside, but I never showed this mob how I felt because that would have given them satisfaction. I returned to my cell, where I lay plotting and planning my revenge on Simmons. The next morning he came into my cell. 'Slop out, Holland,' he bellowed.

'Aye,' I replied.

'Well, hurry up, move it,' he droned.

'Aye, give me a minute,' I said, playing for time.

I put on my training shoes because I knew I was going to be boxing with them. I got my piss pot and sauntered out of my cell. Once I had got to the sluice to empty my pot, I shouted Simmons over to tell him that the sluice was blocked, upon which he came over to have a look.

Once he was in striking distance, I flung what was left of my piss pot over him, then smashed the pot off his ugly little head. The little prick lay on the floor screaming. His pals came running in. I went head-to-head with them. I got a few kicks and punches in, but I wasn't really bothered about the doing I took off them because I got the one I wanted.

I got punched, kicked and hit with sticks until I was black and blue, but I never once asked them to stop because I didn't want to give them the satisfaction. Aye, it was fucking sore, in fact, it was the second or third worst doing over I've ever had in my life.

The next day, my lawyer, Mr Finlayson, came up to see me. He couldn't believe the mess I was in. He took some photos of my injuries, especially of the left-hand side of my face, which was black and blue with a footprint on it. There was a bit of a print on my ear as well. My back and legs had footprints on them, as well as baton marks. My hands were swollen up like Frankfurter sausages from where they had been holding me in the locks. My lawyer asked me if I wanted to press charges against them for serious assault on me, to which I said *no*, but as luck would have it the screw called Simmons charged me with assault relating to severe injuries he had suffered. The lawyer arranged to come and see me the next day, but the screws misinformed him that I didn't want to see him. Funny that.

The five months I endured on the lockdown flew by without any major incidents until a hot summer's night in mid-June. I don't know if it was the heat, but the screws had forgotten to lock the cell door belonging to Steph C from Springburn. Venturing out of his cell, Steph had us pissing ourselves, laughing at the screws' lack of security. He was a funny lad, and he had us all rolling about in stitches. 'Fuck this,' he said to his little pal Taffie from Kirkintuloch, 'I'm going to set the office on fire.'

We all cheered and egged him on as he ran down to the screws' office and set it on fire. Before long, the fire bell was ringing and Steph ran back to his cell and kicked his door over shut behind him. The nightshift screws were running about like a couple of dizzy blondes. They were trying to put the fire out with some fires hoses, but they were too late to save any of the computers or our case files. They were gutted when they came back on shift the next day. They knew someone in the section had done it, but they couldn't pursue the matter as it was their fault for not checking the doors and, most importantly, all the troops on our flat kept their mouths shut.

Relations between the screws and us steadily deteriorated. They started playing silly buggers with a few of the boys down the stairs on the bottom flat. One screw started fucking about with a lad called Adger. The screw would go to his door and wake him up at night to tell him his mam had died and the hospital was on the phone, then the screw fuck would walk away from Adger's door laughing. How sick is that? Although Adger wasn't really liked by the main body of the prisoners, he was still on the bang-up with the rest of us, so, like it or lump it, we couldn't sit back and watch the screws play with his head. One night, Adger couldn't take any more of it, so he started banging around off his door at two in the morning. He kept smashing the solid-steel window frame off his door and, after three hours of non-stop banging, he managed to stick his head through a hole he had created in the door. This man had some strength on him, to say the least. In the morning and in the wake of the damage, the screws shit themselves at seeing his head hanging out of the hole in his door.

But it wasn't just the screws you had to look out for: there were some fucked-up cons as well. There was a deaf and dumb boy in Delta-hall, who had been put in that protection hall for his own well-being, as there's quite a lot of heartless cons in the system that would have probably bullied him if he was in a mainstream prison hall. One day, he was lying on his bed with his special-needs TV, when three protection prisoners entered his cell, and started switching his TV on and off. When the lad tried to tell the three vermin to leave his room, one of them pushed him back on to his bed, while the other two dirty cowards punched him in the face. He couldn't do anything, so he curled up on his bed to protect his face. That's what the scumbags had been waiting for. The three of them overpowered him and ripped his trousers and pants off, before proceeding to gang rape him. I hope these three fuckers rot in hell.

The screws saw Jamie crawl out of his cell, and initially thought he was on drugs, but when they saw the blood running down his legs, they knew something was wrong. Someone grassed up the three cunts and they got brought over to the man-eater to be with all us nice cherubs. Even the screws in this place were sickened at what these monsters had done. One of the boys was English. I asked him what he was with us for and he told me that he'd raped a beast over in the protection hall. I couldn't believe the sick fucker was trying to brag about what they'd just done.

Needless to say, the full section turned on them. We flung piss and runny shit under their doors. When we were going for our dinners, we asked the screws what dinner plates the monsters were getting and we all spat in them. The screws were spot on that way, after all, that's not the normal thing to do to a defenceless boy. The deaf and dumb boy wasn't a beast, as he was doing four years for having seven kilos of hash in his home. A small consolation was that he got out on his appeal, and he also received twenty-five grand of compensation. The three monsters got five years apiece on top of their sentences and were moved up to Peterhead with all the rest of the sex pests.

I had to start watching my own back as the months passed away. One of my fellow prisoners, Geo, suddenly started blaming me for taking two tenner bags of smack out of the stash in the shower room. I was having none of it. I'm no angel and I've pulled some stunts on people in jail to get some drugs, but I've never once pulled a stunt in a digger in my life, as it's not the done thing. Geo was out of his nut on kit and Valium, as I know he wouldn't have pulled me at the door otherwise. He threatened to stab me as soon as he saw me. I said to him to dub his mouth, as there was no point in shouting at the doors, as we couldn't get to each other. I didn't want to be the night's entertainment for the rest of the boys in the section, but Geo kept going on how he would kill me the way he did the boy he was doing life for.

'Aw, is that right, you big hard man,' I shouted, as I'd lost my temper by this stage. 'The boy you killed was only fourteen, so does that make you a hard man?'

Geo had walked into a newsagent's, while drunk and on drugs, and lifted a paper and walked out of the shop without paying.

The boy ran out to ask for his newspaper back. When Geo said no, a fight broke out where Geo stabbed the schoolboy to death. In my eyes, that's a naughty one.

'You're not getting any credit off me or most cons in this jail for that act of cowardliness,' I said, 'so fuck off, you bam.'

By this stage, he was screaming back at me and kicking his door. I left him to it and turned my radio on because I knew I'd brought him down in front of the other boys in the flat. Over the next couple of months, Geo and I started talking again, after all ... a lot of stuff is shouted at doors in the diggers, so I was willing to let it go and he said he was as well, so that was cool. But it seems Geo wasn't so forgiving, as a lad he was pally with later told me that Geo was planning to stab me. I'll keep the boy's name out of this book, but you know who you are and thanks for telling me. Five or six months later, when we were up the stairs on the limited section, I was standing at Chazza Sterwart's door talking to him, when he also told me that Geo was planning on doing me.

That was it, my mind was made up. I went to my little pal's door, Paul S, and asked him for the lockback knife he had. Paul slid it under to me. I went into my own cell, took my white T-shirt off and slipped my brown jail jumper on. I put the knife in my waistband and walked into Stevie's cell, where he and Geo were sitting with cups of tea.

I was asked by Stevie if I wanted one and I said, 'Yes.'

He didn't have a spare cup, so I walked out to get my cup. Stevie walked out to get sugar from Geo's cell. I told Stevie to take his time because I was going to do Geo, at which Stevie turned red. I walked back into Stevie's cell where Geo was sitting on his bed with his feet up. I didn't want to make him feel uneasy towards me, so I started talking to him about football as I edged towards him.

Once I was close enough, I struck out towards him, but he got his hands up to cover his face. I struck out at him again and cut him on the leg. I was trying to stab him in the neck, but I'll give him his dues, he took the worst of it on his hands and legs. Why is it that the way you plan your attack in your mind's eye rarely comes off like that when you perform it for real? Anyway, he was up off the bed screaming his head off. I told him to shut it or he'd get me more jail. He didn't care, as he shot out like a rocket into the section, screaming his head off. I flung the knife back under to little Paul and stood talking to Stevie, nonchalant as you like.

Soon enough, Geo came running out of his cell with a few batteries in his sports socks.

'Come on then,' he bawled bravely, running towards me.

Well, I wasn't going to stand and get belted about the nut with his homemade cosh, so I ran at him. Suddenly, he stopped and swung wildly at me with the homemade cosh. I put my hands up. He got me a belter of a shot on the knuckles of my right hand. I flung a few punches at him before he scampered out of my grip. But the screws were in the section by now, so I couldn't pursue him. They had let this dafty run at me with the cosh because they thought he'd have smashed me up and down the place. Once they seen me doing OK, they came in.

We were taken to our cells and, once in the cell, the top screw said to me, 'Where's the lockback?'

'What lockback,' I innocently replied.

'The one you chibed Geo with,' he responded

'What?' I said to him, 'I never chibed Geo, that prick tried to cosh me and that's all there's to it. Whatever you seen.'

'Well, he's saying you chibed him in Stevie's cell,' the screw said accusingly.

'Well, he's full of shit. Search my cell,' I offered.

'Oh, don't worry we're going to,' the screw said.

The screws turned the full man-eater over looking for this lockback knife, but it was in the safest human stash possible, and they never found anything. I got taken back to Glenochil seg cells after one-and-a-half months in the so-called Shotts man-eater. It couldn't have done its purpose because, three months after I left, they shut it down and moved all the boys back to their own jails' seg cells. So much for Shotts.

CHAPTER FOURTEEN

Smacking it up at a £2m Trial

GLENOCHIL RULE SECTION, A-HALL, BOTTOM FLAT

A ten-strong welcoming committee of screws in the reception area met me.

'Welcome home, Holland,' said the screw I knew as Wilkins with a growl.

'Aye, same to you, you piss pot,' I threw back at him.

Before I knew it, I was down on the floor in the arm locks.

'OK, Holland, listen to me.' I knew this ruthless screw's voice, it was Thompson. 'We're taking you to the bottom flat of A-hall. You'll be pleased to know you'll be placed on a rule, do you understand?'

'Fuck you,' I screamed from the floor. 'Fuck the lot of you!'

'OK, locks and secure, one, two, three.' The macho bunch pulled me to my feet.

Now anyone that's been to Glenochil will tell you, it's quite a distance getting carted in the locks all the way from reception, down the Russian Front and into A-hall. The Russian Front was so-called as it ran about a quarter of a mile from the reception to the real digger, and was as cold as a Polar icecap in the winter. I don't know who started calling it the Russian Front, but I fucking loathed it. Over the years, I've been dragged up and down it countless times.

Arriving at A-hall, I heard a screw shouting, 'Is it all clear to bring this piece of shit in?'

'You're a fucking piece of shit,' I ranted.

I felt the punch hit my ribs; it took the air from my lungs. Fucking hell, Holland, I thought to myself, I was my own worst enemy at times. I couldn't hold back. But the screws wanted me to answer them back because, every time I did, they could give me another punch, kick or slap.

'Right, bring him in,' came the order.

It's fucking sore when four men in riot gear are trying to get through a door space designed for one, especially when you're sandwiched in between them. They crushed me as they squeezed through. That's all part of their fucking torture.

I was dropped on to the floor and stripped naked. Then it was the usual routine: they bend your legs up your back, trapping your hands under them, then they lean all their body weight on to your legs, using you as a springboard to bounce out of the cell, slamming the door shut behind them. I usually just lie like this, the way they left me, for a few minutes, then slowly lower my legs back on to the floor and stretch my arms out at each side of my body like an aeroplane. You can soon feel the blood running back into your arms and legs. I stood up and started laughing uncontrollably. I've asked the shrinks over the years why I do this, but they can never give me a good answer.

'Who's that in there?' the unseen voice from the next cell called out.

I knew the voice; it was my pal, Billyboy Wetheral.

'All right, Billy, it's Jimmy,' I replied.

'Fuck! How are you doing, little man?' Billy enquired.

'Spot on, china,' I replied.

'What happened there?' Billy asked me.

I put him in the picture. 'Oh, just the usual shit. That mob jumped on me up in the reception.'

'Who was it, Jimmy?' he asked

'That Wilkins and company,' I revealed.

I asked Billy when he had come back up here, and he told me the day beforehand along with Ritchy, Sean and Ziggy.

'Little Rab's in the section,' Billy told me. 'So's little Mo Morrison.'

'Is it all right for a charge?' I asked.

'Aye, brother,' Billy told me, then he burst out sniggering.

'What are you giggling at, Billy?' I quizzed.

'You, ya mad cunt,' Billy said, 'that's the only thing on your mind, Jimmy, eh! That rotten mob have just carted you, gave you it stinking and all you're caring about is a charge. Fucking brilliant, son!'

Billy was thirty-two years old, so he was some five or six years older than me. He was a character. He was a lovable rogue, always up to one stunt or another to make sure he had a charge every day. This was the only guy I knew that could write legibly with his two hands, kick a ball competently with his two feet and play any single musical instrument confidently and sing and dance like a Broadway star. Billy was one of a kind, he was so funny.

'Billy,' I said, 'give me a minute 'til I get my clothes in.'

I hit my buzzer on the wall and, a couple of minutes later, three screws came to my door with their riot gear on.

'What is it, Holland?' one of the screws asked.

'Want to give me a pair of pants and denims and a shirt in?' I requested.

The door swung open, and they flung my stuff on the floor and then shut it again.

I got my stuff and put it on. 'Here, Billy,' I shouted to my pal next door, 'what's all that about, with the riot gear?'

'Oh, I know, Jimmy,' he said almost apologetically, 'they've been told to wear it because all of us lot are down here.'

I burst out laughing as I said, 'On you go, you dirty shite bags, eh, Billyboy.' 'Come on the Anti-Screw Crew,' Billy chanted at the top of his voice, then he started yodelling.

Then Little Rab gave me a shout when he came back from his visit. 'Jimmy, how are you doing, little man?'

'Brand new,' I told him.

Rab was a good little guy. He was older than me, and only stood five feet tall. I don't think he liked the fact that he was below average height, but he made up for any shortage of height with his heart. He was quick to ask if I had had a charge that day and, when I told him I never, he swung me a line over. He swung me a sheet over from his window to mine, which I opened up to find a score bag of kit and five blue Valium. I could have kissed Rab. Usually, Rab's bags of smack were the worst in the full system but, that day, he gave me a belter.

I settled into this bang-up easy. There was a good bunch of us on rules. At nights, Billy would keep us all entertained at the doors or windows with his jokes, singing and stories. The screws hated seeing all us happy and they would go out of their way to play with our heads, but we were too wide for them to get caught up in any prison politics. The eight of us would turn our days into nights and nights into days. None of us would even go for our breakfast, dinner or tea. I knew that was fucking up the screws heads, because in a seg unit there's one thing a screw hates and that's to see you sleeping all day, as they get pissed off sitting stuck in their offices with no one to fuck about with.

At night, when the screws went away, we ate like lords because the boys up the stairs from us worked in the cookhouse. They'd bring back cheese, bacon rolls, pies, chips, fruit and milk, all stolen from the cookhouse for us. Little Rab and Mo Morrison would square them up with bags of kit or bits of hash, so overall, things worked like clockwork for us. I lay down there for the rest of that year. Most of the boys got off their rules before I did. I came off my rule along with old Ziggy from Edinburgh.

I got put on A-hall, second flat, where most of my pals were. There was old Bilko from Greenock, Hobo, who later died of a heart attack sixteen years into his life sentence, Little Rab, Sid, who overdosed on kit some years later, and little Budgie. Together we had a great time. I was junked every day of the week on smack, hash and jellies. There were a few bottles of vodka and wine kicking about the flat, but I wasn't really one for getting drunk on spirits or wine, as I've always preferred drugs to drink.

On Christmas Day I woke up to the sound of Pink Floyd booming out of one of the boys' ghetto blaster. Little Budgie was sitting on the end of my bed with the biggest handful of acid I'd ever seen. There must have been at least a hundred of them.

'Come on, you lazy bastard, get up,' he blasted. 'Here take this.' He handed me about ten acids and told me not to take any more than three at a time.

I burst out laughing at him, and told him I detested acid. I gave him them back, but he was adamant. 'Come on, Jimmy, it's Christmas Day. For fuck's sake, take one,' he persisted.

I reluctantly took one. Budgie came up with the idea to spike some guys on the flat. So, off we went, spiking one guy and then the other. We flung them in cups of tea, in bars of chocolate, basically in anything. This Christmas was going to be the best one for a long time. Once we had successfully spiked over fifteen people on the flat, we went into little Rab's cell. We bragged to the rest of the camp about what we'd done, and everyone burst out laughing.

I started to feel the acid I had popped hitting me. My heart started going crazy, like a speeding train. Everything I looked at left a trail and it was freaky. I ran the cold tap and doused as much water round my face and head as possible. I drank a full bottle of undiluted orange, and ate two full oranges, still with their skins on. I was pure freaking out; I hated the feeling altogether.

When Sid and Rab came into my cell, they burst out laughing at the state I was in. Thankfully, Rab asked me if I wanted a few jellies to bring me down. I chewed the life out of them and, within twenty minutes, I was feeling brand new, to say the least. Back to my old self, I started pissing myself laughing when I saw Bilko, Hobo, Rab and Sid tripping out of their faces, drinking vodka and wine. We took a walk about the flat to see the boys we'd spiked.

Eric K was so freaked out that he was running up and down. He was so fucked that he picked up the section TV and hurled it through the screws' office window. Watching him going completely mental was magic to observe. The screws hit the riot bell for what must have seemed like the millionth time. They came running on to the flat, but, for a change, there wasn't any nastiness dealt out from them. They put Eric in his cell and left the flat. I felt sorry for Eric, so I owned up to spiking him with acid, because, if you don't tell someone who's been spiked, it can freak them out. Once I told him what I'd done, the veil of fear lifted from his face. He thought he was going mad. I got two jellies off Budgie and gave them to him under his door, which he chewed right there in front of me.

The rest of the morning was spent in Little Rab's cell. We got our dinner, which wasn't bad for jail food, although we were too fucked to eat it. We got banged up for a couple of hours until the screws went home for their dinner. The nightstand was turned on, a device that opens your cell door for five minutes, only one at a time.

Hobo came out on nightstand and gave me about £40 worth of smack, which he pushed under my door. I could have kissed him. I got my foil out and put half of the smack on the foil. It was magic! I felt the warmth run over me, and the jellies were still giving me a good belt. The rest of Christmas Day was spent grouching – lying on the bed with your eyes shut – drifting in and out of consciousness. I felt on top of the world.

The feeling wouldn't last though, as, a couple of days later, the screws opened my door and told me I was getting a cell search. I was fucking gutted. We were three days to the New Year, when I would have another good party with the lads. I was done with a lockback penknife, three £10 bags of smack and an empty bottle of wine that I didn't even know I had. Someone must have flung it under for a laugh. But I wasn't laughing when I was taken back down the digger and placed on a rule. I was gutted, but I didn't want the screws to know, so I started cracking jokes about the full thing.

'Fuck, you never lasted long, Holland,' one of the digger screws said.

'I know, boss,' I said. 'This fucking mob set me up.'

'Jimmy, Jimmyboy,' my pal shouted from his cell.

As soon as he shouted, I knew it was Ricky.

'What are you down for, Jimmy?' he asked

'Oh, the usual, Ricky boy, the same old shit,' I replied indifferently.

I got put into cell number four in the digger, next to Ricky. He had been sent back down because he had been falsely accused of swallowing something during a visit. It was just a dig out to get him out of the way. So here we were, the only two in the digger, just three days away from the New Year. I burst out laughing and said to Ricky, 'I bet you that a couple of the others will end up down here as well.'

I wasn't wrong. Old Ziggy was brought down on New Year's Eve. Then they brought down Sid, followed by Little Rab and Budgie who came down two days into January. The screws just ruled up everybody that I was pally with, for no reason whatsoever. But, once all the troops were down the digger, we had our New Year's gathering, and partied our heads off for over a week. The screws fucking hated it because they couldn't stop us.

I lay down the digger with Old Ziggy until February. The screws carted Little Rab off to the Wendy House down in Bar L, and Sid and Budgie got back up the stairs.

STIRLING HIGH COURT SITTING, FEBRUARY 1996

The past always comes back and bites you on the arse, especially if you're a con. The time had come for us to stand trial for the hostage taking. I was to stand trial with Ricky, Billyboy, Goofy, Matt, Tam, Sean and Stevie. I was still in the digger when I was informed along with Ricky.

'For fuck's sake,' Ricky gasped, 'that's next week, Jimmy!'

'I know, pal, I know,' I consoled him.

The week flew by and, before we knew it, the day arrived. The security around the court building was like a ring of steel. Ricky and I were driven up in the first jail van, with a second van behind us filled with troops.

'Fuck,' Ricky declared, 'they're going a bit overboard with the security.'

'I know, mate. I think they're trying to make this look worse than it really is,' I said.

We got rushed into the court from the cramped holding cell as if we were terrorists. There were six of us in a cell only big enough for two people, at a push.

'Holland,' one of the turnkeys said, 'your lawyer is here to see you.'

Mr Finlayson was a decent old man. He was your run-of-the-mill lawyer, with his grey hair swept back over his receding scalp. His face was weather-beaten and tanned. My QC was Mr Gebby, who stood 6ft tall and didn't suffer fools gladly. I still have a deep respect for this man of the law, as he knew when people were telling lies.

'Hello, James,' they both warmly greeted me.

I greeted them back. Frivolities out of the way, my QC took the lead and informed me that the Procurator Fiscal had offered me a deal. If I pleaded to the hostage taking, he would drop all the charges against my co-accused. I was taken aback, to say the least. I told my QC that I was not putting my hands up for no man.

'Good,' he said, 'I didn't think you would.'

'Jim,' my lawyer interjected, 'you've got the best QC in the business. Mr Gebby eats and sleeps this kind of case.'

I went back into the cell where all the others were sitting. 'Here, boys,' I said, 'my QC told me the PF offered me a deal. If I plead to the hostage siege, then you'll all walk free.'

'No fucking way.' the troops said staunchly, 'no fucking way.'

Matt held me out a foil with about £20 worth of kit on it. I didn't need to be asked twice, and started sucking a lungful of smack into my system, as if it was going out of fashion. I knew it was going to be a long morning in court listening to one screw after the other telling lies about us.

In the courtroom, the foreman walked into court, with the judge following him. The press area in the court was jam-packed; the public galleries were filled with off-duty screws, coppers, governors and people from the department and, of course, our families and friends.

'All rise,' the foreman announced.

Not one of us got to our feet for the old cunt, and the coppers and screws couldn't do one thing about it. The screws and coppers looked at us with murderous contempt in their eyes. We returned their looks with dumb impudence.

They picked the jury straight away. Then the trial kicked off proper when they called their first witness against us, the fat screw called Sam who had been taken hostage. He was a nervous wreck. He started talking, and swore my life away. Once the PF was finished asking questions, Sam went to walk out of the box, but he was told to stay where he was. I burst out laughing. Little did he know that all of our QCs were going to ask him questions.

The defence ripped Sam apart as if he'd fallen into a shredder. I loved watching my QC at work, as he was so good. He reduced Sam to a bumbling wreck, desperately looking for a friendly face. After the cross-examination, he left the dock a broken man. I loved it: he wasn't the gangster that he thought he was. A couple of the other screws came and went from the box with their tails between their legs. The day was coming to an end when Billyboy's QC stood up and requested that Billy get bail. When the PF granted Billyboy bail, everyone – including Billyboy – was stunned. Little did any of us know that this would be the last time we would see Billy. That night, he was picked up in a motor in Maryhill and murdered. He was shot four times in the body and once to the head.

The next day, before I even went to court, the screws flung the paper into me. I read the front-page. There it was in black and white: JAIL RIOTER AND HOSTAGE TAKER MURDERED IN GANGLAND STYLE EXECUTION. The feature included a picture of Billyboy's lifeless body lying on a stretcher. I couldn't believe my eyes, and had to read it again but it still never sank in. The PF had unknowingly signed Billy's death warrant.

Stories started circulating that someone at the trial had him murdered, and they even lifted one of my co-accused and friends for it, but the truth was that Billy had a contract out on him for some years. He had broken into a house and stole a lot of drugs money and two guns that belonged to a heavy from Liverpool. They got someone that Billy knew and trusted to pick him up, before they took him to the river, where they shot him as an example. None of us troops could really believe what had happened to Billyboy, but it slowly sank in. I would just like to state here and now that Billyboy may have been a drug-taking housebreaker, but he didn't deserve to die like that. No one does, God bless you, Billyboy. R.I.P.

The next five days flew by. On the seventh or eighth day of our trial, Tam, Matt, Stevie and Ricky were told to stand up. The judge then told them that they didn't have a case to answer for and that they were free to go. So that just left Sean, Goofy and me in the dock to face the music.

The day after, I took to the box to answer some questions put to me by my QC. He asked me if I took the screw hostage.

'Definitely not,' I replied emphatically.

Once my QC sat down, the PF stood up and asked me the same question. I gave him the same answer. He called me a liar. Then the four boys who had been let go came in one after the other and told the packed courtroom that they were responsible for taking the screw hostage. The judge and PF went bright red in the face; if the ground could open up, they would have jumped down the hole headfirst. I loved it. The Crown had left open a legal loophole for all of us to jump through. The judge asked Goofy to stand and told him he didn't have a case to answer and was free to go. He walked out of the shadow of the court a free man.

But I was left stewing in the dock for the next two days along with Sean. The jury retired for their verdicts. As we waited for the jury's verdict, we started burning a couple of bags of smack. We knew we were walking as well. We were called back into the court, and I knew it was over as soon as I saw one of the jury smile.

The judge told me to stand up, and he read out the jury's verdict, which was 'not proven' on all charges.

I pounded the air and then sat down.

Sean was also found not guilty of all charges. I jumped out of my seat and gave him a huge hug. We looked round at the public gallery. The screws, governors and people from the department were all gutted. Sean and I stuck our middle fingers up at the lot of them and swaggered back down to the cells.

My lawyer and QC came in. We shook their hands, and thanked them. Sean and I were then both taken down to the waiting jail vans, where the cameras and people from the media and newspapers were rushing over. I stuck my fingers up at them and shouted, 'Anti-Screw Crew.' The next day, the newspaper headline read: HOLLAND STICKS TWO FINGERS UP AT THE SYSTEM. They were going to take out a civil case against us, as the public had just been robbed of £2 million in court costs to convict us. But nothing came of it.

CHAPTER FIFTEEN

Double Hostage Siege Drug Hell in Glenochil and Perth Prisons

BACK TO THE HILL

I was on a high with the result at court on the van back to Glenochil. The five screws in the van with me were so gutted you could have heard a pin drop. The van pulled to a halt outside the front gates of the jail. I looked out of the window of the van into the gatehouse. I was astonished: the screw Sam was standing there with a couple of his henchmen. The greasy bastards were expecting me to have got a sentence at court. They were there to growl menacingly at me, but the result gave them no option but to look depressed with no wind in their sails. I looked straight through him and his pals, never once blinking or averting my gaze from them until the van drove me through the gatehouse and around to the reception area.

Once in the reception, I got the banal welcoming committee of seven or eight screws and two governors.

'OK, Holland,' the top governor lectured, 'don't think that you are going to get an easy ride from my staff. We all know you are as guilty as sin. Some of the prisoners in this jail think you are special because you got off with the hostage charges, but we don't. In our eyes, you are a scumbag,' he spewed at me from his crumpled old mouth.

I laughed in his face, and asked him, 'I'm an innocent man, so why are you still hounding me?'

The governor cut me off by telling me I'd be going back to the digger on a rule for good order and discipline. I told him to do what he wanted, as I'd still sleep like a log, as I was just an innocent man. I started singing, something they couldn't do anything about. I later heard when I was back in the digger that most boys in the jail cheered for me when I walked out of the court and stuck my fingers up at the system. I felt as if I'd just jagged a gram of the best. The hairs were standing up on the back of my neck, and the sweat was running off me. I was so high that night, I couldn't get to sleep. The next morning one of the digger screws opened my door and told me the governor wanted to see me in the office. I leisurely swaggered into his office, just to let him know that I didn't give a fuck what he did or said, as I felt invincible. I took a seat on the chair at the other end of his desk.

'OK, Holland,' he said dryly, 'we have decided to put you back up the halls, but let me tell you, Holland, if you step out of line once, you will be back down here for a very long time. Is that clear?' he said.

'I'm not giving a fuck; you can keep me down here until I get out, mister!' I went on to unleash a further outburst: 'Your threats don't carry any weight with me, so, if you're finished talking, I'll just nip back to my lovely warm bed.'

'Get that animal out of my office,' the old prick ordered at the top of his voice.

'Have a nice day,' I shouted back over my shoulder, as I tottered off to my cell.

I burst out laughing when the screw slammed my door shut behind me. I lay down the digger for the rest of that day, until the next morning, when the top screw in the hall came down to see me and told me he'd like to give me a fair crack of the whip on his flats. I took a chance and went up the stairs that day.

Little Budgie and Sid were still on the flat, and gave me a hug and a slap on the back for walking at the court case. The rest of that day was pretty nippy, as every second guy would want to wish me well. I did appreciate what they all said, but I just wanted to get in behind my door for the night to spend some quiet time by myself in reflective thought.

Things soon returned to normal. I got put on the pass in the hall, a privilege that usually goes to boys that have earned it working in the sheds. I didn't ask for the job, but the governors decided that it would be better to keep me in the hall where the screws could keep their eyes on me. My day consisted of getting up at 9.30am, brushing and mopping the flat with a couple of other passmen. I got on really well with one of the guys, called Mark. He was some nine or ten years older than me, and came from Barmulloch, in the north side of Glesga. Believe it or not, he was doing seven years for robbing a bank with a cucumber! He wasn't your run-of-the-mill jailbird, as he was articulate and very well mannered and never had a bad word to say about anyone. It's not very often you come across someone like that in jail. After we had finished our work, we'd sit in my cell or Mark's and have a cup of tea and a burn of smack or a joint. I would just sit and listen to the stories Mark would relate to me about his early days growing up in Glesga. He told me how he and his pals would jump on the trams down to the city centre, where they would take bundles of old newspapers round to the chip shop, whereupon the owner would give them free chips.

I used to love sitting with Mark, as he never had any airs or graces about having this or having done that. Most prison chat is just pure shite. I don't know why people say such things, but I've come to the conclusion that many cons say this or that to impress some of the hard men in prison or some guy that's holding smack. But you don't need to say you've got money or drugs for me just to like you. That's why Mark made a refreshing change, as he never said anything except his good old stories and a bit of innocent patter.

My work on the pass, however, didn't last long, as I started losing the plot a few months later in November 1996. I was, by this time, on 65ml of methadone a day, while still partaking of the delights of smack. I got booted off the pass as I couldn't even find the energy to drag myself out of my bed. The only time I did have any energy, I would use it to smash things up. One day about twenty-five of us smashed our cells up. My pal Porkie was doing a life sentence with his co-accused, Big Wull up on the top flat of A-hall. They'd blitzed their cells up along with Tessy and Arthur, so we were banged up for a couple of weeks in the cells we had smashed with no windows or beds, just a poxy mattress on the floor. Their case has since been sent back to the appeal courts, so they should win it this time, after falling foul of this country's corrupt justice system in the past.

But our hi-jinks didn't end there. We were soon moved over to C-hall, where we could all indulge our drug habits. We had recently been joined by one of my best pals, Steph, who had returned from his open-prison conditions for taking drugs. One day Porkie and I went for our methadone, when, to our horror, the nurse told us we weren't getting it until we gave her a urine sample. We knew we were done out of the park, as we had needle marks on our hands, arms and necks. But the smack had already run out, so we really needed our ration of meth. When we returned to our cells empty-handed, Porkie and I decided to storm down to the screws' office. Once in the office, I blew my top with the screw sitting behind the desk. I can now look back and safely say I was out of order doing and saying what I did, but in the heat of the moment I didn't have anything else on my mind except getting methadone. The screw told me he couldn't do anything for us, so Porkie and I proceeded to smash things up in his office. But give the screw his dues, as he never pressed the riot button.

On a mission to trawl for drugs, Steph and Sean were scampering about the hall, but no one had anything. I put it to Porkie on the way back that we should consider taking a screw hostage.

Porkie sparked, 'Aye, fuck it, I'm up for doing that as well.'

I told him I was only kidding, but he wasn't. He was up for doing it.

My stomach churned with nausea. 'Fuck the screw,' I ranted, 'why don't we get the nurse when she's down giving out the nightcap medication.'

'Naw, fuck that. We could get the doctor in and take him and his bag,' suggested Porkie.

I burst out laughing, but had to admit it sounded great. 'I'm up for that Porkie boy,' I said to my friend.

We jumped about the flat looking for someone to kid on to the screws that they were sick. Not long after, we found somebody. I'll call him Stig. We primed Stig with our plans, but he didn't really want to go through with it. But he had no option, as we threatened him with violence if he never did it.

One of Stig's pals told the hall screw that Stig was lying on his bed in pain. The screw went down and assessed what was wrong with him, to which Stig replied that he was getting shooting pains in his abdomen. The screw phoned the nurse, who came down and looked Stig over and told him she was going to phone the doctor out.

Once the nurse left Stig's cell and went up to the screws' office, Porkie and I went into Stig's cell and told him that we would be standing in the cell across from his and that, once we spotted the doctor, we'd run in and take him hostage.

'You just keep cool and stay lying on your bed, have you got that, Stig?' Porkie put to him.

'Aye, aye, I've got it,' Stig answered anxiously.

I followed Porkie back over to the cell to wait for the doctor to come in. We waited and waited. The time was getting on. The nurse came down and told Stig the doctor wouldn't be in until 5.30pm. But we were desperate, so as soon as another screw, who I will call Pete, walked into Stig's cell we decided to take both the nurse and the screw hostage.

HOSTAGE TWO, 3 JANUARY 1997

'OK, brother, are you ready?' I asked my pal, Porkie.

'Yes, let's go, mate,' he replied.

The rush on running into the cell was fantastic. I hadn't felt anything like it since my robbery days. The screw and the nurse didn't know what hit them. All they knew was that two junkies strung out on meth were holding knives to their throats. Pete tried to struggle with me, so I stuck the nut on him and flung him to the ground.

But everything was happening too quickly. Porkie made a pig's ear of closing the cell door, as the other screw up in the office came running down and shoulder-charged it open. He was very, very lucky that Porkie didn't stab him in the head, as he pulled his head back out of the door just in time.

'Get to fuck, you prick!' Porkie screamed out of the door at the screw. 'If you try and come back in here, we'll kill the screw and nurse, do you understand, you bam?' Porkie warned.

'Yes, I understand,' the screw shouted back at us through the now locked door.

'Good,' Porkie said, 'you better get me and Jimmy our meth or we'll be here all night.'

The screw told us that he would need to phone his boss for approval. Meanwhile, I'd cut strips off the bed sheets and trussed the screw's hands and feet up behind his back. I don't think Stig could believe his eyes. His face was a picture. But I was more interested in the sight of the nurse's bag, which contained a cocktail of drugs that Porkie and I quickly gulped down. There was Valium and DF liquid and handfuls of anti-depressants. We didn't care what we took, just as long as it took away the horrible pains and feelings we were having. I can't really explain in detail what these symptoms of withdrawal feel like, but imagine you had toothache all over your body, hot and cold sweats, and buzzing in your ears, with the shit flying out of you every twenty minutes, and you would be pretty close. I can now say that this still didn't give us the right to take a screw and a nurse hostage, but we were so hooked at the time that we would have murdered anyone for drugs if they had them.

The little nurse was crying her eyes out. She kept mumbling, 'If I knew you were that desperate, I would have given you a full bottle of meth.'

'Well, you're a bit late telling us now, you fucking cow,' I screamed at her.

I was starting to feel better. The Valium and DFs were kicking in. When the feelings of euphoria took over, we started laughing and singing. We heard the boys up the stairs from us getting moved on to the other side of the hall, so we couldn't shout up to them. The screws also emptied D-hall, the side that was facing us, so we couldn't shout over or in case any of them shouted over words of encouragement to us. A couple of trained negotiators came and stood outside the door trying to strike up some conversation, the usual routine. The negotiators always tried to get you talking because they can distract your mind from the current situation. I told Porkie to blank them, as this was his first hostage siege.

I pulled the screw, Pete, out from under the bed and untied his hands and retied them at the front so he could sit with his back more comfortably against the wall of the cell. I'll give Pete his due, he kept calm all the way through, and would talk to the nurse to keep her calm. What is more, when Porkie and I fell asleep from the effects of the drugs, Pete refrained from tying us up. I was asleep for three hours or so, and then I woke Porkie up. Pete was still sitting with his back to the wall; Stig and the nurse were sitting on the bed.

The nurse, who I'll call Sandra, had calmed right down by this time. She asked me if I was OK. She was worried that we had overdosed on the cocktail of drugs. Not a chance of that happening, as our habits were sky high. On becoming more alert, Porkie and I started talking to Pete and Sandra. The cocktail of drugs had done the trick; we were settled within our minds. I told the screw and nurse that it was nothing personal, as we only wanted the drugs. We also told them about the doctor and what we planned to do if he'd come in on time.

The screw, Pete, couldn't believe what we had just told him.

'Jesus, fuck, you must have really been desperate for drugs,' he said. 'Once this is over with, Jimmy, I'm going to take a drugs course and take a more active role when I see people rattling or coming off drugs. If you two madmen can do this, well, what will stop other people from doing the same or even things worse than this?'

The conversation went on. We found out that Pete used to be a professional football player for Hibs. He started talking about the games he had played against our two teams, Rangers – my team – and Celtic. The hours cooped up flew by and, before we knew it, it was three in the morning. At this point, we'd been holding them hostage for nine hours. Sandra must have broken the world record for holding in a pee, as there was nowhere for her to go. Eventually we let her go from the cell.

We let Pete go soon after. Pete had remained very, very calm. I'll give him his dues: after being head-butted, tied up and having a knife held at his neck for many, many hours, he coasted through the ordeal. If you're reading this book, Pete, I'd like to say sorry for what we put you and Sandra through, but I now think you understand that it wasn't personal – it was the drugs that we needed. You were in the wrong place at the wrong time. I also hope you're still doing the drug work with recovering addicts in the jail.

Once Porkie and I had come out of the cell, we were taken away, one at a time by the riot screws down to the digger. I was amazed that we never got a finger put on us. Once I was in the digger, a screw shouted through and told me I was going to Perth Prison in twenty minutes. But before I was to leave, my next-door neighbour, Big Tin from Govan, gave me one of my funniest memories. The governor, who I'll call Mrs R, opened his door to see how he was. Well, over the weekend, Tin had been saving up his piss pot, full of piss and shit. Well, need I say any more? He flung the lot round her face and body. Mrs R let out a blood-curdling sound I'd never heard before or ever since. Covered in excrement and piss, she fell to her knees and started crying. The screws jumped on Tin and gave him a severe doing, but the big chap took it all in his stride.

PERTH PRISON HOSTAGE, JANUARY 1997

I'd never been in Perth Jail before. The only other time I'd been in Perth before was when I had been through it on the stagecoach going to Dundee to watch my beloved Rangers play when I was fifteen years old. The sun was shining on the way up from my last prison, even though it was a cold winter's afternoon. But, once we had passed through Perth town, the sun went down on us and was replaced with menacing-looking, dark rain clouds.

I felt as if the powers from above had given me the worst welcoming committee possible. I saw the turret-like roofs jutting out forebodingly from the jail, like the devil's horns. I was apprehensive. When we drew up closer, I could take in fully the sinister-looking old castle that would have been more suited to Transylvania than the middle of Scotland. As we pulled up to the prison gatehouse, two screws came out and opened the van door to talk to one of the escort screws. They whispered a few words to each other, then one of them shot me a glance as if to say, *you scumbag*. I just kept looking at him, not once averting my unblinking gaze. The van door slammed shut.

'OK, Tam,' the head screw said to the driver of the van, 'take us down to the Rule 80 unit.'

The diesel engine kicked into life once more and we drove out of the gatehouse to the prison side. The place reminded me of the movie *Village of the Damned*. I spotted an old con in his late sixties, with an orange-coloured plastic shovel and a black bin bag in his hand. He was scooping up shit bombs that the prisoners had discarded out of their tiny cell windows the night before. The van stopped outside of a blue-coloured door. Again, it was like clockwork. As soon as the door opened, eight screws in full riot gear came out to meet us at the van.

One of them opened the van door and said, 'OK, let's be having him.'

The two screws I was handcuffed to moved off their lazy arses, and I moved with them. A screw came up to me, standing at 6ft 4in tall, and told me how the unit worked. After a few minutes, I was escorted to a unit by a party of screws, and put in cell number six, right at the end of the row of cells.

The screws took the cuffs off me and asked me to strip naked, all in front of twelve screws. I was past being embarrassed. I stood there naked in the freezing cold before one of the riot screws flung me a pair of pants and an ill-fitting jail uniform, which I gladly put on. The cell was so cold that I was starting to shiver and my breath was turning to mist that hung upon the air. All the screws left and the thick steel door slammed shut behind them. Then a steel-grille gate slid over in front of my door on the inside of the cell. It was a fucking cage for an animal in a zoo!

I suddenly heard a voice calling my name. 'Jimmyboy, are you OK?'

I knew the voice, but couldn't figure out who it belonged to. 'Aye, mate. I'm brand new,' I shouted back through at him. 'Who's that, anyway?'

'Me, Andy,' he said, 'Andy from Barhead, Glasgow.'

'Fuck, how are you doing, mate?' I shouted through to him.

'Did that rotten mob batter you, Jimmyboy?' Andy asked.

'No, did they fuck, Andy. They never put a finger on me,' I shouted back.

'Just as well,' Andy informed me, 'because if they had touched you then us five boys down here would be rolling about with the screws, riot gear or not!'

I soon found out from Andy the names of the other four cons: Frazer, Spike, Fat Cunt and Grass. To top it off, Robert Mottan, a child rapist, was here with me as well, in his own cell just around the corner. There was another character with us called JD. He'd sawed through the bars of his cell window on New Year's night and climbed on to the roof of the hall he was in and partied the night away. You don't get many like JD, he was, and still is, a very good laugh and a great pal of mine.

The rest of that night went by slowly for me, and, as usual, I was rattling. I never had any methadone or smack, so the night was a torturous affair. I had shit my bed and thrown up over my bed and floor, and the sweat was dripping off me. I was very, very ill. Of course, the loving and caring screws never gave me anything, and informed me that the doctor and the nurse wouldn't be round until the morning.

When the screws opened my cell door for breakfast in the morning, they put their hands up to their noses and mouths, as the smell of my bodily fluids and puke hit them like a steam hammer. I told them I was ill and needed my methadone or something to help me out. Finally, after what seemed like an eternity, the nurse and doctor came down to see me. The doctor went through his usual quackery and told me I was fine. He never wrote me up for anything at all, not even a detox! I told him I was tripping, to which he told me I would get over the worst of it within a week. Here I was coming off 65ml of prescription methadone, plus a smack habit on top of this, and he told me I was fine! I called him a prick and the nurse a cow. They slammed the door shut behind them.

Some two hours or so later, three screws opened my door and told me I could take a shower and change all my bedding. But doing all this was like running a marathon. The sweat and pain I was experiencing was unbelievable. I'd never felt so cold turkey in my whole life. If I could have hanged myself to escape this turmoil, then I would have done. I was talking to people who I believed were sitting on my bed. I spotted some tin foil lying on the floor, so I made it into the same shape as a razorblade and started trying to cut my throat, but it wasn't working.

I don't know where the time went, but after a while a screw told me that my lawyer was up to see me. 'Get your trainers on,' he bawled.

But I didn't have any trainers. I had no footwear at all.

Six screws were standing at my door. One rubbed me down and another one ran a metal detector over my body.

I had secreted the tin foil in my mouth.

'Right, let's go,' one of the screws ordered.

'No! Hold it,' another screw exclaimed, 'where are your shoes?'

'I've not got any,' I told him.

'You can't go up to see your lawyer without footwear,' he remonstrated.

I was given a pair of slippers to wear, which were two sizes too big. I only needed a red nose to complete my attire and I would have looked like Coco the fucking clown.

Once we got to the room where my lawyer was, my cuffs were taken off. As I went into the room, my eyes feasted on a very attractive woman sitting there. I didn't recognise her.

I said, 'I'm so sorry,' and I started to make a sharp exit. A first for Jimmyboy Holland to make a sharp exit from a stunningly good-looking woman, eh!

'Just a moment, Mr Holland,' she called out.

This eye-catching woman told me she was representing me and that my lawyer had sent her up. I immediately told her I was rattling and I needed my methadone, but she told me she couldn't do anything for me. In a hopeless act of desperation that was doomed to failure, I looked at the door and, on seeing that the screws weren't outside, I got up, turned my back to her, and pulled the tin foil from where I had secreted it in my mouth. I swung round and told her to shut her mouth. I was taking her hostage. She froze to the spot and then let out a snigger. 'Look, James, put that down, stop carrying on with the tin foil,' she said apprehensively.

I told her I wasn't carrying on. I grabbed the table she was sitting at and put it at the door, before I grabbed her and held the tin foil at her neck. When they heard me shouting, the screws came running to the door.

I told them, 'If you come in, I'll kill her. You better get me my methadone fix or I'll fucking kill her.'

I let her go and sat at the table with my legs cocked out on the chair so they couldn't push the door open. The six screws told me not to be daft.

'Come on now, Holland, let your lawyer go,' they appealed.

'Fuck off,' I yelled at them, 'get me my methadone.'

My heart went out to her, as I didn't really want to keep my lawyer hostage, but my need for methadone was too strong. The standoff with the screws lasted two hours. In an effort to break the deadlock, one of the nurses came down and showed me a bottle of meth through the little glass window on the door. This elicited the same reaction from me as dangling a carrot in front of a donkey. The screw told me to smash the window and they'd fling the little bottle of meth into me. Little did I know they were only distracting me so they could set up the automatic jack at the bottom of the door. I didn't know a thing because it happened so quickly. The door snapped in half, the table shot up in the air and my legs flew up, hitting my chest. I fell off my chair and, before I knew it, the screws were jumping on top of me, throwing punches at me. The last thing I can remember was a bright flash of light. I was totally knocked out.

Later, I found out that a screw had kicked me full force in the face, and had broken my nose. The blood was everywhere and I was taken to hospital. I couldn't walk, so I was getting pushed about in a wheelchair. I had cotton wool padding stuffed up my two nostrils and a sling around my nose with it tied at the back of my head.

Later that night, I came back to the unit and was put back into my cell. I was given some DFs at hospital, but they only helped dry up my shit. A con called Robert Mottan looked through my cell-door spy hole and asked if I was OK. I told him to get the fuck away from my door. I also told him if I got the chance I was going to stab, slash or scald him. I spat at the spy hole where his eye was, but there was a bit of protective glass to separate us. I started calling him every name under the sun. I also dissed him up on his life sentence and told him that I wished he never ever got out, as he's was not a criminal, but a beastie, a monster bastard. He had raped little boys, and is hated in the prison system. He's a dirty fucking beastie, poofy, grassing, shite, boy bastard. But just thinking about him makes me ill, so I'll not mention this monster again.

I lay in that cell for the next nine weeks, gradually getting better and better. The boys in the unit with me helped me the best they could, but there isn't really much anyone can do to help when you're coming off drugs. I went to court twice, once to get fully committed for the Glenochil and Perth hostage sieges and once for battering the screw in the Shotts man-eater. I went through a five-day trial and was found not guilty of battering the screw, but I still had the jail hostage trials to face. My witnesses in the assault trial were Rose, Lynn and Lizzy, and my lawyer. Thankfully, the jury took my side and found me not guilty. I would like to thank Rose, Lynn and Lizzy and my lawyer for standing in court and telling the truth, as the screws always seem to tell lies in court, for some reason.

CHAPTER SIXTEEN

Jingle Bollocks at the High Court

I hope that, by now, a trend is emerging from this book. Every stupid incident of violence that I have been involved in comes down to one thing: drugs. I've wasted my full life up until this point because of drugs. I've been stabbed and I've stabbed, coshed, battered, slashed, taken hostages and scalded people because of the lack of drugs or money to get drugs. I've had guns fired at me and I've fired guns for drugs, so if this book can help even just one boy or girl to give up the drugs, drink or solvents then it will have been worth it.

Drugs are addictive not just because of the substance, but also because of the lifestyle that goes with them. A few of my pals and I started off like most other young boys, experimenting with drugs from chipping in our pocket money on a Saturday to buy a bit of hash, but, before too long, we had tried acid, then speed, then smack and coke. Most people I have known who have died through taking drugs started off through hash. Some do just stick to hash, but most move on up the classes, to B- and then to A-class drugs. I've done every single drug at least once. I've done all the solvents in the modern world from glue to petrol to fire extinguishers. I've drunk spirits and beers I didn't like. So I know what I'm talking about.

But there is no glamour in taking drugs. There is no glamour in being in and out of prison. It is a waste of life. Don't be like my pals and me. If most of us could change our lives and live our teenage years again, then we would and, you can bet your life, we wouldn't be taking drugs. So I really hope this helps you to at least think about not taking drugs. I'm currently on methadone for the fifth time. I'm determined to beat my own demons and finally live the rest of my life drug free, but I can only take it one day at a time, so never plan a week ahead, because you never know what might happen in a week's time. So please think long and hard about what you're doing.

Meanwhile, back in prison, the weeks were turning into months and I was finally back to my usual old self. As usual, a couple of screws were on mine and JD's case, so, one Sunday night when the screws opened the door to give us our water, JD and I stuck our heads through the bottom of our cage-like door. The screws were mortified, as they couldn't shut the steel door owing to our heads poking through the cage grille gate.

We lay like that all night, until the next morning, when our necks were so stiff we couldn't move them at all. Just as we were chatting, the governor came down with a couple of works screws. This cunt hated us being in the unit. The bastard had a bucket of green liquid like household washing-up detergent, which the cheeky old cunt proceeded to pour over our heads. He then tried to push our heads back through the grille gate, but we weren't having any of it. I could hear JD shouting to me a warning that they were going to use what's called a motorised Stihl saw to cut through the bars above our heads.

I started sniggering. 'No, they wouldn't, mate, they're just trying to put the shitters up us.'

Well, wasn't I wrong? The Stihl saw revved into life. The fizzy-buzzing sound of the two-stroke motor was deafening. The screws flung a soaking wet towel around our heads and sawed one gate and then the next with the high-power cutting disk. The cunts didn't fuck about. I was deaf in both my ears for days after because of the noise from the saw being so close to my head, and I still suffer ringing in my ears many years on.

They moved JD down to the seg unit in Bar L. I was left on my own to stew. I was so fucked off by the old cunt's actions that I went totally mental. I set fire to my cell. I got dragged out unconscious and put over in the category 'A' cell, in the surgery, and then I got taken back over to the Rule 80 unit. I flung my piss pot of piss and shit round a screw. I was put in the silent cell, where I covered it in wall-to-wall shit. I stayed in that cell, with the shit, for twenty-seven days. When I came out, I'd grown a beard and was covered in green spots. I had a cold and felt so weak.

My aunty Rose, cousins Lynn and Lizzy were coming to visit me on the Sunday, so I didn't want to let them see me in such a bad way. I shaved, got my hair cut, ate all my food and took the antibiotics the doctor had prescribed for me. To make matters worse, I'd developed pleurisy and a bad infection from the shit. I was put into the closed visit room to see them. As I was on cat 'A', the screws kept the cuffs on me. I was gutted, as my visitors were upset at the way the screws were treating me. My aunty Rose pulled one of the screws aside and asked him why I was getting treated like a caged animal, to which he told her that I was too unpredictable and they couldn't take any chances. He said that, because I had taken people hostage in the past, I might do it again with family members. Can you believe that shit? This is what they do, they make out that you'd even hurt your own family and friends, when, in all likelihood, these are the very people you would least hurt when in confinement. My fight wasn't with family members. I felt as if the screws were defiling my visitors, so I never put any more passes out. Well, the screws got what they wanted, and I had played right into their hands.

The remainder of my time in Perth Prison was spent fighting with the digger screws, digging holes in my walls and barricading myself into the phone room. Despite my behaviour, some screws were OK with me and treated me humanely when they were on shift. I can publicly thank them here: Big Kev, Jim, Paddy, Old Pat and Old Sandy. I don't think I ever once had any trouble with them and they never showed any towards me. I'm not a screw lover, far from it, but, if a screw shows me a bit of kindness in a digger, I'll show them a bit back.

My trial was set for 23 June 1997 at Perth High Court. The three hostages from two incidents were put on to the one indictment against me. The two weeks leading up to my trial flew by, as every day in the digger flies by when you're on a long-term bang-up. I was looking forward to the Big Day in my own perverse way of thinking. I didn't give a fuck about getting a sentence. I was going to make sure the judge never forgot my name in a hurry!

Meanwhile, I wanted to give the screws as much bother as possible. A screw came and took me to the reception so I could put my suit on, which I did, but then another one came down and told me to strip again for a search. I had already been searched with a metal detector in the seg unit.

'I don't give two fucks,' the bastard with attitude said to me in a threatening manner.

I blew my top and warned the cocky bastard, 'If I take the clothes back off, I'm not putting them back on again.'

'Fucking do it,' Bastard Face ordered, 'I don't care.'

I took off all my stuff, even my pants and socks.

'OK,' the fuck pig screw said, 'put them back on.'

I told him to get to fuck and never to talk to me in that manner again. He slammed my door shut in the dog box. I was adamant that I wasn't putting my stuff on. Ten minutes later, the screws opened the door to take me to Perth High Court for my hostage trials and I was standing there naked.

'Right, boss, I'm ready,' I said.

'What do you mean, Holland?' asked a gobsmacked screw. 'You need to put your clothes on.'

'Will I fuck. I'll sit here all day if you don't want to take me to court,' I said.

The fucking screw who had ordered me to strip came back and said he was sorry for talking to me the way he had and asked me to put my clothes back on.

I told him to get the fuck out of my face. 'It doesn't work like that, mister,' I told him.

The screws phoned the governor, who came down and asked me to put my stuff back no. I told him *no* as well. The old daft cunt told me I'd be put on report if I didn't. Here I was, going up for three hostages and he's shouting about a report! I burst out laughing in his face. They eventually decided to put a blanket around my waist and bring my clothes with them in the cat 'A' van. I must have looked like Gandhi in the van on the way to court.

I was put in a cell once we arrived at the court. Twenty minutes later, my pal, Porkie, arrived at the court with his cat 'A' escort from Bar L, and was put in the cell a couple down from me. When I told him what I had on, he burst out laughing.

The court's duty lawyer came down with a message from my aunty Rose: 'Tell the little bastard not to embarrass me at this court or I will fucking kill him!' The lawyer told me what my aunty had said, word for word. One of the screws had told her that I was down the cells, naked. Now I hate the system and most screws and the law courts, but I love my aunty Rose and the family and I would walk over hot coals for them. I didn't want to embarrass Rose, so I got the screw to hand me my suit in.

Once Porkie and I were taken up into the courtroom, I looked round and gave aunty Rose a smile, to which she smiled back. My uncle Macky was there too and so was my big pal, Alan, who's stood by me through thick and thin as well. I couldn't believe the amount of coppers and screws in the dock with Porkie and me. Once the judge came into the courtroom, Porkie and I started calling him a poof and baming him up. The judge was Lord Abernethy, who was known to be a bit of a hard judge, but that reputation didn't carry any weight with us two.

The snooty lord ended up sending us back down the stairs for over two hours. When we were brought back into the court again, we started singing 'Jingle Bollocks' and a bit of the 'Whole World in Our Hands'. The old judge blew his stack and told us we were going to Edinburgh High Court for the trial and sentencing.

'So fuck,' we shouted, 'you're still a dirty old dog.'

'Get them animals out of my courtroom,' he screamed.

I looked up at my aunty, uncle and Alan. Their faces had the look of thunder on them. I knew I was going to take it stinking off them at my next visit and on the phone, but Porkie and I just wanted to let the judge and screws know that we didn't give a fuck about anything they could do to us.

I got a couple of minutes to get a snigger with my mate before I got whisked away in the cat 'A' van back to the digger in the jail. Once back, I got carted badly down to the Rule 80 unit. The boys in the digger started banging their doors and shouting for the screws to leave me alone. To be honest, I've been carted about that many times off the screws I was used to what they did. When anyone gets put in the locks and carted, for the first time it's sore, but, over a period of time, you get used to anything they fling at you. The boys in the seg unit had calmed down once they knew I was OK. The rest of the week went by without any incidents.

But, for some unknown reason, the beginning of the next week saw every one of us go totally ballistic. We dug holes in the walls, smashed up everything in the cells and ripped up all the linoleum on the floors. The cells were smashed to bits. Sure as fuck, the mufti mob came in and carted us off one at a time. Some of the other screws cleaned the cells out and then we got flung back in them.

I kid you not, we never even had a mattress and the cell was totally bare of all contents, apart from the dirt on the floor. It was decided we'd start pissing on the floors and wiping our shit on the walls, something known in the business as a Shit Up. The screws kept us in the cells like caged animals for three or four days. We had phoned the newspapers and our lawyers to tell them the way we were being treated, as it's supposed to be against the law to leave you overnight without any bedding or a mattress. Did the screws care? Did they fuck! They said we'd ripped our bedding and mattresses up, which was a lie. We never got any to start with. We slept on the cell floors covered in our own body waste for three fucking nights. It was freezing cold, and the only reason we did eventually sleep was through pure exhaustion. Eventually, the screws asked us if we wanted our bedding stuff back. Of course, they didn't have our prison welfare at heart – it was in case they got collared breaking the law. They were protecting their own fat arses.

The day was set for my next trial at Edinburgh High Court on 9 July 1997. I never really managed to get a good sleep the night before the trial, so I decided to put my prison-issue clothes on at 3.00am. The seg unit was so quiet I could hear one of the other boys snoring. I lay there in abject silence, with the light outside my jail window shining through, but it was still pitch black in my cell. I wondered what the other five boys were dreaming about or if any of them were still awake, lost in their own little world, thinking about the future and what lay ahead for them.

I must have dozed off again, as I came to when the screws opened my door to give me my breakfast.

One of the screws who I was all right with said, 'Big day today, Jimmy.'

'I know, boss,' I replied dryly, but without malice.

'The escort that's taking you will be here in thirty minutes,' the friendly screw said, shutting my door.

'Aye, brand new, I'm ready,' I said.

'Good, good,' he said.

It must have been habit, but I stripped off all my jail clothes and waited naked in my cell for my escort to come. The door finally opened for them to take me to court, but once they saw me naked they asked where my clothes were.

I told them, 'I'm not wearing jail clothes or civvy clothes, I'm going like this.'

A couple of the screws burst out laughing at my remarks, which also made me laugh.

'Come on, Jimmy. Put some clothes on,' they pleaded.

'No, am I fuck. I'm going like this,' I snapped.

'Oh, have it your way, Holland,' the head screw ranted, as he stormed off.

Off we went to Edinburgh High Court in the cat 'A' van with the usual police cars and bikes, but also with a helicopter overhead for good measure. Fuck knows what they needed that for. I don't know what it is with High Court buildings and me, I always seem to strip naked. I hate the full system of law and what it stands for, so I didn't feel as if I needed to show them any respect. They were raping me of justice, so I might as well be prepared.

Once I got to the High Court, the screws with me covered my modesty with a couple of their hats, one at the front and also at the rear. I was laughing and shouting that they'd abducted me out of my bed. 'I'm innocent,' I cried out. I was rushed through to an area where there were five cages on each side. This was the first time I'd been in the new cell area at Edinburgh High Court. Again, Porkie was brought through from Bar L and put in the cell around from me, but we weren't allowed to see each other.

I had a visit from Porkie's lawyer and QC, as I never had legal representation because no one wanted to take me on in case I took them hostage. So, when Porkie's lawyer and QC came round and saw me sitting naked in the cell, they didn't know where to look.

I told them, 'I'm not going through with the trial, as I haven't got anyone to represent me.'

Porkie's lawyer said, 'Porkie didn't want to go through the trial either, as he felt it was a waste of time and, to be honest, you're guilty as sin, nothing can change that.'

Fuck, so it was decided! My pal Porkie and I would plead guilty, as, if we continued on our present course and took it through to a full trial, we'd have got twelve years each at the very least.

I still refused to put any clothes on, so was marched into the courtroom in handcuffs with a screw holding a blanket around me. The look on my aunty and uncle's faces was a picture. I don't know how they felt at seeing me like this, but it was too late. Porkie came up a couple of minutes later, swearing and singing Republican songs. Even though I'm a Rangers man, I took my hat off – metaphorically – to Porkie's show of defiance. Nice one, mate.

Lord Hope entered the room, whereupon everybody rose to their feet except for Porkie and me.

Once the case was under way, the judge asked me, 'How do you plead, Holland?'

I swore at him saying, 'Fucking guilty.'

Porkie did the same. I think the judge knew he was dealing with a couple of guys that simply didn't care what the fuck happened to them. He gave me six years consecutive to the six years I was already doing. I only had three months left on my current sentence. It came to Porkie, who got six years on top of his life sentence. But I don't know how that would really affect him on top of a life sentence. As for me, the drugs had taken a hold on me, so I didn't care about my sentence. When I look back, I can see now that I was a nut job for doing such daft things in life, but you can only learn by your mistakes. My problem is that I don't listen to anyone when I've made my mind up about doing something.

From the court, I got flung back in the cat 'A' van. We made it back to Perth Jail from Edinburgh in double-quick time. I never got to say cheerio to Porkie, and I've still not clapped eyes on him since that day in court in 1997. However, I have read of his later hostage-taking exploits in the paper and received a letter from him. He was sentenced to another fourteen years on top of his life sentence for more hostage takings in prison.

I lay in Perth's Rule 80 unit for a further eight months. Then I was transferred back down to Bar L seg unit, the Wendy House.

CHAPTER SEVENTEEN

The Bar L Wendy House isn't for Kids

THE BIG HOOSE IN BAR L, WENDY UNIT, 7 AUGUST 1997

I could smell the smog when we drove into Glesga. The sun had been beating down all morning. There's no place else in Scotland like Glesga on a hot, sunny day. The dazzlingly depressing vista of the jail recumbent on the panoramic landscape came into view from the prison motor. My heart skipped a beat as a feeling of comfort came over me. I was excited to be coming back to the Big Hoose after so many years away from it. I suddenly felt closer to my aunty Rose and the girls, plus a few of my old pals. Fucking hell, I could nearly reach out and touch them all! I knew it wouldn't be a problem for my loved ones and friends to visit.

Once the high-security cat 'A' van was inside the prison and had checked in at the gatehouse, it made its way past all the work sheds, turned to the right, past the big education block, and there it was, in all its glory ... the famous so-called Wendy House seg unit, in between E-hall and A-hall. The last time I was in this seg unit, I'd been battered, kicked and punched until seven different colours of shit came out of me. But this time was to be different. The MUFTI mob screws were conspicuous by their absence in the VIP welcome lounge. Instead, the screws that were there had friendly smiles on their faces! Strange, I thought, they must have been members of a syndicate of lottery winners.

I didn't know any of the new screws that were now working in the seg unit. Once I was settled in cell number four, the door opened, with three screws parked outside. Surely there was a beating here.

But one of them simply asked, 'Do you prefer to be called James or Jimmy?'

I told him, 'Jimmy.'

'OK,' he said, 'you're going to be here for a few months, so let's hope we all get on well, Jimmy.'

'I'm not down here to cause trouble, but I'm not going to be head-over-heels in love with you either,' I replied glibly.

'That's good, Jimmy,' another screw with a shaven head and goatee beard replied. He was called Wullie, and he told me that they were told before I came here that I'd just cause them trouble and give them a sore head.

I told them, 'If you treat me like a human being, I'll treat you the same way. But, if you treat me wrong, then I'll be like a bear with a sore head.'

'Good, son. I get your drift,' the older screw, whose name was Davie, acknowledged.

I liked the way Davie spoke his mind. Wullie handed me a phone card so I could phone my aunty Rose and arrange my visits. Now, in all my years in any seg unit, I'd never been given a phone card off any screw, so this was a nice surprise. On the surface, I played it cool, but, underneath it all, my mind was wondering what this was all about. I was paranoid about what any of the other cons would think of me if they heard or knew I'd got a phone card off a screw. I needn't have worried, as most cons that came down to this seg unit were offered or helped out with things from the new lot of screws. Things had changed, and the days of the MUFTI squad were in the past. The governors finally realised that they just fuelled hatred on both sides.

Once I came off the phone, a big screw called Rab I'd never seen before asked me if I wanted hot water to make a cup of tea. I took the water and then shut my cell door. I then heard my name being shouted at the window. I asked who it was.

'Brush,' the boy said.

I hadn't seen Brush since Longrigend, all those years ago. He was originally from East Kilbride. The little man was brand new with me; we were like two long-lost brothers. The little chap's got one of the worst scars on his face I've ever seen. At least the poor cunt got the guy back that did it to him. In Bar L Prison, there were more boys with chib scars on their faces than not. Chibing is the favourite pastime of the Glesga culture, especially in the jail. I don't think any other prison in Britain has more people getting slashed down the face than in Bar L. I'd safely put a bet on there having been more than 500 slashings there since 1980.

Brush asked me if I needed any tobacco, to which I told him I was OK, but, when he asked if I wanted a charge of smack, I accepted right away. I thanked little Brush and told him I'd be back up to talk to him once I'd drunk my tea and burned a bit of smack. I hadn't had a bit of kit for about six or seven weeks, so, as soon as I took the smack, I whitied up. I felt nauseous, as if I was at death's door. When Brush heard me puking into my piss pot, he started sniggering out aloud. Most people don't throw up on a tenner bag of jail kit after all.

After a while I felt better, and well recovered enough to go to the window to talk to Brush. I asked him who was down the seg unit with us. Brush told me we were with Little Rab L from Port Glesga, JD my mate from Perth seg cells, Little Laurence T from Greenock and Moose from Paisley. I knew every single one of them, so the Wendy was soon jumping with patter. We all used to lie down at the doors talking and singing, playing quizzes until three or four o'clock in the morning, as we never had anything better to do with our time. My mate Danny B from Govan was in A-hall, and he used to shout down to me at nights. My other pal John Simpson used to shout down from E-hall at nights as well. I hadn't seen John or Danny since Dumfries YOI, so it was good to talk to them at nights from the windows.

Even though we were isolated from the outside world, we were still in touch with goings-on through the radio. I'd been in the Wendy House just over three weeks when I heard of Princess Diana's sudden death. Moose shouted me to put my radio on. Sure enough, every radio station was reporting the story. I'm not shy to admit that I had a tear in my eye, as she was the people's princess, and was stunningly beautiful. It didn't matter if you were Catholic or Protestant; everyone in this seg unit was gutted at her death. On the day of Diana's spectacular funeral, everyone in Bar L got passed a slip of paper, which asked us to stay quiet for one minute's silence to show our respects for the princess. There was a couple of arseholes shouting and kicking their doors, but over 1,000 cons showed their respects.

After that, things started to go back to normal pretty fast.

Other prisoners came and went. One guy, who I didn't know personally, but had heard a lot about, had come down to the Wendy House on remand facing a murder charge in Paisley, in 1996. His name was Stu Boyd. His co-accused, Stewart G, had been found guilty of the same murder and got sentenced to life in prison. Stu's trial went on for eleven days. At the end of it he walked out of the court, scot-free.

There was also another boy down on remand for murder called John Ferriar. He came from Clydebank. I got to know him over the months, but before long he went to court and was found Not Guilty. The best of luck to him and his wife after all those months of heartache. It's sad to see innocent people having to go through the heartache of a murder trial, but it must also be some buzz to be found Not Guilty.

However, being let out of the Wendy doesn't guarantee a life of happiness. I think the Wendy has some sort of curse on it, as four or five boys that have been in the seg unit have been murdered soon after being released. Some people will say that they were more than certain candidates to face death, because of their lifestyles, but the number of murders was nevertheless very high. My little pal Rab Leslie was involved in a fight with a couple of other boys in a pub, in Port Glesga. During the fight, Rab had his throat cut and bled to death in his girlfriend's arms.

Then there was John Simpson. John came down to the Wendy on November for slashing Fritz McGraw, the brother of Tam 'The Licensee' McGraw, in E-hall. John didn't miss him with the chib; he gave Fritz a very sore face. You know, John had the heart of a lion; he was scared of no man ... a real daredevil. Most of the big-time gangsters had heard of John. He was only twenty-four years old. He was Stu Boyd's cousin, so was well known and respected. Having a kind side to his nature, John got his girlfriend to buy me a pair of Nike trainers. John also told me he would buy me a TV and tracksuit once he got out and started working again.

But a few days after his release, John's face was splashed all over the newspapers. He'd been shot in his aunt's house at point-blank range on New Year's Eve. Two of his so-called pals did it, but I'll not mention their names. They thought they'd killed John, but, somehow, he survived and went to hospital. They kept John in hospital for two weeks or so, and then he signed himself out. By this time, John was on the warpath, but the problem was, he wasn't fit to be out of the hospital, never mind on the warpath! He should have gone down to England and got himself fit and lay low, but that wasn't John. He wanted revenge at any cost and he wanted it now.

I don't know if being shot fucked up his sense of judgement, but he started making insane threats to people. He threatened to murder one of the boys he knew, who then went to a well-known Southside gangster. The gangster gave him a gun and told him he'd better murder John. The boy waited for John as he went to get a taxi. He pulled a gun out and shot John in the chest a couple of times at point-blank range. John's lifeless body fell to the ground like autumn leaves falling from the trees. He may have been hated by a lot of people in the city and in every jail in Scotland, but these people hadn't seen the kind-hearted, sensitive side to the big man's nature. God bless you, big man. I hope wherever you are, John and Rab, that you're all doing OK. Love and respect to you from your little pal here. R.I.P.

CHAPTER EIGHTEEN

Screwbirds and Killing the Junkie

PETERHEAD SPECIAL UNIT, JANUARY 1998

It wasn't long before I was sent to the Peterhead Special Unit, which was designed to allow disruptive or unruly prisoners to adjust back into mainstream prison life after being on long-term bang-up in cell blocks up and down the country. The main jail housed every imaginable depraved sex beast in the country, since the prison ran an allegedly world-class 'stop' programme for sex offenders, supposed to help the most elite of the sex monsters to stop raping and murdering innocent women and children. The unit was totally separate from the mainstream prison, and had protective walls right around it to keep us from getting at the monsters.

The prison had had a lot of money spent on it. There was a concourse area, visits room, a state-of-the-art gymnasium and work-shed, a pushbutton digital fitted kitchen, living room and music room. All in all, the unit was a very worthwhile project. All very nice, except for the presence of a screwbird.

The screwbird is a funny sort of creature. So far, I've identified three types.

Screwbird Do-Job: the first woman screw in history to work in any special unit. She came up to collect me from the main reception of the jail; she introduced herself as 'Terri'. In a way, Terri was quite attractive, with shoulder-length brown hair, but she differed from the other types of screwbird, in that she never flung her feminism in my face, and just did her job. A rare collectors' item.

Screwbird Lead-On: this one really bugs most prisoners. There are tell-tale signs to look out for: smart appearance, flirts with the cons and leads them on. As soon as the con says or does something, the screwbird puts them on report.

Screwbird Predatory User: beware! This type gets really pally with certain cons. They're predatory creatures. They wrap the con around their little finger by showing a bit too much cleavage or talking dirty. Once the con's hooked, she gets him or them to bully and batter the cons she doesn't like.

As I was saying, Terri didn't use her beauty to intimidate or get her way with any of the prisoners, as she was fairly androgynous. She'd play football and tennis with us. Terri would also help the teachers that came in to teach us English, maths and art. Most of the prisoners liked Terri, and there were also a few male screws that were spot on with us. I never thought that I'd admit it, but I now have a different outlook on certain screws. For the first time in my life, I looked beyond the uniform of the screw and saw the person behind the mask of mystery.

Some of the screws from Peterhead that treat me with dignity are listed here: Big Sinky (not the Glenochil one, the one from

Aberdeen), Old Lee, Adrian, Big Kev, Malky, John B and Mikey G (who have both left the job now), Toasty and, of all people, a governor called Bob. Yes, a governor! He's left the job now. These people talked me out of leaving the unit, which was a wise decision.

There are also a few special people I want to mention that spent a lot of time helping me. Grace, who was our cookery and arts & crafts teacher, and a wonderful woman. Helen, our ceramics teacher. This little woman was so strong, she was amazing and so was her family. Helen also helps out a bit with underprivileged children. Keep up the good work, Helen. Janice, our drugs worker, who started up Gram Plan Addictions Programme Services (GAPS). She and some friends have done more to help the addicts of Aberdeen and Frazerburg than anybody else. Her pure raw determination is overwhelming. She had breast cancer, and was in hospital for over a month, but that never held this brave, brave woman back from helping me and many other recovering addicts. I've nothing but a deep respect for this wonderful woman.

Then there was Father Coyle, the Chaplin at Peterhead Prison for over twenty years. This man has probably seen more human suffering than most, but he always had a smile on his face. He could tell a great joke, and is a credit to his faith. And also Big Pamela, who was just starting out in her profession as a psychologist under the watchful eye of Dr Ian Stevens. Pamela was a joy to look at and she was good at her job too. Lastly, Ian Stevens, probably the best psychologist in his field of work in Scotland. I was at Ian's school, The Douglas Inch Clinic when I was younger, and I've known him most of my life. The BAFTA-award-winning TV programme *Cracker* is based on Ian Stevens. It was Ian that suggested I write a book about my life, so here I am. Ian has now since retired from the SPS.

All these people I've mentioned gave me a chance, whereas beforehand I was totally out of control. Before I met them, my life was hardly worth living. I was that far gone, I didn't even care if I lived or died. All I wanted was my next fix of drugs. But, when I'm off drugs, I'm a different person. The unit showed me what I could do when I'm drug-free. But others are not so lucky. The prison doctors often can't see these people in prison for two and three days. In a last-gasp cry for help, and in desperation, they hang themselves to escape the sheer pain of rattling. I would say that most prison suicides are caused by drug-withdrawal symptoms or bullying. Then you get others, like the nurses that are supposed to care for people, telling people that are rattling when they come off the streets not to swear at them or they won't get any treatment. Come on, the system's a pure joke!

I started to look at drugs differently when I started talking to my drug worker Janice. I started to see the bigger picture. I learned that the screws in the unit were there to help us. There are a few cons that go into the units and come out of them thinking they're King Kong, but that's the wrong attitude to have. People should understand the unit wasn't built so you would come out and think you're harder than you went in it. If you thought that, you would get battered, stabbed or slashed from the mainstream cons, and quite rightly so, as no cunt likes a smartass who walks about thinking he can batter everyone because he was in a special unit.

For the first time in my life, I gave the screws 100 per cent respect, because they gave me respect. I started to learn things I did not know before. My reading, writing and spelling improved, as did my skills at woodwork, ceramics, painting and brickwork. My newfound maturity soon attracted the attention of the governor, Bob, who asked me if I would like to do some work for a handicapped charity. I gladly took this responsibility. Bob took some old bikes that no one had claimed from the local police in Peterhead, and asked me to put them back together again. Over the next three months, Bob and I put our hearts and souls into fixing the bikes up. I was surprised when Bob sprung it on me that some people from the charity were going to come in with a couple of handicapped people to collect the bikes. I was over the moon, as I wanted to see their little faces light up when they got their bikes. I got my photos taken with Bob and three or four of the handicapped children; their smiles said it all.

I'd like to mention some of my pals that were in the unit with me at this time. There was Rab T, from Maryhill, in the north end of the city, who is doing twenty-five years for a shootout in Paisley. The boy's a diamond. We were as thick as thieves. We used to love it when the Rangers vs Celtic game was on, as we were the only two Rangers supporters in the unit at that time. Then there was Paul G from Govan. Paul was some boy, a laugh a minute. He was doing six years for robbing an off-licence. Would you believe that, even though Paul stays a stone's throw from Ibrox Stadium, he supports Celtic? Even though he's out of prison now, he still writes to me and visits me from time to time. About two years ago, Paul was jumped upon by a gang of youths. One of them slashed Paul's face from his forehead down through his eye, lip and chin! The scar is ghastly to look at, but, underneath that scar, he's still the same old Paul I know and respect as a friend.

Then there was Popey from Perth, who was doing nine years for stabbing a guy to death in a street fight. Although Popey talked with a stutter, he could sing like an angel. I was taught by Popey, who was a wizard at bricklaying, how to build fishponds and fireplaces out of granite rock. Popey could also talk fluent

Norwegian, as he stayed over there with his family until he was seventeen. Then there was Stuart G, from Paisley, who is doing a life sentence for a murder he didn't commit. Also, Old John C, who was an amazing man. John was an old-time bank robber, and has done fourteen years of a life sentence, although he never killed anyone. John was in the special unit with me, and could do anything he turned his hands to. Last, but not least, is Old Dougie T. He was doing twelve years. He comes from a little place to the south-east of Glasgow called Cambuslang.

Even though life in the unit was going well, as in all prisons there is no such thing as a completely stable atmosphere. Just one event can spark it all off. On one fateful night in November 1998, Old Dougie got into a fight with a boy in the unit. Dougie battered him, but, since violence was not tolerated in the unit, he was sent back to the mainstream jail. Another boy called John was also involved. John was doing a life sentence for killing his girlfriend, something he couldn't live with. When he went back to mainstream prison, he hanged himself. The guilt of killing his girlfriend had taken its toll on him.

Most of the prisoners were gutted about the departure of Old Dougie, but the screws weren't going to listen to us or change their minds.

This was to cause a siege of gigantic proportions.

CHAPTER NINETEEN

Shoot to Kill Prison Siege – Back to the Wendy House

HOSTAGE SIEGE NUMBER FOUR, ARMED RESPONSE UNIT

We'd made up our minds; Stuart, Popey and I would take the governor hostage in retaliation for Old Dougie being shipped out. Hell, I liked this little governor as well, but it was down to him to bring Dougie back, and he was too stubborn to consider budging. I went into the kitchen and lifted three huge steak knives, before returning to my cell where all the boys were sitting. We then went through to the back visit room where a steel-grille gate separated us from the governor's office. Stuart and me tapped at the door and waited for one of the screws. We told him we wanted to see the governor, but the screw told us Bob wasn't in, so we went back to my cell.

But I was so hyped up with rage by this time that I just ran out and stuck the knife at the throat of one of the other prisoners. For some reason, Stuart P did the same to another con. We dragged the hostages into Stuart's cell and slammed the door shut. Popey was already sitting in the cell when Stuart and I dragged Old Sanny and the Hobbit into Stuart's cell.

Once the door was shut over, we let our captives go. We were all sniggering our heads off, as we could hear the screws on the other side of the door running about all over the place. One of the screws, Malky, who was hated by most cons, was shouting through the side of the door asking us what was wrong. I shouted back through to him, 'If any of the screws try to open the door, I'll shoot the hostages!'

I just said it for a laugh, as we never had a gun, but the screws took what I said as gospel. Everything went deadly silent outside the door of the cell. It continued like that for some five or six hours. By three in the morning, we were all tired. We'd a problem, as there was only one mattress between five of us, so two of us would take forty-minute sleeps at a time while the other three stayed awake. After a succession of sleeping sessions, at six in the morning a voice shouted my name from outside the cell. I didn't recognise the voice, but I knew he must have been from the north-east of Scotland or Aberdeen.

The voice said he belonged to a member of the Grampian Armed Response Firearms Unit. They had taken over from the Prison Service. We thought it was some kind of joke and burst out laughing at the cunt. We all started making sheep sounds, just ripping the piss out of him. Stuart asked him to show us some proof of identity. The guy told Stuart to uncover the spy hole on the door. Sure as fuck, the copper was standing there with a black helmet on, sunglasses and a submachine gun. As soon as we saw this guy, the laughing and carrying on stopped dead.

Stuart swiftly covered the spy hole back up. Unknown to us at that time, armed coppers were simultaneously looking for guns in

Stuart's wife's house, in Paisley. They thought that his wife, Lynn, had brought a handgun up to the visit. Remember, Stuart was a cat 'A' prisoner and was involved in all the Paisley gang wars at the time. Added to this was the fact that some MPs in Paisley had received death threats, so they didn't take this lightly at all.

The armed copper stuck a sheet of paper under the cell door with instructions on how they wanted us to come out. They wanted us to strip naked and come out one at a time with our hands on our heads. I had to come out first, followed by Stuart, Popey, the Hobbit and Old Sanny. We were still shattered from being in a cell all night without too much sleep.

'Fuck this,' I said to the rest of the guys, 'let's just get this over with.'

We all stripped naked, then Stuart shouted out of the side of the door and told the armed copper we were ready. About five or ten minutes later, someone put the key in the cell door and a guy's voice shouted my name and told me to come out slowly with my hands on my head.

I shook the rest of the boys' hands and opened the cell door, all very slowly. My heart was racing like a dragster's rev counter. Once out of the cell, I was the focus of attention. Two armed police marksmen were standing at one end of the section. They wore black air masks, black helmets and black boiler suits. They had little submachine guns, just like the ones you see in the movies. They even had infrared target dots on them; two little red dots were now merrily dancing about on my chest like errant measles. There were another two armed cops standing at the other end of the section, one of whom had a handgun pointed at me. The other was unarmed, and he was shouting out instructions to me, telling me to walk very slowly down towards the coppers with the submachine guns.

When I was about five feet away from them, they told me to sit on the ground, cross-legged with my hands on my head. The other four prisoners from the cell all did the same. Once the five of us were sitting in the corridor, the copper who was doing all the talking told me to stand up slowly, with my hands still on my head. But I was so weak that I had trouble getting up. Every time I tried, my flabby belly would just wobble. So I had to roll over to the corridor wall and use my shoulders to help me up. Once I got on my feet, I was out of breath and sweating like a Turkish wrestler's jockstrap.

The copper told me to walk backwards, towards him. Just as I was doing this, disaster struck. I fell over Popey, landing on my arse and back. As soon as I fell, I lost my temper. I shouted at them at the top of my voice, 'You fucking pricks, if you're going to shoot me, well, fucking shoot me! If not, I'm coming towards you, face on!'

The copper didn't seem to mind me walking towards them, but once I got within a couple of feet of the grilled gate, they told me to turn around and take a couple of steps backwards. I froze.

The copper with the handgun stuck it at the back of my head. He told me to slowly put my hands behind my back, one at a time. As soon as I did this he handcuffed the rest of my fellow prisoners. After I was handcuffed, I was quickly moved out of the area round to the PT room, where I was photographed, videoed and then handed back over to the Prison Service riot screws. They rushed me out the back door of the unit into a van where I was transferred up to the main part of Peterhead Prison. In typical Holland style, I was stark bollock naked.

I was taken into A-hall where some of the worst sex monsters in the country were being held. The riot screws put me in a cell on the second flat. Once I was safely in the cell, a nurse asked me if I had any injuries. I told her I didn't. I was given prison clothes to put on and then the door slammed shut. Once the screws had left, I jumped up to the window of the cell. A-hall looks on to the main gatehouse of the prison. Outside there were three ambulances, two fire engines, umpteen police cars and vans. For fuck's sake, I thought, they'd taken my threats deadly seriously about us having a gun. They would have shot us if we made any moves. One of the riot screws who brought me in my dinner later that day told me they wanted to shoot us and ask questions later. It just shows you, eh! You're not even safe in prison.

The guy next door to me banged on his wall and asked me to come down to the pipe that runs through every cell. I told him, 'Get to fuck,' because he was a sex monster. I also told him, if I got the chance, I was going to take the screw hostage, take his keys, open his door and kill him. I was just spouting this out to the monster to give him a fright, but he shouted that he didn't care and he told me he was the top man of the jail. His name was Gavin. I'll call him The Kilmarnock Monster, as he had abducted a fourteen-year-old girl and raped her. He had then decapitated her. This monster was only a couple of feet away from me, with only a brick wall separating us. If I could have got to him, I would have.

These monsters sicken the normal mainstream prisoners. They shouldn't get protection; they should be flung in with all of us so we can give them our own kind of instant justice. I don't think Peterhead Prison should be kept open with all the beasts in it, as they all boast to each other who they've raped or murdered. There is a programme that's supposed to stop them from reoffending, but most refuse to take the programme, so they should shut it down.

The funny thing is, these monsters can get away with all sorts of heinous crimes, such as rape, incest, touching up little kids, buggering young boys and the like, and they get all the help in the world. But, hey ... the minute you do over some high flyer's house to feed your drug habit, you get locked up for years and they throw away the key! What they're saying is, it's OK to drag my daughter up a dark alley and shag her up the arse, but don't burgle my house!

At about 4.40pm that day, I was taken down and put into the back of the prison's cat 'A' van. Stuart was already in the van. The screws cuffed us together, and told us where we were going – Stuart was going to Shotts digger and I was going to the Wendy House digger, in Bar L Prison. It was starting to get dark. Stuart and I were just sitting in the back getting a laugh between us and smoking roll-ups. The trip from Peterhead to Glasgow usually takes three to three-and-a-half hours. Well, we got to Shotts in two-and-a-half hours. We'd done an average speed of well over 100mph with the coppers driving in front and behind us with their blue flashing lights and sirens blasting. The motorbikes were always a couple of miles in front of us, clearing the road ahead.

I quite enjoyed the journey down from the north, as it was a little change. The last time that happened to me was in Perth when I was being taken to Edinburgh High Court. We arrived at the digger, and the same screws as the last time I'd been there were on duty. They were friendly enough: Big Rab, Wullie, Little Andy, Old Davie and Spoony. I was given some food, a radio and a flask full of coffee.

BAR L WENDY HOUSE, NOVEMBER 1998

I was here just over two weeks when a big pal of mine, called Paddy Mc, came down from the halls. Paddy is from Barrowfield, in the Eastend of Glasgow. He was coming off drugs at the time, and was in a very bad way. I scored a bit of kit off two of my pals, Brian and Bungy, to sort Paddy out. Paddy was the sort of guy to get smack in and help everyone out, so I knew he would source Brian and Bungy back up once he got himself sorted out. Later that night, I heard Paddy being violently sick in the cell next door. I lay there helpless; there was nothing anyone could do for him. I was lying there wondering what Paddy was thinking about in the nightmare he was so obviously stuck in, poor cunt. Over the next couple of days, Paddy just lay on his bed being sick, sweating, not sleeping and having the runs. The guy had been through it a hundred times before, so I never had any doubts he'd get through this as well.

My birthday was coming up very soon, on 10 December. I'd booked a visit for my aunty Rose, my big pal Alan and my little cousin Lynn, as they always visited me on my birthday. I couldn't believe I had reached my twenty-eighth birthday, and was still in prison. The years seemed to fly by too quickly for my liking. I always get nervous when I go on a visit with my aunty Rose, as she doesn't take any shite off me. That's what I love and respect about this wonderful woman. She always starts off by saying the same thing: 'I hope you've been changing your pants and socks and taking showers, and that you're keeping your cell clean.' I've been known to live like a tramp. I never used to clean my cell or empty my bin, and used to only change my pants and socks once every three days and take one shower a week. I just never cared about my personal hygiene. But my aunty hated that. She's been known to slap me round the ear and tell me off in front of screws. But, when I'm in the right, she's very protective of me and won't hear a bad word said. That's what I call real love and respect, so, when I go on the visits, I make sure I'm clean as a whistle so I don't get a slap.

This was my first visit since I came back from the Peterhead Special Unit. I was confident I would not get slapped, as I was as clean as a whistle. But, when I sat down, BANG! I didn't see it coming. Rose slapped me clean across the lug. She went to do it again, but I pulled my head away just in time.

'Right you, ya cunt, what did you do that up the unit for?'

She was talking about the recent hostage taking. I tried to squirm and bluff my way out of having anything to do with it, but Rose knew me too well. But once I told her the truth, I had a great birthday visit. That's the way it goes with my lovely aunty and I love her for being so strong-minded towards me. My big pal Alan was a good friend and still is. He has done a lot to help me over the years. What can I say about Alan except you're a 110 per cent top man and so is your lovely family, big chap. I can't wait 'til you read this book, Alan, as I know you'll understand completely.

The visit finished and, as always, I got a lovely warm cuddle from my aunty, who, in my eyes, is the closest thing I have to a mother. I love holding her tightly and, if I could, I wouldn't let her go. That also goes for my two little gorgeous cousins Lynn and Lizzy. I would love to just hold you for ever, in my arms, as I've been brought up in an all-male environment, so am not very confident around girls and women. I tend to shy away, but, with my family, I love being in their company, and they know that. I've watched them grow up from two little teenage girls into two very mature confident women. Lizzy has now got a little baby boy called Lee, who is totally amazing. I've had Lee up at lots of visits. I love holding this small bundle of joy in my arms. David, Lizzy's husband, is a real top man. I think he knows that anyway.

Once I go back to my cell after the visit is over, I always lie on my bed and have a lingering smoke. Most people in prison are on a high when going to a visit, but, once it's finished, most people feel a little bit down and I'm no different from anyone else. I may be called a nut job or a danger man from the screws and cons, but people in prison who know me will tell you that's not true at all. I've hundreds of feelings just like anyone else does.

Brian, Bungy and Paddy invited me to come down to the door to do a crossword and get a chat. I told them I would be down in half an hour or so, as I just wanted to savour the last moments of my visit with my family and friend. I then went down to the door and got a good snigger. About ten days after the visit, my two other pals came down to the digger: Little Besty from Greenock and John H from Port Glasgow. At this particular time, John was doing a life sentence and had an ongoing appeal in at Edinburgh High Court. They made out that John had shot his lovely stunning girlfriend in the head, two or three times at point-blank range, but he didn't. Just to clear the record, John won his appeal after seven years. In 2001, he walked free out of the High Court. But, in 1998, a lot of cons still had John down as a beast.

My pal Besty was in Dumfries YOI with me all those years ago and this was the first time since then I'd seen him. It was good to see all the lads again, but there was only four days to Christmas and no one had any smack! I asked Paddy if he would get someone to take some smack over to a pal's house, who would arrange to get it to me on Christmas Eve. Paddy was true to his word, and got a ¼ oz of smack dropped off for me. I hid the package in my mouth but it was so big I could hardly talk. A screw came over and told me to follow him. Because I was being held in segregation, I wasn't allowed to mix with the other prisoners. Once through in the holding room, the screw asked me to open my mouth.

I mumbled with my mouth full, 'Fwuck owff.'

There wasn't much he could do himself, so he went and radioed for assistance. There was nothing else for it: I had to swallow the parcel. After gulping, gasping and gagging, I managed to swallow it. The screw that had pulled me told the other screw I'd swallowed something. I told him he was a fucking liar. I got taken back to the digger. Once safely back in the cell, I tried to get the parcel back up by sticking my fingers down my throat to make myself sick, but I couldn't get it, no matter how much I tried.

I went back to see the boys. But nothing was doing. Here we all were on Christmas Eve, Christmas Day, Boxing Day and then 27 December – still no parcel! I went through every single shit with my bare hands. I'd all but given up hope and then, on 28 December, just after dinnertime, the screws had gone on their lunch break. I felt a pain in my belly, and needed a shit. I pulled my boxer shorts right off and bang! The parcel had a late delivery. I ran over to my window in jubilation and told Paddy, who let out a celebratory, 'Yee, hee.'

I was standing naked at my window screaming with excitement about getting the parcel. I made up everybody's bags, took my cut of the smack and gave Paddy his. We might not have had a good Christmas, but we certainly made up for it over the New Year.

The whole place was fucking jumping. It's amazing how a little bit of powder can make people react. I gave John about ½ gm. Best, Paddy, Sean all had some too, but, sadly, Brian and Bungy had got back up the halls before I had the parcel out, so they couldn't have any. Everyone was however soon rattling, as there wasn't any smack left. But then good old Paddy gave me a £20 bag he had stashed to share with John. After we'd done the bags, a screw from the MDT drug unit came over and told me they wanted me to give a mandatory urine sample for a drugs test. I told him to fuck off, so he went in and asked John, Besty and Paddy as well. They all told him to bolt, so we all got put on report. We stood in front of the governor and he took our wages off us, but that was all he had the power to do.

Besty had finished his sentence by 14 January, and John was soon moved to the Glenochil digger. Paddy was sent back up the hall. So I was left there on my own, until the Scottish Office decided to put me back to the Peterhead Special Unit. I had to go in front of two of the men in grey suits from the Scottish Office, plus a governor and doctor, Ian Stevens, and my personal officer in the Wendy House. I felt a bit intimidated going into this high-powered meeting, but I had to if I wanted to get back up to the special unit. When I took my seat at the meeting, there was a barrage of questions flung at me, such as, 'Why do you want to go back to the unit?' and 'Will you take a drug test every week?' and, 'Will you go on anger management courses?'

I agreed with everything the people at the meeting said to me. I just wanted to get out of that room, as I could feel all of their eyes burning into me. I didn't want to have to stay in a segregation unit for the next year. Once the meeting had finished, my personal officer, Old Phil, came into see me in my cell. He asked me how I felt about the meeting, and I told him I felt it went OK. Old Phil was brand new with me. He told me it would be better if I got back to the unit, and I agreed.

About a week went by. I was called back in for a meeting with Dr Ian Stevens and Phil. They told me the unit expected me back and I'd be going at the end of that week. I was only banged up for four-and-a-half months in the Wendy. I was now on my way back to the special unit. I'd better not fuck up this time, 'cos they'd throw away the fucking key.

CHAPTER TWENTY

Holland Takes a Hostage for a Sausage Roll

PETERHEAD SPECIAL UNIT, FEBRUARY 1999

I believe destiny controls our lives, so it was no surprise to me when the prison van I was in, heading for Peterhead, was involved in an accident. A car ran into the back of us as we were going over the bridge in Aberdeen. I saw this as a sign that the car shunting us from behind was pushing us away from the Bar L Wendy House and towards Peterhead. I felt good about going back to the unit, even though I was only away from it for four-and-a-half months.

On entering the unit, Popey, Rab and Little Paul greeted me with a hug and a slap on the back. I felt as if I'd never been away from the place. I quickly settled back into my old routine. I got myself off the drugs, and provided three clean sheets on the drug tests, which I was happy about, as it was the first time that I'd ever managed that in prison. I also flew through my anger-management course with flying colours. I was also attending

English classes, as I wasn't the brightest of spark plugs when it came to grammar. I had a wonderful teacher called Denise, who spent a lot of time with me. I learned that Denise had just been through a hard time with her husband dying, so I admired her for coming in and being so professional about her job. I believe Denise is now the head teacher at Shotts Prison. Good on her.

Not long after coming back, the unit was to host an Open Day for Easter where us cons could meet our families and friends and invite them into see how we lived. The screws had ordered a big bouncy castle for the kids to play on and clowns to keep them entertained. Popey and I built a six-hole crazy golf course and a barbecue out of bricks. The screws brought their wives and children in as well. This was the first time that I've ever seen the children of the cons playing with the screws' children in harmony. Watching the kids playing together without any malice really brought it home to me that this is the way it should be.

I showed my aunty, two little cousins and my big pal Alan around the unit. I think they were happy at what they saw. Rose told me to behave myself and to stick it out here, as it was better than the mainstream. We went outside and, not wanting to miss the moment, Rose, Alan, Lynn, Lizzy and I took our trainers and shoes off and jumped about on the kids' bouncy castle. It was so much fun. We were all like big kids and then I started playing the drums, as the unit got me a premier drum set to play on.

My aunty Rose tried to do a somersault on the bouncy castle, but she never managed to get all the way over, and ended up landing on her head and neck. After assuming Rose was OK, we were all rolling about with tears in our eyes, as it was so, so funny. Then we learned that Rose couldn't move her neck! The sniggering stopped there and then. I was just going to tell the screws that they'd need to get a nurse to come down and see to Rose, but she'd have none of it.

'Don't bother, son,' this brave woman said, 'I'll be OK. Give me a few minutes.'

After getting to her feet and walking about a little bit, Rose found a chair where she sat for the rest of that day talking to Terri, my female personal officer. I was off walking about the unit and then playing crazy golf with Alan, Lynn and Lizzy. We were having a whale of a time, while stuffing our faces with the best of foods. Some of Popey's pals came up, one of whom was a wizard on the guitar. My two little cousins, Alan and I sat and listened to Popey's pal play some Pink Floyd and Bob Dylan stuff, as well as some Travis and Oasis numbers on the guitar.

The day flew by a bit too fast, but what a day it was. Where else can you take your visitors and have a great day with them like that in prison? It was a great idea. That was one reason for keeping my head down in the unit.

Once everybody had left, all of us cons would take whatever food was left into our cells. I tried to be sly and bag four fancy ice-lollies. Without looking, I grabbed the box out of the freezer and stuck them down my jumper and went and hid them under my pillow. Then I went and got crisps, cakes, nuts and bottles of ginger beer and went back to my cell for the night.

Later on, when we were locked up and my cell door was shut, I lifted my pillow to get my ice-lollies. I took a double take. They weren't ice-lollies in the box at all. It was a box of four frozen fish! I was gutted. I shouted to Little Paul and Rab and told them what I'd done, and they burst out laughing. I saw the funny side of it as well, but I was gutted at first, as I badly wanted the ice-lollies.

We whiled away the time after the Open Day by watching some videos and by playing pool or table tennis. After a week or so, everyone in the unit was back to their normal selves. Old John and Sanny would be down the wood shop all day, every day, making some really nice stuff. I didn't really know much about joinery or woodcraft, but, when I saw Old John making a coffee table out of mahogany, I wanted one as well. He told me he'd help me make one, but I would need to stick in at it, as it was going to take about a month or so to make. I reassured John that I'd stick in at it and learn what I could from him, and that's what I did. Every day for the next month, I was down the wood shop at half-past nine in the morning until five o'clock at night.

Rab and Paul were trying to wind me up saying things like, 'Are we not good enough to run about with any more, Jimmyboy?' But I took this good-natured banter in my stride. After the month, when they saw me carrying my lovely coffee table, that was also a chessboard, up to my cell, they wanted one as well. I'd started something off, and that was it! For the next few months, they were down the wood shop helping make their coffee/chess tables with Old John and Old Sanny.

The summer had finally come. The sun was splitting the sky. Everyone in the unit was out the back, lazily lying about with only shorts and vests on, including the screws and governor! We had a barbecue going and some good Rolling Stones and Beatles songs were blasting out from the CD player. Some of us were kicking the ball about between us. We were waiting for the Red Arrows aerial display team to do a flyby. They did it every year; it was the business standing in the hot sun with a sizzling barbecue going while watching the Red Arrows. This year was special, as the *QEII* had docked on its world tour and was just anchored out of the bay in Peterhead.

Overall, this was a special place. The views were stunning all the year round; you could look out to sea on a hot day and see the oilrigs. I loved watching the fishing boats fighting with the elements on a windy and rainy winter's night. You'd see a tiny little boat being flung about like a cork, which would then disappear, making you think that it had been sunk, but, then a few minutes later, it would pop up on the crest of a wave. Anyone who thinks fishermen don't deserve the money they get should just watch them going out to sea on a winter's night. These people are either very, very brave or they've totally lost the plot.

I started to learn more about the Peterhead area. The local people call the place the Blue Toun. The winds there are legendary. You can stand and lift your jacket over your head, and use it like some sort of a kite: the wind catches it and blows you backwards for twenty feet. We used to play this game all the time to see who got blown back the furthest. I was always last, as I was four or five stone heavier than any of the other boys. The screws told us that the locals all had a special brand of ginger hair. I thought they were pulling my chain until a little screw, Hutchy, that I knew from Bar L came up on detached duty. After a heavy weekend on the booze, he came in one Monday morning to the unit, and told us that all the local girls had red hair and webbed feet! We burst out laughing when he told us they had webbed feet and smelled of fish from the factory they all worked at.

The seagulls in the area are massive. Bins with wings, I called them. When you throw stones at them, they try to eat them! They are the biggest seagulls I've ever seen in my life. These things can eat for Scotland. When the fishing boats come back in from the sea to the harbour, it's like a squadron of WW II bombers flying overhead, all squawking at a deafening pitch. Now I'm not a fan of seagulls, but their eggs are lovely to make omelettes with. I've eaten seagulls' eggs for months on end in the unit. They are an acquired taste, as they're a bit strong and salty, but they're perfectly fine to eat. One egg covers the full frying pan!

After the summer had passed, it was time to look forward to the Celtic vs Rangers game on the TV. In readiness, Rab and I would set our chairs out for the game away from Paul and Popey and most of the screws. Rab and I were the only two in the unit that supported Glasgow Rangers. We wore the only two football tops and draped ourselves with the Union Jack flags as well. When the game kicked off, we got a goal within the first ten minutes. We went fucking mental. Then we scored another goal halfway through the second half. We had the game won, but Celtic got a goal back with about ten or so minutes to go. Paul, Popey and some of the screws were jumping about mad, screaming at the TV, but it was too late, as we'd won it. Rab and I jumped about the unit, which the others didn't like one little bit, but we never cared.

So things were going well down the unit. But you can never relax, as, not long into the winter, a tragedy happened. The governor brought us all together to tell us that the unit was shutting down for good. None of us could believe it. The unit had only been open for five years. We initially thought that it was a joke, until it was on the TV news later that day. If we were sex offenders then they'd have kept the place open!

I was gutted, as the unit had helped me so, so much. I had just got back into being a normal human being. Most of the boys were gutted with it. A lot of screws were gutted too, as Adrian and Banksy had just moved their families up to the north-east of Scotland when they got the unit jobs full-time. Old Lee had taken it bad as well. Then there was big Sinky, who was really a good, big cunt as far as screws went; he didn't want to see it shut either. This would be like a family breaking up! Nothing anyone could do or say could put a stop it. So, everyone in the unit, the screws and us cons, went out of our way to make sure we would all have a good time before it shut.

Christmas was drawing closer and we were to have one last Open Day with our families. It was great; the kids were all over the moon because Santa was coming. Well, guess what? I was Santa! I told my family that I needed to go and change into my Santa suit; they all gave me a big hug. I went into the governor's office where the Santa suit lay, I put it on along with the big beard, and slung the heavy bag of kids' presents over my shoulder. When I walked into the room, cameras flashed and a big cheer went up.

I started shouting, 'Merry Christmas. Ho! Ho! Ho!'

All the kids, the screws and the cons were jumping about me shouting, 'Santa.' That's when Terri, my personal officer, came to my rescue and told all the kids to sit down. After they sat down, I shouted out their names from off the presents. When they came up to me, I sat them on my knee and gave them their present and their respective mums and dads took photos. It was some buzz.

I was totally shattered after I took the Santa suit back off through in the office. Terri told me I was great and had made all the children's day. When she told me that, I felt on top of the world, as all the cons wanted to make it the best Open Day yet for the children. And it was.

Christmas and New Year came and went like an express train. January was upon us once again. Everyone in the unit was gutted, but also a little bit excited about moving to the other jails. I was going to Saughton Prison, down in Edinburgh. My little friend Rab was going to Shotts Special Unit. On the way down to

Saughton, Rab and I were transported in the same prison van, in which we sat and laughed our heads off all the way to Edinburgh. But, once we got inside the prison compound, the laughing stopped. I wished my friend all the best and told him I'd keep intouch with him by letter.

The jail van's door slid back over. That was the last time I'd see Rab for over two years.

SAUGHTON PRISON, JANUARY 2000

The reception area in Saughton Prison was by far the newest and cleanest I've ever been in. I found the screws that worked on the reception desk to be quite polite towards me. I was allocated to Pentland Hall, which was for people serving twelve years and over. Most prisoners there were lifers. I knew about fifteen prisoners in this hall that I'd been pally with from the young offenders down in Dumfries. There was Big Tosh and Mark from Edinburgh, Little Nobby and Little Logie from Glesga, Old Jim from Springburn, Bilko from Greenock, Smuger from Glesga, Ramie from Glesga, Tam from Cambuslang and Tam B. Tam B had got a name for himself over the years for being Arthur Thompson's hitman. A lot of people didn't like Tam and called him this or that, but no one dared call him things to his face. I got on with the guy from the very start, so, Tam, if you ever read this, you know I've nothing bad to say about you. You were, in my eyes, a good pal. I wish you all the luck in the world and hope you're still sticking out your oil paintings.

I hadn't been in the hall for one day before one of the screws told me I had to go to the drugs unit and give him a urine sample for a drug test. Well, you all know what my reaction would be to that ... it was like a red rag to a bull! I went totally ballistic and raged at him, 'If you don't get out of my face, I'll fucking stab you. You may have a few of the boys jumping through hoops, but don't think you're going to try your shit on with me, mister!'

He got the message, and did an immediate about turn. I didn't know it then, but the screw went away to see the PO, the top officer in the hall, to tell him to remove me from the hall and put me in the digger.

A few of my pals who were doing life sentences gave me a slap on the back and told me they loved it when I put that awful animal of a screw in his place. The funny thing is, if it were any of them that had said it, they would have been on the first bus back to whatever jail they had come from, so I felt it was my duty to bring that rotten screw down a few pegs.

Not long after, I was sitting with my pal Big Tosh when a screw came over to inform me that the governor wanted to see me back in the hall. I told Big Tosh that I'd be getting taken to the digger. He said he didn't think so, but I knew I was. I took my work boots off and put my jail shoes on, got up and told Big Tosh I'd see him about some time.

On the way to the hall, I never once talked to the screw, who was trying to make small talk with me. I've not got any time or respect for that kind of prison warden. Once we entered the main office in Pentland Hall, I knew my fate before the governor even told me. There were four or five screws standing in the office, so they must have been expecting me to blow my fuse and fly into a rage, but I never gave them that satisfaction. Instead, I just smiled in their faces and said to them, 'Let's go, I'm choking to lie in my bed.'

As soon as I walked through the digger doors, it was like walking back in time to the early 1900s. The stench of dampness hit my nostrils like smelling salts. The actual cell doors were just five feet tall, which shows you how tall the average prisoner was when they built the prison. I kid you not, it was the smallest cell door I've ever seen in my whole life. I spotted a puddle of murky-looking water, as some of the roof had been leaking like an old woman's bladder ... and it had the same pungent smell!

Since it was early January, the cell was the coldest one I've ever been in. The mattress was sopping wet, and there wasn't a chair or table. Rather bizarrely, there was a little stump from a tree that had been painted and stuck to the cell floor with concrete. It looked like something Madam Whiplash would use in sadomasochistic whipping sessions. The screws left the cell and slammed the door shut behind them, and then I heard their voices getting fainter and fainter, until I couldn't hear anyone's voice at all.

I walked up and down the cell, trudging through the puddle of water. I only had a jail sweatshirt on, so I soon felt the wintry cold creeping in and, within twenty minutes, my body was starting to spasm into involuntary shivers, so I decided to jog up and down and jump about to keep myself warm. I was starting to get a bit paranoid. The more I walked up and down, the more I was convinced that the screws had deliberately flung water over my mattress. I was wild in my mind at the thought of them trying to break my spirits. I don't know how long went by, as you lose track of time when you can't hear anyone. I felt as if I'd been here for hours, and I was right. These are the same techniques meted out by the Americans to those poor cunts cooped up in Camp X-Ray at Guantanamo Bay. I'm pleased the last of the four British boys were shipped out of that place after three years of being tucked away.

I picked up on the screws laughing and talking, their voices were getting closer and closer, before I heard a key clank into the lock of my cell door. I told them I wanted to see the PO. One of the screws radioed the PO on his walkie-talkie, so he came down. I knew the PO from my time in Glenochil. His name was Mattie, and he'd always been brand new with me. I told him that I hadn't been fed. Mattie wasn't very happy, and he ordered one of the screws to go to the cookhouse and get me some food. I also told Mattie that my mattress was soaking wet and I didn't have any blankets or bedding. He soon made sure I got everything. The screw came back with my food, which was fish and chips. I'll tell you, it was great, and I finished my meal off with a nice hot duff – a cake – and custard.

After I got everything, Mattie left and I jumped into my bed with my clothes on, as it was too cold to stay outside the bed. Little did I know, but the digger had been condemned and no one had been in it for over a year, as they'd just opened a brand new high-tech digger, but, for some unknown reason, I was put in the old one.

The next day, around about ten or eleven o'clock in the morning, my door flew open. Two screws, followed by Mattie the PO and a governor I hadn't seen before were standing over me. The governor told me I'd be going into Fourth-hall. He apologised for me being put in the cell. I told him, 'I don't care where you put me, I'm easy. I'll stay here, as I'm quite liking it.' I just never wanted to let the screws know I was bothered by it, but I was over the moon when the governor and screws left, as I knew in reality I could have become very ill if I stayed for much longer in that cell.

I moved into Fourth-hall that afternoon. The heat of the cell hit me like a Sahara breeze and there was a nice bed with a quilt and a good mattress. This place was a five-star compared to what I'd slept in the night beforehand. That night, when I was lying in my bed, I lay there and listened to faceless voices shouting to each other. The hall was buzzing with activity until midnight, and then it just went quiet. I could hear someone's radio playing Diana Ross's 'Chain Reaction'. I turned to face the wall, pulled the quilt over my head and drifted into my own little world of abandonment, leaving behind all my worries and fears.

The next day, some of the Edinburgh boys I'd met through my years in prison, and some I didn't even know, were coming to my door and passing tobacco and bars of chocolate beneath it. I'll never forget the kindness of the troops. I was really glad that the boys in the hall helped me out, as the governor had taken my wages off me. I even got a couple of bags of smack and some DFs off Little Davie.

The PO I knew, Mattie, was in seeing me every day for twenty minutes at a time. He gave me a couple of phone cards so I could phone my aunty Rose and some of my pals. Overall, I was kept on my rule for two-and-a-half months, and then Mattie got it sorted with the governor to put me into D-hall.

I'd like to mention a few boys that I met in D-hall: Little Nessy from Edinburgh, Old Shug from Edinburgh, Alan from Clydebank, Little Shug from Glesga, Jim C from Cumbernauld, Little Pickles from Glesga, Piggy from Paisley, Old Faff from Glesga and a couple of other boys. The hall was sparkling clean, as far as short-term jails go, and each cell had its own toilet, washbasin and TV, so I was happy with being there. I got put in with a little boy called Billy, from Greenock, who was mad, had red hair and always made me snigger. I don't know if it was because he had a Westcoast accent just like me or if it was his mad red hair, but the little guy was some buzz.

I heard a lot of Edinburgh boys saying that they hated the Fifers, as they're just like rats with legs. But I didn't find the Fifers to be like that. Some of them were my pals, including Big Jacko,

Big Bob, both of whom came from Methil, a town in south Fife, and Neilly from Cowdenbeth.

My time in D-hall was spent mostly with me keeping my head down and just getting on with my time. I mostly sat with Piggy from Paisley. Piggy had got twelve years for his part in the infamous Paisley Gang Wars, along with Goofy, Bazil and Stuart. I didn't really know Piggy at first but, when I got to know him, I found the guy to be a diamond. Over the next couple of months, Piggy showed me how to play backgammon, a game that I thought I'd never master. I watched and learned every move Piggy made when he was playing Old Jinx, an old man in the crucible of his early years. We sat at a little table on the third landing, outside Piggy's cell, where we ate our dinner and tea. Sitting at our little table, we could see over the full hall. It was just like the hall on the TV prison drama *Bad Girls*.

One day out of the blue, I was called down to the PO's office and asked if I'd like to go back into the gardener's shed. I started work that Monday. By now, Tosh was head bin man, which basically meant he could walk about the full jail with a big trolley, collecting all the rubbish from every hall and office building in the prison. As soon as I got in the shed, Tosh told the gardener that I was to be his second helper. The highlight of our day was going down to the main office block where all the pretty young civilian girls worked in the prison administration department. Tosh fancied this one, really pretty girl, who was about twenty-two years old.

He would get all hot and flustered when he spotted her. The fires of passion were fuelled in Tosh when, one day, she innocently gave him a big Cheshire cat smile and offered him a fag when she was standing at the front door of the prison office block smoking. From thereon in, Tosh was loved up with her.

As for me, I go all quiet around women. I'm no virgin, far from it, but, when it comes to birds, I go all shy. I love looking at pretty girls as well, but, when I need to talk to them, I go all red. I know a lot of my pals will take the rise out of me for saying this, but I'm writing about my life. I'm not going to say that I'm a fanny magnet and that the birds all love me.

Anyway, every day, Tosh, Frankie and I would take a smoke break outside the offices on the chance that the stunning girl with the lovely big teeth and perfect hair and body would come back out for a fag, but she never did. Tosh was that desperate to get a little glimpse of her that we even washed the outside of the office windows. We hadn't got permission from the governor to do so, but we did it anyway.

One day as we were doing this, an older woman in her fifties opened the window of the offices and asked us what we were doing. Quick as a flash, I told her that I was her new Diet Coke man. She burst out laughing. I started walking backwards like Michael Jackson. I had her in stitches, and a couple of her pals came over to the windows to see me doing the moonwalk and telling jokes. I had all the women giggling, and Tosh and Frankie were gutted. After that day, Tosh, Frankie and I would get waves from the women and we'd wave back at them. That made our day, even though Big Tosh was gutted that the girl he fancied never came out to smoke any more fags, but she'd give him a little wave.

Around about this time, I got a letter out of the blue from Lisa, my girlfriend from all those years ago when I was in the children's home in Carluke. I was stunned, to say the least, as I hadn't heard from Lisa in years. I didn't even know how she knew I was in this prison. She basically told me she still had feelings for me and she wanted to come and visit. I hadn't seen Lisa in over ten years. I didn't even know what she looked like, as people can change a lot in ten years. What I remembered of Lisa was that she had gorgeous, come-to-bed brown eyes and long, blonde, curly hair.

I read her letter, over and over. Time had certainly passed, as she told me she'd had a baby. I think Lisa just told me all of this in her letter just to clear her head, as I don't think anyone was really listening to her in her own household. I was in two minds to write back to her. I was doing years in prison, and my life was going nowhere. Lisa was at a crossroads in her own life and relationships, and I was a shoulder to cry on.

Ah, what the hell, I thought. I put pen to paper and wrote her a four-page letter telling her that I wasn't doing too well in my life and wouldn't be the best role model for her or her baby. In reply, she told me that she didn't care what I'd done and why I'd been in prison for so many years; she just wanted to come and see me. Cunningly, she also gave me her mobile phone number. I sat and stared at the number for some twenty minutes or so, deliberating whether I should call her. Whatever I thought, I decided I'd phone her that night.

Before calling Lisa, I snorted two Temgesics, which are little white tablets the same size as a Sweetex. Waiting half an hour until the buzz from the tems kicked in, I put the phone card into the phone and punched Lisa's mobile number into the chrome-plated keypad. The phone on the other end was ringing and my heart was racing like a bongo drum.

Just about ready to hang up, a girl's voice on the other end of the phone stopped me when she said, 'Hello.'

The voice was so soft and sounded sweet as honey.

I asked if I could speak to Lisa. She said, 'I'm Lisa.'

I told her who I was, and she let out a little laugh and then thanked me for phoning. Not knowing what to say, I just froze up, as I hadn't spoken to Lisa in all those years, but she led the conversation along, asking me how I was doing and all the usual stuff. Talking about people we both knew, Lisa shell-shocked me with the news that one of my pals from my childhood had killed himself. Barely managing to hold the conversation together, I couldn't believe it.

Down to my last five units, I told Lisa we were running out of time. She asked me for a kiss over the phone. Although my face went bright red, I gave her a kiss all the same and then she told me that she really, really wanted to visit me. I told Lisa that I wasn't the same slim, full-head-of-hair boy she'd last seen. Lisa told me that she didn't care if I looked like the hunchback of Notre Dame.

After the call, my thoughts went back to when I took Lisa to the movies in Wishaw and then on to a small intimate café. Reminiscing on other thoughts took me back to times of lying on her bed for hours on end, watching videos when all my pals would call me a 'little sissy' for spending time with Lisa instead of with them. Startled out of my relaxed state, Billy came into my cell and asked me if I wanted a pipe of hash. I took a pipe. The rest of that night was spent just lying on my bed stirring up more memories of my early years with Lisa.

The next morning came a little bit fast, and I woke with a stonker of a headache. Taking that hash was a bad idea, as it always gives me a sore head the next day. After eating my breakfast, I slowly staggered over to my workplace like a zombie. Once in the shed, I slumped down into the chair and closed my eyes. The next thing I knew, my Tosh gave me a shove, and exclaimed, 'Look at the nick of you, Jimmyboy. What the fuck have you had?'

I told my big pal that I only had a couple of tems and a pipe of hash the night before. Twenty minutes later, or so, my body clock finally kicked into life. I was ready to go and get 'em. Anyone will tell you, it's a struggle to get up with the larks at 6.45 every single morning, but in prison it's even harder to do so if you've been smoking hash the night before.

The screw that ran the gardens came up and told me that I was getting a new job for the next couple of days away from Tosh and Frankie. He told me to take the ferret up the backfields to track the rabbits down. I couldn't believe my luck. Everyone loved taking the ferrets out for some rabbiting, most of the boys had done it at one stage or other and now it was my turn. I ran down to where the little ferret was kept in its little cage. Opening the cage and putting my hand in made me recall how everyone said that the little thing was very nasty, but it didn't bite me. I put it in the left-hand pocket of my donkey jacket. It sat upright with its head peering out of my pocket and, to my surprise, it didn't make any effort to jump out.

Making my way up to the backfield of Saughton Prison to the rabbit burrows, I let the little ferret out of my pocket to go down the hole, but it came up with nothing. After two hours of the same, I was a bit pissed off and put the ferret back in my pocket and took a walk around the jail.

Once at the back of Pentland Hall, I let the ferret run around so he could tire himself out on a bit of spare ground. After about twenty minutes or so, a screw came out from the hall and asked what I was doing. He told me to get the ferret and take it back round to the gardener's shed. My blood was boiling at this screw's stinking attitude. Knowing myself, if I didn't walk away from him, my lid would have blown and the nut would have been stuck in the rotten bastard's face. I mean, there I was, not doing anything wrong, minding my own business when the screw went out of his way to cause me some grief. That's the way a lot of them work.

Once I walked back round to the gardener's shed to put the ferret back in his little cage, the head gardener asked to see me in his office. Slowly walking back to the guy's office, I knew full well that it was about the screw round at Pentland Hall and that I shouldn't have been there. Struggling to hold my temper in, I asked him to phone D-hall and get them to send someone over to collect me from the works shed. When back in D-hall, the feelings going through me would soon be washed away by a charge of smack or two. I visited my pal Alan, and asked him to sort me a hit up.

As I hadn't taken a hit of smack in a few years, Alan said, 'Are you fucking serious?'

I told him, 'Yes.'

After I dropped my trousers, Alan stuck the needle into my groin. The rush of the smack hitting my bloodstream was like a speeding bullet shooting through my veins. I pulled up my trousers as the smack started taking full effect, and wandered to my cell where I flopped on my bed in a fluffy, dreamlike state. After that, feeling on top of the world, all the shit that had happened with the screw earlier was wiped out by my smacked-up journey.

The next morning the screw stuck his head into tell me I wasn't required at the gardens that day. I punched the air with my fist, and turned over on to my left-hand side. I put the quilt between my legs and pulled it over my head, as that's the only way I can usually sleep. Most people that have been on drugs for some years can't lie in their beds with their feet and knees touching together at the skin. Most will put a quilt or a pillow between their knees to cushion them. I know it sounds mad, but that's what most of us do.

Having the day off work gave me the time to start thinking about escaping. I thought about the tractor that took the outside work party out of the prison. The prisoners would sit on the back of the blue tractor on two steel benches. I developed a plan to lie inside a metal toolbox until the tractor came around and hooked it on to it, which I carried out. But I had told one of my pals about the plan, which was a big mistake. As soon as I was in the toolbox and attached to the tractor, one of the boys tapped on it to tell me to come out, as the gardening screw was asking everybody where I was. I was fucking gutted with the con tapping the box. Coming out of the box rather hurriedly, I told the con I'd see him at dinnertime for tapping the box and giving the game away. I quickly jumped out and got back to my post. Planting flowers, I was fucking pure gutted. There was going to be a slashing at dinnertime.

Around about eleven o'clock, two screws and the PO from security came round to me, and told me to go back to D-hall. They took me into the office where the hall governor was, who told me he'd received information that I was trying to escape on the back of the jail tractor. To cover myself, I burst out laughing.

'Escape,' I said. 'Aye, right you are, is this some sort of joke?'

'No, Jim,' the governor replied, 'it's no joke. The garden screw was told from a couple of boys that you were lying in the trailer.'

'Fuck off,' I replied, 'that's just bullshit so he can sack me from the gardens.'

The governor told me that I'd never get to go back out to the gardens. Instead, I was made a passman in the hall, which turned out to be a good job. All I had to do was feed the fish that were in the five fish tanks in the hall. Although I really wanted to be in the gardens, I was happy with that job. The boy who chapt me out for the trailer malarkey was in a different hall from me. Nevertheless, he got slashed down the face some two or three weeks after the garden thing happened, which was poetic justice and saved me a job.

Time was passing, and my visit with Lisa soon came along. Upon reaching my visitor's table, the woman that sat there looked nothing like the luscious Lisa I had once known. Holding back my shock, I did my best to summon up a smile, of sorts, to conceal my alarm. As we went through the frivolities of greeting each other, my eyes couldn't help but take in the full extent of the damage caused to this once beautiful girl by the ravages of time. Gone was the once silky smooth skin, only to be replaced by furrows of worry and creases of torment. The once shiny, flaxen, well-groomed hair was now dishevelled, uncombed and untidily out of place. To be honest, she looked like she'd been pulled through a hedge backwards and then spent the rest of the night sleeping under it! When she was younger, she used to be able to get away with it, but now it showed.

This was going to be tricky. Lisa told me she'd slept over at her pal's because she'd been arguing with her dad. He'd slapped her round the face. My blood started to boil and my heart went out to her. I hate to see any man hitting any woman, more so when it's someone's dad doing the hitting. I consoled her best I could. At the end of the visit, Lisa pulled out a bundle of cash; there must have been over £700 or so. On seeing this, one of the visit screws came over and told Lisa to put the money back in her purse or he'd have to terminate her visit, as you're not supposed to have money in the visit hall in Saughton Prison. Now, give the screw credit, as he could have stopped the visit for that breach of security, but he never did. At that, Lisa flung her arms round my neck and started kissing and cuddling me. She told me she didn't want to leave me. Calmly and firmly, I told her that I had to go back to the hall, and that's when the tears started running out of her little eyes.

Rather than return home that late at night, Lisa told me that she'd decided to stay in a hotel in Edinburgh for a few days, as she didn't want to go on the train back through to Glesga, as the journey would involve getting the adjoining train to Lanark.

'Book another visit for us in a couple of days' time,' Lisa threw at me. Then she disappeared out of sight with the rest of the visitors.

I kept in touch with Lisa and got her back on a couple more visits, so things were going OK, until one day when I got shouted down to the PO's office. The PO told me I'd need to give them a urine test due to me flouting my drug taking in the screws' faces. Hell ... having just taken a burn of smack that morning, I was going to fail the test. After telling the PO that I wasn't giving them a sample, he told me had no option but to downgrade me to the jail's A-hall for failing to provide a sample.

The hall was black, smelly and dirt poor. There wasn't any toilet or washbasin in the cell. There wasn't even a chair or locker. The place didn't even have heating. The hall should have been razed to the ground, as it wasn't fit for animals, never mind humans. Ah well, as ever, you've got to adapt to the surroundings you're being held in because, if you don't, you'll go off your rocker! I knew a few boys that were also in the hall from Edinburgh: Finny, Mark and Tam. I fixed in with them very fast. By this time, I flung all caution to the wind, with my smack habit becoming bigger. I knew this was going to end in disaster and, sure as spring follows winter, I was totally off my head on drugs, once again.

HOSTAGE SIEGE NUMBER FIVE

I can remember the day as if it was yesterday. It was 4 October 2000, a Sunday and Celtic were playing Kilmarnock at Rugby Park. Along with the boys in my clique, I was down the recreation room. We were all freezing cold, and were rattling, as there wasn't any smack in the hall. I spread the word to Tam and Finny that I was planning on robbing the nurse who came down to the hall with the nightly medication. I was told that the nurse had already been and gone, and I was gutted.

I was banged up with a boy I'll call Den, who was usually OK, but being without smack was driving me mad. Seeing how I was rattling, Den asked me what I was going to do.

I said, 'Take you hostage and demand a bottle of meth or some difs.'

'Hey,' he replied, 'that's a great idea. I'm up for that, Jimmy.'

I grabbed Den by the throat and stuck a knife at his neck. I told him straight, 'OK, pal, you've asked for it.'

I violently flung Den to the floor and tied his hands behind his back and then pressed my panic button on the wall so that the screws would come along and see what was up. Once the screw opened my cell door, he iced over and froze stiff. I made a lunge at him to drag him in the cell as well, but he must have had his three Weetabix that morning, as he escaped my grasp and ran down the hall. He was screaming, 'Holland's got a knife, he's got a knife!'

All the screws quickly gathered on the bottom flat of the hall. I threatened them, 'If you try and come into this cell, I'll cut his throat!'

One of the screws shouted up, 'Why are you doing this, Jimmy?'

I jokingly shouted back to him, 'Because you never gave me an extra sausage roll, what do you think I'm doing it for? I want drugs from the surgery, DFs or methadone, then I'll let the cunt go.'

Finishing my spiel, I walked in and slammed the cell door shut. I covered the spy hole with toothpaste before cutting little Den free. The two of us then smashed the cell to bits and had some fun. After we burned ourselves out, the sweat was dripping from us and we sat and laughed our heads off.

Soon enough, a couple of spare screws wearing riot gear were standing by the door. This sent the shivers up little Den and made him a bit jittery, so I told him he had nothing to worry about, as they did that all the time. One of the screws shouted my name and asked me to talk to him. I told him about my need for methadone and how bad I was rattling, and he replied that he'd need to ask his boss for permission to get me something.

By this time, Den and I were bitterly cold, as the windows had been smashed out. The sweat on our bodies had become our enemy and was cold to the touch. Finally, a gruff voice at the cell door told me that, if I were to let Den go and come out peacefully, they would give me some DFs.

'Look,' I said, 'I've heard that same old record played a good half-dozen times in the past, but OK, I'll do it. I'll let Den out and then I'll come out, but if I don't get the tablets in the seg unit, then the next time I take a screw hostage I'll cut his throat, no questions asked because you fucked me about, OK?'

'OK, Jimmy,' one of the screws pacified me, 'there won't be any smart business.'

The screw asked me to fling the knife out of the window. Instead, I bent the knife shut and stuck it back up my arse, the safest hiding place. Then I told him that there was no knife, just a bit of aerial for my radio that I was holding in my hand.

'Look, Jimmy, we need to be sure that it is what you're saying it is,' one of the faceless hobbits shouted.

I told them to stand back from the door and I'd push it under the door.

'OK, Jimmy, we're going to open the door very slowly. Den, you come out first,' the same faceless screw ordered.

Five minutes later I walked out of the cell with my hands behind my head. I then felt a screw pull my hands down hard and fast from my head, which they cuffed. They then took some video and snapshots of me for their album before taking me to the seg unit.

Once in the unit, I asked them where my tablets were. The nurse was standing there with four 30ml DFs, but I had to take a shower first then go into my cell. Once done, the nurse gave me the tablets. I thanked her and then told the screws that, if they'd given them to me in the first place, I wouldn't have done what I'd just done.

The PO told me he didn't know what I was talking, which was something the governor later repeated. As far as they were concerned, they'd never issued me with any tablets from the prison surgery. Whatever, I didn't care, as I got what I wanted out of the whole thing. The next day, a headline in the *Sun* read: 'HOLLAND GOES MAD FOR A SAUSAGE ROLL'. The screws told the papers that I had done all that for a fucking sausage roll, and tried to make me look like a dafty in the national press, so I'd be the laughing stock of the prison. Well, it backfired on them, as all the boys in the hall and jail were saying to the screws, 'We knew you gave Jimmy some DFs to end the hostage thing quietly and quickly.'

The cops came into ask Den to press charges against me for taking him hostage, but the little man told them he just smashed the cell up with me for some fun. Then they came and told me I'd be getting done for taking Den hostage, but I told them to prove it, before walking out of the office back to my cell.

Later that day, I was transferred to Shotts seg unit, accompanied by a ten-man riot squad. This was a bit over the top, if you ask me, but what can you do? I was destined for pastures new, but where was I to go next?

CHAPTER TWENTY-ONE

Transitional Suicide

SHOTTS SEG UNIT, 5 OCTOBER 2000

I've been in Shotts seg unit more times than a whore's dropped her knickers. But for the first time they decided to use a metal detector on me. They stripped me and handcuffed my hands behind my back. Then they ran a metal detector over my naked body. Every time the infernal thing went over my arse, it would start screaming. The screws asked me why the metal detector kept going off. I told them it must be faulty. But they had another theory: there was a lockback knife concealed up my arse. I laughed in their faces and told them to stop talking shit. The digger PO, who I'll call Sandy, told me that they would strip-search me every time I came out of my cell, even when I went for a bath or shower, as they didn't want to take any chances with me in case I did have a knife. Every time they came to my door, the only time they would open it was when they made me stand with my hands on the bars facing the window. If I never did that, I wouldn't get fed. They were taking this very, very seriously, indeed.

My good pal Piggy was in the seg unit with me, as was another pal, Hammy. Most people in Scotland have heard of Hammy, even if they haven't met the guy. I got on OK with Hammy. The guy gets a lot of bad press and other cons make some horror stories up about him. I can't deny or stick up for Hammy or the guy's sexuality, but everyone to their own thing is what I say.

My little cousin Gordie, from Glenochil, sent me letters to wish me all the best and to keep my chin up. I started thinking about my family, so I phoned Aunty Rose. As soon as I heard her voice, I knew there was something very wrong. It turned out that Uncle Macky was seriously ill in hospital. His liver had been failing him over that last two months or so.

Rose said, 'I don't know if Macky will make it through the night!'

At hearing this, my throat went out-and-out dry. I didn't know what to say to this dear lovely aunty of mine.

My units had ran out, so I gave Rose a kiss over the phone and hung up and went back to that cold, dark cell and lay on my bed. Closing my eyes, I reflected on all the good times I had had with Uncle Macky. He was a very funny man and I know he'll be looking down on his wife and children, and Gordie and I. God bless you, Macky boy.

The next day, I got my canteen, bought a phone card and phoned aunty Rose, who confirmed that Macky had passed away. Tears came to my eyes, but my inner resolve wouldn't allow me to cry in front of the screws. I locked away my emotions and regained my composure. I kissed Rose goodbye and hung up the phone, went back to my cell and had a little cry in private.

After being in this seg unit for six-and-a-half weeks, the

governor came into my cell and informed me that he would allow me to have open visits back. I booked a visit for my cousin, Sam, who came up to see me with Marie, Big Wall's wife. The visit went great. It was good to see Sam again, as I hadn't seen him for years. He was doing really good, making money and, most importantly, staying out of jail.

I also got Lisa up to visit me, as she only stayed about six miles away from Shotts Prison. At one visit, Lisa told me she wanted to marry me. She had everything planned for when I got out of prison. I told her to slow down. To be truthful, I didn't want to marry her, or any other girl for that matter, as I know I wouldn't be a good husband. And in this case I didn't want to be tied down in some mad spur-of-the-moment marriage. Well ... she didn't take it too well, but she bounced back from it and told me that we could still have kids together.

I firmly told Lisa, 'No!'

After that, she went away from that visit and wouldn't answer my phone calls or letters. Thinking that was that, I just stopped writing and phoning. Then the next thing I knew, Lisa had tried to take her own life with a drink and drugs cocktail. I sent her a get-well card and a letter, but she never replied to it, so as far as I was concerned, our friendship was over.

I had been in the seg unit for nearly ten weeks when the screws came in and told me that I was going to Glenochil seg unit the next morning. The date was 23 December, just two days before Christmas and I was going back to the worst digger in the prison system.

CHAPTER TWENTY-TWO

The Seven Oafs of Glenochil Hate Factory

DECEMBER 2000

When I landed in the reception of Glenochil Prison, there was a seven-man-strong terror team waiting to play with me in the reception area. They had a look of murderous contempt in their eyes. They all dwarfed me; not one of them was shorter than six foot tall. I hadn't been back here since January 1997, so they must have missed me, the cunts. It looked like a scene from *Reservoir Dogs*: I hoped they weren't going to slice my ear off and pour petrol over me. In the background, blaring out from a CD player, was Bing Crosby's 'White Christmas'. Explain that one.

'OK, Holland, strip,' one of them ordered coldly.

This crew meant business. I did what they demanded, as I wasn't going to give them the satisfaction of battering me.

'Right, Holland, don't think we've forgot what you did in this jail, so don't think you're going to get an easy ride or any favours off us,' the screw with the ice-cold stare spat out.

'I know that,' I said in an attempt to pacify them.

But I wasn't taking any of this crap for long. As far as I was concerned, these were the seven oafs. Many of you will think that I should have just shut my trap and took it, but if you don't make a stand against these breaches of human rights then we'll eventually be overrun with dictators.

'I don't want favours from you, anyway. What do you think I am, some sort of fucking dafty that can't handle your seg unit? It's a piece of fucking piss,' I blasted at them.

'Oh, is that right, Holland?' came the sarcastic reply.

At this stage, I wasn't scared and replied scathingly, 'Yes, that's fucking right!'

They quickly moved me on, down to the seg unit, which is quite a walk, all in. On the way down, the screws surrounded me in an attempt to make me feel insecure, but I was having none of it and told them so. Just as we were coming to the end of the walk, the screw Porky and I had taken hostage in '97 appeared. Some malicious rodent in the reception had phoned the wanker down the hall to come out on to the Russian Front to meet us. Once he was in front of me, he stopped and threw me a hateful stare.

I asked him if he liked being at the mercy of Porky and me, which instantly wiped the cockiness off the bastard's face.

Then, he chided, 'Have a nice Christmas, Holland!'

I sickened him, 'Just think, tosser, just over two weeks from now, it'll be your hostage anniversary. Goodbye, prick.'

I don't think any of the screws were expecting me to say anything, but I wasn't going to let them break me with their mind games. I've been through far too much for some daft screws to think they can beat me mentally, no danger of that. Once I walked into the digger, I was greeted by another half-dozen screws.

'Happy Christmas,' I snarled at them.

They didn't answer back. They were all standing glowering with their legs apart and their arms folded like some sort of motherfucking bouncer you'd see outside a seedy backstreet nightclub.

'Are you trying to make me paranoid, boys?' I said in a pretend gay voice. 'As that's what you are, just little boys, then!'

'Follow me, Holland, you're in there,' the big butch one said, as he pointed to cell number five.

I walked in and said in my take-off gay voice, 'Jesus, fuck! This cell is better than any other digger cell I've been in. Thank you, boys, for giving me such a nice cell. I thought you would have put me into a cell that was dirty and cold. What can I say? You aren't half as bad as you're trying to make out, fellahs.'

Once I was in the cell and the door shut, I heard the screws in their office talking to each other, calling me a scumbag and a prick. One by one, they called me every name under the sun. I must have done something right for them all to be having a go at blacking my character.

I heard someone banging on the wall and shouting my name.

'Aye, hello,' I said, 'who's that?'

'Me, Jimmy, it's John,' the voice replied.

John was the chap who got done for shooting his bird dead, although he was innocent. He was in the next cell. He told me that it was only him and another boy down here. John told me about how they weren't getting fed until seven o'clock at night whereas the rest of the jail got fed at four o'clock. Most of the things the screws were doing were just trivial things designed to niggle you, as they knew it would get you upset enough so you would shout at them or kick your door in protest.

I, on the other hand, tried my best to just blank the screws, totally. I gave them dumb insolence, not bothering even to talk to them when they asked me if I wanted a shower, exercise or hot water. Nothing! Every time they opened my door, I lay on my bed with my eyes shut. This seemed to get at them more than people banging on their doors or calling the screws cunts and bams.

The next morning was Christmas Day. The door opened like any other morning in the digger. 'Holland, do you want a slop-out?' one of the screws asked.

I never answered him.

'I take it that's a no, then?' he said walking out, slamming the door shut.

I jumped up to my door and shouted to John, 'Happy Christmas, pal, hope you have a nice day, mate. There's a good play on the radio this afternoon.'

'Cheers, Jimmyboy,' John shouted back, 'I hope you have a nice Christmas as well, Jimmy.'

'Aye, don't worry, brother, I'll have a great day. I can't wait for the Boxing Day sales to start,' I told my pal, and then lay on my bed again.

I knew the screws were sitting in their office, gutted that we were still showing them that they would not affect us one little bit. You'd have to spend five years in segregation without it showing any ill effects, and I think you know by now that I'm a pretty strong character myself. There was no way they could get through our defences and into our minds.

The rest of that morning, I just lay on my bed and daydreamed. I dreamed of all the nice things that had happened in my life. I must have dozed off, as the screws were soon standing at my door with my Christmas dinner. I looked at it. The dinner looked invitingly nice, and I did all that I could to stifle any signs of sensory emotions as I looked at the mouth-watering inviting meal. It took all my inner willpower to turn my back on the Christmas dinner. As I lay on the bed, I could feel my belly rumbling with hunger pangs. I was totally famished ... I could have eaten the hind legs off a donkey. I wasn't on my own; John shouted down and told me that he didn't eat his dinner either. We both burst out laughing. Once I walked away from my door, I paced up and down the cell. The cell wasn't very long, five steps then you had to about turn and walk the five steps back to the door again.

I eyed up an uninviting packet of cornflakes, which must have been lying in my cell for weeks. Whoever was in the cell before me had left them; I ripped the plastic bag open and scooped a handful of dry flakes into my mouth. I chewed them for all they were worth, before making an effort to swallow them down, washing them down with a bottle of cold water. What a Christmas dinner that was.

When the screws came back that afternoon, they changed their approach. The PO that ran the seg unit asked me why I wasn't talking to his staff. I told the PO that he must be wrong. 'I have been talking to your staff.'

'Well, Holland,' he quizzed, 'the staff have told me you are being very negative towards them.'

'Not at all,' I told him.

'Do you want a shower?' he asked.

'No, boss,' I told him, 'I've already had one.'

A screw butted in and told the PO that I'd not taken a shower since I'd been in here.

'Oh, you must be wrong. I have had a shower, every day,' I gushed.

I knew I was fucking the screw's head up and making fun of him in front of the PO of the digger.

'If you don't mind, boss,' I said, 'I'd like to get into my bed and listen to the play on the radio.'

He contorted his face, turned and stormed off out of my cell. Really, it was great. I was lying in my bed on Christmas Day when the screws could have been in their houses with their wife and kids, but, instead, they were sitting in a little, poky office, freezing cold while clockwatching, with no cons to play around with.

It may not sound like a big deal to you, but, believe me, it was a moral victory over the nazi screws that were looking after us. The rest of that Christmas Day was spent lazing in my bed. Once I knew that the rotten mob had left the digger, I got up and stood at my door, where John and I talked and talked for hours.

Of course, I couldn't forget my annual Christmas and New Year prison party. Over the next week, leading up to New Year, John and I got something sorted out between us. I went on a visit and smuggled in a shed-load of smack. A new boy called Dessy had recently joined us down the unit. Over the next five days, the three of us were off our heads on smack. The screws were gutted, as they couldn't do a single thing about it.

On New Year's Eve in Glenochil, a screw walks about the jail playing his bagpipes from twenty minutes to midnight until ten minutes past. Up the hall, everyone was up at their windows, shouting at one another, wishing each other a Happy New Year. But, when the phantom bagpipe player came round to the digger, we gave him it stinking. Here was this bastard trying to cheer us up when he knows that his screw pals have us locked up like animals!

Around 5 January 2001, we were joined by an old pal down the digger. Chuck from Hamilton is a diamond. Chuck was doing a life sentence and had only come back up from a jail in

England some six months beforehand. The screws don't really like Chuck, so they went out of their way to stop his visitors from getting into see him up in Shotts. Trudging through knee-deep snow, Chuck's bird and child took a chance when they braved the inclement weather and hiked to the prison, as the roads were blocked off. When they eventually succeeded in beating the elements, the rotten, heartless screws turned Chuck's bird away, telling her that she was too late for the visit and that she should have been ten minutes faster. Now, if that isn't a bam up, what is? Not surprisingly, Chuck went off his head and told the screws that they were out of order for doing that to his bird and kid. The screws told Chuck to calm down and that he would get another visit the next day.

The guy and his family got fucked about for nothing. We all helped calm Chuck down at the doors. The boy isn't any mug, and has got a reputation for violence. We didn't want to see Chuck getting any more time on top of his life sentence for doing something daft that he would regret later. Once we'd calmed Chuck down, we all jumped into our beds, as the heating had suddenly packed in. It was really sub-zero cold, even an Eskimo would have frozen. The next day, the screws gave us a couple of extra quilts and socks and sweatshirts to try and help keep us warm. I kid you not; a cup of tea went cold within two minutes of leaving it on your floor. There was no way, in the depths of winter, that we should have been kept down the seg unit with no heating.

The screws were so cold that they had to sit in their big, thick woolly jumpers with their uniform coats and hats on. They were all sitting huddled around a portable gas fire to stay warm in the crowded office, as all the water pipes had burst. They took us, one a time, to A-hall for a shower. This went on for over a week before the heating finally got fixed.

The governor came down and said sorry to us for keeping us in the seg unit in these conditions. By way of compensation for our good behaviour in the face of such harsh conditions, he allocated us each a ½ oz of tobacco and a phone card. He also ordered the cooks to send us down more food and plenty of hot chocolate. Overall, it wasn't too bad, apart from the cold, and it was good to see the rotten nazi screws suffering the same as us, for a change.

But all things come to an end. On 26 January 2001, I was moved from Glenochil seg unit up to Perth seg unit. I was so glad to be getting away from that hate factory to somewhere a little bit more human, to say the least. They sent Dessy and Chuck to the Wendy House, in Bar L, and John went to Shotts digger. The Glenochil hate factory lay empty for a few months so they could fix the place up a bit.

CHAPTER TWENTY-THREE

In and out of the Wendy House like a Fiddler's Elbow

PERTH SEG UNIT, JANUARY 2001

This was the first time I'd been in the newly purpose-built Perth seg unit. The last time I was up here, I was in the old Perth Rule 80 unit, over beside E-hall. When I had left they were only just digging the foundations for this now completed seg unit. How time flies, I was thinking to myself as the prison van pulled to a halt. I was walked into the new unit. I suddenly thought that I had been here before, but of course I hadn't. I quickly saw that Perth seg unit is the spitting image, right down to the last nut and bolt, of its sister, the new Saughton seg unit.

'Hello, Jimmy,' a screw said. It was Big Kev from the old seg unit back in 1997. He said I was looking well. The guy was spot on as far as screws go. He was only in the job for the money. But of course he is a rarity, and I soon saw a stereotypical screw, who kept looking at me with a growl embedded on his twisted face. I knew at some point that he and I would be falling out.

The first thing I sensed on being put in a cell was the heat. It was hot enough for me to strip my torso down to just a T-shirt. Now if I just wore a T-shirt down in Glenochil, I wouldn't be here just now writing this book, as I would have probably died from hypothermia. Big Kev opened my door and asked me if I wanted any of my civvy clothes to wear instead of prison-issue clothes. I knew he wasn't pulling my leg, so I asked Kev to get me my Rangers tops, my tracksuit bottoms and a couple of sweatshirts. As any prisoner will tell you, it's much better wearing your own clothes instead of the ill-fitting and humiliating prison stuff that half the prison population or so have worn before you. When Kev came back, he handed me my civvy clothes. He also gave me a CD player and CD. I was a prisoner with all the mod cons: curtains, quilts, a kettle and a CD player in with me. As a result, my weeks started to fly by. I started going to the gym every day to get myself fit in the PT room.

A couple of boys I hadn't known before were in the unit with me. There was young Gavin from Drumchaple, who was a twenty-three-year-old boxer on the cusp of the pro circuit when he was copped for a ten-year prison sentence. Thankfully, Gavin's still got youth on his side and I know he'll become a world champ if he turns pro on getting out. Then there was Little Mick from Drumchaple, who is well known in the Glesga underworld. Mick once got shot in the face with a shotgun. Incredibly, Mick got up afterwards and pulled his own gun out and chased the guy out of the pub and shot him back. There was also another boy called Jim from Aberdeen. He would eat razor blades. It got to the stage that he cut his throat and wrists. He was rushed into Perth Royal Infirmary, where he was very lucky to survive. He ended up being taken up to the state mental hospital, in Carstairs.

One day in Perth digger, we heard the riot bell going off. All the screws ran over to A-hall where they found the young offenders that were on remand smashing up the hall. Some screws had been hurt. In the end, it took the screws over nine hours to win the hall back into their control. Once they restored order, they started bringing the young offenders down to the seg unit. A boy called Scott from Dundee was put
next door to me, with his brother, Darren, a couple of cells away. I got on really well with these two young brothers and am pally with them to this day.

I was moved down to the Wendy House seg unit in early April. The clock was ticking: I only had three months left of this twelve-year sentence.

WENDY HOUSE, APRIL 2001

All the screws down the Wendy House were brand new with me: Old Phil, Big Rab, Wullie, Old Davie, Big Brian, Little Gary, every last one of them. I also got on well with most of my fellow cons: Little Besty from Greenock, Little Gerry from Tollcross, Little Mitch from Maryhill and a couple of other boys. But not everyone in this world is sound, and sure enough we had to share the place with a dirty sex beast. He was a policeman from Dumfries that was done with raping some women. He got it stinking from all of us ... little pots of piss were flung under his door and we kept him up all night by banging on his cell wall. I used to spit in his dinners when I went into the pantry, as he was on a special diet. By the time the lads had finished wanking their semen into his fish, well, he didn't need tartar sauce!

The dog went up to court where he got twelve years up his arse. On his return we all started singing and shouting in tune to the song that Tom Jones covered, 'Sex Bomb'. We'd sing: 'Sex case, sex case, hang him, hang him.' After that, he tried to cut his wrists, but sadly he did a bad job, and survived. He was moved over to the surgery for his own safety, and then he was taken to Peterhead mainstream prison where all the rest of Scotland's worst sex monsters lived. This was the best place for him, as he could swap stories with his fellow sex offenders.

But I had my own life to think about. Time was ticking. And I was going to be released. The day before my release, I was taken on the mandatory walk to see the governor.

I playfully told him, 'I'll shoot you in the head one night next week when I get out.'

Of course, I was only kidding, but he took it pretty serious and the coppers were called in. They came in and told me that, if anything happened to the governor, I would be the prime suspect. I laughed in their faces.

WALKING OUT OF BAR L PRISON FRONT GATE

The big day had finally arrived. I'd spent nine years and three months out of a twelve-year sentence in prison. So, you could say, I was fevered up. This was truly magical and I was over the moon at being released. With each step back out into the open world, my heartaches and memories of being immersed in a world of shit were being lifted, but, for those I was leaving behind, my heart hung heavy. I was both saddened and exhilarated. The treatment I'd endured during my incarceration was unjust, but I was just another faceless person denied justice.

I walked out of the front door of Scotland's biggest prison, a free man. I was, however, to be under supervision from a social worker on what is known as a non-parole licence, like any other prisoner that gets out after a long-term sentence. He picked me up in his car and drove me to his office in the middle of

Glasgow city centre. His office was straight across from the Central Station, completely the wrong place for it, as that's where most drug dealers and prostitutes hang out. I mean, all it would take to get back into crime was for someone to bump into an old prison chum.

Anyway, I was with my social worker, as I didn't trust myself to make it to my brother's house without stopping or getting into some sort of trouble. I could already feel the need for a hit. My stress levels had shot through the roof, and beads of sweat were on my forehead, which were starting to flow down on to my eyebrows.

'Here we are, James,' my social worker announced, 'we're here.'

Once I got out of his motor, I was greeted by my brother, his wife and my girlfriend, Lisa. My eyes locked intensely on to Lisa. She looked a thousand times better than when I'd seen her on that first prison visit. She came running into my arms and gave me a kiss and cuddle. My brother shook my hand and his wife gave me a cuddle.

We all went into the house. The social worker only stayed for a couple of minutes then told me he was leaving. He told me he hoped to see me some time the following week. I told him I'd be there and not to worry. I'd need to report to this social worker for the next two years. Once he left, my brother gave me a bottle of Buckfast out of his fridge, but I gave it back to him, as I'd given up the booze. He was stunned, to say the least, but I told him I didn't drink. I asked Lisa if she'd got me some smack. She nodded and told me she'd got me ½ gm in her purse.

I didn't waste any time. I wrestled the much-needed contents from the purse and put it on the foil. After three or four lines, I felt the neat heat of the heroin cruising through my system. Without resisting, I submitted myself to its familiar electrifying warmth. I asked Lisa if she wanted a burn, but she declined my offer, as she 'didn't take that shit any more'. I never even offered my brother or his wife any because I didn't think they still took smack, but my brother, Bert, wasn't slow in coming forward and asking for a burn. I took another six or seven lines and handed the lot over to him.

After that, Lisa and I went to our bedroom. Once in the bedroom, we were like a couple of teenagers, but I never had sex with her, as the painters were in – she was on her period. You'd think after being in prison for so long and only having the five fingered widow for company that sex would be the first thing on the mind but, in my case, it wasn't. No ... I hadn't turned gay! We just kissed each other and stuff. Some while later, my brother tapped on the door and asked me if I wanted to go down the city centre for some new clothes.

The four of us went on a shopping spree. I got some army-style khaki pants, a pair of trainers, some sweatshirts and a leather jacket. Then we all went for a McDonald's and on to see my dad, who I hadn't seen in years. After the visit, I told my brother that I needed to phone a couple of people. I phoned a few of my pals and arranged to meet up with them some time over that week. I told Lisa that I had to go and see a pal of mine and that I'd be back later that night.

I got my brother to give me a run over to my pal's place. Once we were at my pal's house, my brother couldn't believe the money that was scattered about in his bedroom. There must have been twenty or thirty grand. My pal was doing well through the drugs. He took me into the bathroom and gave me a grand and a mobile phone. He told me not to get mad with smack or crack, as there was a power of money to be made. I eagerly told my pal that I wanted to make as much money as I could.

Once I finished the chat, I went to see my other pal, Steph, who was out of his face on crack coke. I had never really tried it until that night. But BANG! That was it. I was addicted. The rest of that night, Steph, my brother and I smoked the grand I had in my pocket and the £400 of crack that Steph had.

The next day, Lisa and I went up to see her dad. He was an old man, and was sat on a chair, not at all looking the epitome of health. He told me he didn't want me going out with his girl. I told him that was up to Lisa, as she wasn't a little girl any more. Lisa told her dad that she loved me. I butted in and told him, 'Don't you dare ever hit Lisa, ever again. If you do, I'll hit you, understand?'

He called me every name under the sun, so I told him to shut the fuck up and went back up to Lisa's bedroom. We stayed there for a couple of days, then one of my pals gave me the key to a little flat that he owned, up above the hotel in Carluke. It was just a one-bedroom flat, but he told me I could stay in it as long as I wanted to, rent-free.

I soon developed a keen eye for other ladies. I met a little bird who was working in the saunas in Edinburgh. I had marathon sex with this bird for three days, while at the same time getting out of my face on crack. When I returned to the flat, I was dirty, as I hadn't changed my clothes in five days and I stank like a sumo wrestler's jockstrap! I was totally skint but, as ever, Lisa took me in.

I had a bath, food, sex and then bed. I stayed with Lisa for the next two weeks.

I really wished I could have got a grip of my drug taking, but I simply couldn't. That was my downfall. To make things worse, at the time I believed that I never had any problems with drugs. I never took in a word of what Lisa told me about ending back up in prison. I was, by now, sick of Lisa nipping my nut to stop taking drugs. So one day I told her to fuck off and walked out of the flat.

While I was waiting to get the bus back into Glasgow, I spotted a boy I hadn't seen since primary school, all those years ago. It was Rab, the boy who'd battered me on the school bus. I shouted him over. He didn't remember me until I told him my name. When I told him, he stuck his hand out to shake. I asked him if he would like to smoke a joint with me. I won him over and off we went.

Leading him to the slaughter, I took him back to the flat where we found Lisa sat crying. I shouted Rab into the bedroom. Once he came in and sat down, I told him to lean over and to give me the hash out of the drawer. He leaned over to open the drawer. BANG! I kicked him full force in the head. Then I hit him over the head with a glass Irn Bru bottle.

Once his head and face were burst open, I kept trying to smash the bottle into his face, as I needed to satisfy my thirst for vengeance. I was going to smash him into oblivion. On hearing the critter screaming like a banshee, Lisa came running into stop it. I believe she may have been trying to get my attention, as I was lost in abandonment to this blood fest of revenge. I gradually came out of my delirium. As he left, I took great pleasure in telling him that I gave him the doing over for battering me on the school bus all those years ago when I was in the children's home.

'If I see you again, I'll shoot you, understand, you prick?' I blasted.

Then I told Lisa, 'I'm going back through to Glasgow.'

I went and stayed with Steph for a few weeks. I met a guy called Foy, who I'd been in prison with. He was doing the odd job, and asked if I wanted to join him. We did chemists, jewellers and pubs. I'll not say where, but by this time I was totally out of control. I knew my days were numbered, and that it would only be a matter of time before the coppers got me or I ended up dead. I'd been out of prison for six weeks by this time. I was totally fucked up on drugs. I stopped going to see my social worker and told Lisa to get the fuck out of my life.

I woke up one morning, sore from a heroin-induced sleep to see my pal Steph sitting eating a bowl of Sugar Puffs with the TV at full volume. The date was 11 September.

'Fuck's sake, Jimmy, look at this,' Steph said.

When I looked at the TV, I thought Steph had a video on. I told him I couldn't be bothered watching the film. 'I'll watch it later, Steph,' I whined.

'Nah, it's not a video, it's for real,' Steph told me.

Terrorists had struck New York. I shot up and sat next to my pal and watched the news. I couldn't hold my hands steady to empty the smack on to the silver foil. Steph had to do it for me, that's how bad I felt at not having any drugs in my system.

Once I was sorted, Foy came round and chapt the door. I let him in and he excitedly told me about a drug dealer with £20,000 in a stash. So that was that, I was going to rob the dealer later that night with Foy. We went round and stood outside the drug dealer's door. I had the gun in my hand, Foy had a knife and another boy who was with us had an axe. We looked like something out of Madame Tussaud's waxworks! When the people inside opened the door, I stuck the gun at the dealer's head. Everything happened really fast after that. We never got the £20,000, in fact, all we got was some smack.

Once we were safely back in the motor, we made our way back to Foy's flat. I was gutted that the turn never went to plan. I lost my rag with Foy, and belted him across the face with the gun, bursting his nose and lip. I then made my way back over to my pal Steph's house with over an ounce of smack. I knew that would keep us going for a few days, but not forever.

On the Sunday morning, Foy and I robbed an RS McCall's out in Lanarkshire, taking just over a grand in money, five grand's worth of mobile top-up cards and 30,000 fags. I knew that would have kept me going in crack and smack for the next two weeks or so. But only a few days after we'd done the robberies, I was getting a lift in Foy's car when the police pulled us up in Tollcross.

Hell, I had a handgun on me! I told Foy to put the boot down so we could try and get rid of the handgun, but he said he couldn't get rid of the coppers. That was that, the game was finally up. I lasted for two lousy months after being freed from prison. When we were getting questioned in the police station, my so-called pal, Foy, stuck me into the cops so he could get himself a detox off drugs. The grass told them the lot. The two of us appeared at Glasgow Sheriffs' Court on 18 September 2001.

We were sent to Bar L for seven days, and then we got fully committed for trial. The two of us were charged with armed robbery, assault and robbery and a firearms charge. I was also recalled on the December of that same year to finish the rest of my twelve-year sentence, as I had breached my licence. I had been out of prison and back in quicker than a fiddler's elbow.

CHAPTER TWENTY-FOUR

Suicide isn't Painless ... It Kills

DECEMBER 2001

The remand hall in Bar L hadn't changed for years. It was still decrepit, old, smelly and damp in the cells. The whole of the second flat was full of prisoners, all on detox to help them over their drug problems. Both Foy and I got put in the same cell. I still wasn't 100 per cent sure at that time what Foy had told the coppers at the station, so I planned to keep my cards close to my chest and to quiz him over the coming weeks and months.

There was a boy who was down at court with us called Graham. He'd been fully committed to stand trial at Glasgow High for being in possession of a kilo of smack. He got put in the cell next door to us. This was his first time in prison. He came from Shettleston, in the east end of Glasgow. I was down at the pipe talking to him. After a while, I told Graham that I was going to try and get my head down for a few hours' sleep as well. That was the last time anyone ever heard the guy talk, as he hanged himself that night. I really wish he'd told me that he didn't feel too good, as I would have sat at the pipe all night with him.

The next morning, the screws broke the news to me that he'd hanged himself. At first, I thought the screws were kidding on. I expectantly banged at Graham's wall, hoping that this would be a sick joke, but there was no answer. When we never got let out of our cells for exercise, I knew it was for real. I've witnessed and lost a lot of friends to drugs, murders and suicides in my life and, please believe me, it does play on your mind. You never completely recover.

After Graham's death, Foy went down to court for some other charge that he was out on bail for when the police picked him up with me. He never came back to C-hall; instead, he got twelve months and he ended up in A-hall as a convicted prisoner. I was moved in with a boy called Brono from Haghill, in Glasgow's Eastend. Brono was in for murder, but he was brand new with me and we were as close as two peas in a pod. But our friendship was to be short-lived, as I was soon moved over to E-hall to finish serving my existing sentence.

Here I was, back in prison, with not much having changed. Christmas morning hit me in the face like shit off a stick on a hot summer's morning. Most other boys got visits and presents from family and friends, whereas I never even got a visit. I felt more down than ever, but didn't show my feelings, as too many bullies would have jumped on you and vented their hatred. By all means, when your door's shut over for the night, you can do whatever the fuck you want. Most people take their masks off and hang them up for the night. All prisoners act hard, bad, strong, paranoid, shy, happy or daft to help them by each and every day in prison, but, after the lights go out, it's a different world.

I went down to recreation the next day to chat with my pals, play some pool, watch TV and walk up and down to stretch my legs. I didn't know I'd end up jumping into a full-blown, violent fight between my pal and another prisoner. I didn't know the other prisoner but, when I saw him beating up on the man I was pally with, I just saw red and jumped into the fight to help my friend out. The other boy came off second best that Christmas Day, but it just shows you, violence is always lurking about at the surface of most arguments in prison. After that day, my time in E-hall kept running faster and faster, until it was mid-March 2002.

PAYBACK

One day I phoned Lisa's house. Her father picked up the phone, and I asked to talk to Lisa. The words he said to me will never go away until I die. He told me that Lisa was dead.

'She died last night, suddenly, and without warning,' he sombrely told me.

I told her dad to stop fucking about and put Lisa on the phone.

'I've told you, Jimmy, she's dead,' he said one more time.

I didn't know what to do, laugh or cry. I didn't believe him, as he had always hated me even when I was just a boy of eight or nine. I completely flew off the handle with Lisa's dad and called him every name under the sun, then hung the jail phone up on him. I wish now that I could take those words back, but I can't. What's done is done.

I phoned my brother, Bert, and asked him to drive through to Lisa's house and see what her dad was playing at. My brother went through and found out that Lisa really was dead. When I phoned him back the next day, he told me Lisa had dropped dead in her bedroom, but no one knew what had happened. He later told me she'd swallowed a cocktail of drugs and drink. I lay in my prison-cell bed, in abject mourning, day in and day out for some weeks. I couldn't get Lisa out of my head.

In between all this personal stuff, I was moved back to Shotts Prison, after I was sentenced to nine years at Glasgow High Court for allegedly taking part in two armed robberies in Lanarkshire: one supposedly on a disabled couple in their home and the other on the manager of a shop. The woman who was attacked in the first incident, and the shop manager, both identified me from police mug shots. Eventually, at trial, the woman and the manager both identified me as being one of the robbers in each incident. This is important to remember for later on, this 'dock' identification was a joke!

Now this is where I make my stand, as the 'dock identifications' were crucial to the prosecution's case against me. Without them, I wouldn't have been convicted due to the farce that went before. A challenge to the 'Dock IDs' was simmering, and it was decided to use my case to mount a legal attack. Going back to 1975, the Thomson Committee examined trial procedures in Scotland and concluded that identification at a parade should be preferred to identification in court. In my appeal to the Scottish Law Lords, it was argued that dock identification was unfair, owing to it being obvious in court who the accused person was. In a submission to the court, Margaret Scott, QC, proposed that, in future, only evidence of identification made before a trial should be admissible.

However, Lord Gill, the Lord Justice-Clerk, said, 'The submission for the appellant challenges a fundamental and long-standing feature of Scottish criminal procedure. If it is correct, the practice of dock identification has been unfair to the accused, whenever it has occurred, for at least two centuries.' He continued, 'The essential question is whether an identification of the accused is, by the mere fact that it is made when he is in the dock, unfair in every case, no matter the circumstances and no matter that the witness may genuinely recognise the accused and would do so wherever he saw him.'

Lord Osborne supported the views of Lord Gill, and my old mate, Lord Abernethy, said, 'Every dock ID was subject to safeguards. Scottish law demanded corroboration before there could be a conviction, and it was open to the defence to contrast an identification in court with a failure to pick out the same person at a parade.'

So there you have it, I made legal history by being a failed test case. This meant that all the other appeals awaiting the outcome of mine would fall by the wayside for the same reason. Meanwhile, I was in bits, my head was nipping and I had to face Shotts Prison. But, I had an ace card up my sleeve. See the final chapter for the happy ending.

SHOTTS, MARCH 2002

I got into the swing of things right away in A-Hall, as I knew everyone there. Most of the prisoners had been in young offenders or other prisons at the same time as me, so we were all pally. But at nights when all was quiet, I would still sit looking out of my window up at a starless nightsky and think of my Lisa.

I don't know if I believe in ghosts but, since Lisa passed away, there's been mad things happening in my cell at nights, like toothpaste falling from my sink, and the radio going all static. Photos fall off my walls, but they don't scare me one bit, as I know that it is Lisa or Sash or Billy that's trying to get through to me. Once, when I was talking to my little friend Scott Phin, my toilet flushed itself. Scott shit himself and, when I told him about all the other stuff, the hairs on his neck stood on end. Keep your chin up, Scott, OK. Tell your son I was asking for him, if you ever read this book, as I know you love him to bits.

Wherever I go, trouble follows. I was only in Shotts Prison for two weeks before the riot started.

CHAPTER TWENTY-FIVE

Screwing the Screwbirds and the Shotts Riot

A-HALL AND B-HALL

Most prison wardens say that the riot started because there was a power cut in the jail that night. They say all the cons went mental because Liverpool were playing a game in Europe which they couldn't watch because of the power cut. Well, that may have taken place in B-hall, but it wasn't the case in A-hall. The fundamental cause was the lack of kit. But, of course, you would never find that explanation in a Home Office report, as everybody knows that there are no drugs in British prisons.

It only took us thirty minutes to completely smash and wipe out the hall. The screws had no chance of getting the halls back under their control, so the SAS were called into control the jail. Believe it or not, the army has a duty in law to respond to such incidents if called in by the relevant authorities. One of my pals was trapped in his cell, so we ripped the doors off the hinges. When we did eventually smash the door down, it fell down on

Petesy's head and burst all his head and eye open. Looking back on it, this was so funny that it could have been a sketch out of *The Benny Hill Show*.

I'd just like to give a mention to a few of the boys that were up for it enough to be united against the screws: Petesy, Drew, Jonesy, Big Scott, Dunky, Davie, Matt S and Tam F. I hope you're all doing brand new. The riot lasted for nearly twenty-four hours. At one stage, near the end, we were all jam-packed in one cell, which are only designed for one person, but we had sixteen of us in it, squeezed like sardines. I think that's a new record in Shotts Prison.

We ended the siege the next day. As soon as we all came out of the riot-torn hall, we were moved all over the place. I was moved back like the prodigal son to Bar L's seg unit, which was by now my second home. For once I wasn't alone, as I was moved over with Big Andy S from the Forth. Andy is doing twenty-five years. I call him the bionic man, as he was shot in the chest three times by a police marksman, but still managed to crawl away into the woods before he was arrested. Andy told me about the carry-on in B-hall with him and Sammo getting dug out for their hall rioting, as per usual. Time after time, it's the same faces that get pulled out if anything ever happens in prison, even if the guy has really nothing to do with it.

In reality, the grasses had control in Shotts. The governors and screws turned a blind eye to the prisoners that grassed on their fellow prisoners. The grasses can have mobile phones and sell smack freely in the halls, whereas someone like me gets flung in a seg unit for years on end because you were done trying to bring a parcel of drugs in at a visit or had a phone in your cell. That's what I hated about Shotts Prison. Dirty fucking grasses. Well, wake up and smell the cappuccino, you dirty pricks. You deal in human bodies, getting guys in your hall stabbed for fuck all. You know who you are. I don't need to lower myself to your standards, no cunt in the system likes you, but they don't say it up front because you'll stop giving out their drugs.

So, I was glad to see the back of Shotts Prison, as it's a poison factory of pure hatred. I lay down in the seg unit in Bar L for some three months and then got moved back up to Perth seg unit, once again.

PERTH PRISON SEG BLOCK, JULY 2002

When I arrived, it felt as if I'd never left the place. I had that deja-vu feeling. This time, the screws gave me a portable TV in my cell. At first, I smelled a rat and told them I didn't want their rotten TV, and that they could shove it, but within one week, I had it on twenty-four hours a day. I know, I'm a weak bastard, but why fucking not, that's what I say. After all when you're in a seg block, you're as well to make it as best for yourself as you possibly can. If you don't, you'll end up going mad and becoming bitter.

I was only in this seg unit until 4 October before being accepted back into the special unit for violent prisoners down in Shotts Prison. But, in the meantime, I had to sit down and talk to professional after professional about my aggression, violence and communication skills. All in all, it was a total waste of time for me. As you know, if someone hits you, you hit them back – you don't tell them to go away just 'cos you've done a fucking anger-management course. What good is that when someone pulls a knife out on you? Fuck, it's a jail. We're not in some holiday camp.

What we needed more than anything were lessons in how to deal with the fucking screws. Screws will try, and sometimes succeed, in driving cons to the brink of madness. I've been at the brink of madness myself, where the shrinks had to be brought in, but thankfully I never got flung in the mad house. There was one boy, whose name I won't mention, who started prison around the same time as me, and has been in the nut house no less than five times. Never mind Mark 'Chopper' Read, this guy cut off his own finger at the knuckle because he didn't like it. He has also cut off his eyebrows, slashed his own face and body, been on forty- or fifty-day hunger strikes, where he ate bits of his radio. As soon as he was released from prison, he became a normal guy again. I get so angry sometimes at the way our system turns normal boys and girls into nutters, when they should be helping them.

Never believe that screws treat people the way they would like to be treated. But you don't need to take my word for it. You could read other jail books like Jimmy Boyle's *Sense of Freedom*, Charles Bronson and Stephen Richards' *Silent Scream*, John Steele's *The Bird that Never Flew*, Paul Ferris's *Ferris Conspiracy*, and many others. Every single one talks about and documents hard-handedness from screws. The system fucking stinks.

A couple of my friends were in this seg unit with me that I'd like to say hello to. Firstly, there's Cammy, Paul T, Kev M, Punter and Hendie. These boys would sit for hours at the door talking and getting a good laugh. I also need to thank Steph and Sharon, my very close pals who visit me most weeks in prison. These two have done loads for me, thanks again. You know I love you.

The big day had finally arrived for me to leave the seg block and go back to Shotts Prison. Ah, fuck it, I thought, a change is as good as a rest.

SHOTTS SPECIAL UNIT, 7 OCTOBER 2002

Back to Shotts again. This time, I thought I should try and learn a bit more about the place that had become a home-from-home for me. I learned that the unit had been built on a spare bit of ground within Shotts Prison compound in 1991, to house the most violent men from the old Bar L Special Unit, which was shutting its doors for good. Some of these cons had real attitude: Jimmy Boyle, Bally, Larry Winters, Shug Collins, Toe Elliott and Ronnie Nelson. Its most famous resident after Jimmy Boyle was T C Campbell, who was wrongly convicted of six murders with his friend Joe Steele. By the time I went into Shotts, some twelve years after it had been open, there wasn't so much of the hardcore nametag to the place as there once was, but still we all had our moments.

One moment in particular was to change my life forever. We were told in November 2003 by the governor and screws that the unit would be shutting down, as the Scottish government had decided to house Scotland's worst ever mass murderer, the Lockerbie bomber, in the unit by himself. After that, no one really cared about the place. Some of the screws that I can't mention by name were even bringing us drugs in. Some screwbirds were even giving prisoners sexual favours. It was good to see us prisoners and the screws singing from the same hymn sheet.

Things were going fine until the morning of 7 January, when a big argument started over one of the screws not bringing drugs into the unit that he'd been paid £300 for. One thing led to another, with the result that a screw ran at me with a pool cue to snap it off my head. He missed. And that set off a whole chain of events that ended in four screws being rushed to hospital with multiple stab wounds.

After that, there was a major smash-up of the unit. There were some five or so running battles with the mufti mob. These hostilities went on right through the night before the screws won control of the unit back. Once we got carted out, Danny, Billy and I were taken to Kilmarnock seg block and charged with four attempted murders on the screws in the unit.

In the morning, we were taken to Hamilton Sheriffs' Court. In typical Holland style, I refused to wear any clothes. I was freezing my bollocks off, my hands and feet were blue, as was my penis. I pissed on my legs and toes in the security van to heat myself up. When I went into Hamilton Sheriffs' Court, the turnkeys put me in a cell on my own. I was in there all day from eleven in the morning until seven at night, freezing my bollocks off.

I asked to use the toilet but the screws wouldn't open the door of my cell, so I done a shit on my hands and rubbed it all over my head, face and body. Talk about face painting! I knew it would fuck their heads up before mine. What put the icing on the cake was when they brought the woman judge and PF down to my cell door. They were nearly sick from the smell! I lay at the bottom of my cell door and pissed at their feet. If I was getting treated like a dog, I was going to act like one. That soon took the grin off the screws' faces.

When I got back to Kilmarnock seg cells, I got a shower and came off the dirty protest. I got put next door to one of my pals, Leo, who I hadn't seen in years. We had a good laugh until one in the morning, when the screws decided to come into our cells in their mufti gear to give us a cell search. But I can't say much about this, as we still have an outstanding court case against the screws for sexually assaulting me. Take it from me, it's not just some prisoners that are gay, there's a lot of screws as well. Two screws in particular were manhandling my privates.

I only lasted another three weeks in Kilmarnock Prison before I came back up to Perth seg. I was still waiting to go to court for the four attempted murders of the screws with my two co-accused, Danny and Billy. Now we should have been at court within six months, but for some stupid reason we had to wait more than ten. But that's the fucking Scottish prison system for you.

CHAPTER TWENTY-SIX

Attempted Murder of Four Prison Officers

Well, there I was, up on a charge for the attempted murder of four prison officers, and a charge for assaulting and abducting a hostage during the course of the riot. Perhaps it would be useful if I gave you another view of my situation, that of my lawyer, as detailed in his files:

I'm in receipt of papers in this case and note that the accused is due to stand trial at the High Court Edinburgh in the sitting commencing five January 2004 along with his co-accused, all of whom were prisoners at Shotts at the time of the offences, being housed in a special unit for difficult prisoners.

He faces six separate charges in total, all related to a riot at Shotts Prison. Four charges are of the attempted murder of four prison officers, another relates to the assault and abduction of a hostage taken during the course of the riot. The charges can only be described as a catalogue of offending of an extremely serious and violent nature and are aggravated by the number of charges involved, the use of weapons, and the locus and the status of the complainers assaulted in the course of their duty.

Any one of these offences would, in itself, attract a substantial custodial sentence. However, the very recent, lengthy and analogous record of the accused exacerbates matters. The record discloses a number of convictions for dishonesty and violence and, in particular, convictions relating to assaults of prison officers during a prison riot and the carrying of offensive weapons and firearms.

He has been convicted on indictment on six previous occasions. Of particular significance are the three High Court convictions in respect of assaults and robbery and contraventions of the Firearms Act 1968. In the last ten years, he has received custodial sentences of six, two, six, six, six and finally nine years.

In these circumstances, it is axiomatic that, if convicted, a very lengthy custodial sentence will be imposed. Indeed, I am of the view, standing the degree of violence and the course of criminal conduct alleged in the present offences together with the appalling record, that this is a case where, if convicted, the court is likely to impose a discretionary life sentence.

So far as the conduct of the trial is concerned, there are a number of complex legal and other issues which arise. These relate to both the application of the doctrine of concert in the particular circumstances of this case, but more particularly to the instructions given which disclose a background of prison corruption involving, inter alia, the wide-scale supply and distribution of controlled drugs by prison officers and sexual activity between prison officers and prisoners.

Standing the nature of these allegations, it is self evident that complexities will arise both in respect of the preparation of the defence case for trial and that difficult and sensitive cross-examination of some senior prison officers will be necessary at the trial itself.

The final difficulty, but perhaps, in practical terms, the most significant in what is already an extremely difficult case, is the accused himself, so far as the conduct of proceedings are concerned. As described by the prison authorities, he, like his co-accused, is an extremely volatile and difficult prisoner to manage. He has spent much of his prison life in segregation and, indeed, at the time of the alleged offences was being held in a special unit.

He has a history of disrupting court proceedings, of having to be removed during the course of his trial and, indeed, in the present case for committal proceedings, the court had to be convened in the back of the police van, as the accused was in a state of undress and was conducting a 'dirty' protest in which he covered himself in excrement.

The accused will, therefore, be required to be managed and carefully guided by his legal team if proceedings are not to be extended and disrupted in a significant way.

I cannot overemphasise how important it will be to have a very experienced counsel leading his defence team if significant delay and, ultimately, possible desertion of any trial is to be avoided.

In other words, I was all but dead and buried.

CHAPTER TWENTY-SEVEN

Kangaroo Trial

EDINBURGH HIGH COURT, 5–28 JANUARY 2004

I'd been waiting one whole year to stand trial with my two co-accused. The whole thing was a total farce, to say the least. When I finally appeared in court on 5 January, things didn't start as they should have done. Firstly, I sacked my legal team who were representing me. If that wasn't enough, the trial got put off once again.

The Scottish prison system knows fine well that the charges the courts have got us on will not stick, and that's why it took a full year to come to court in the first place. If I were found guilty of the charges, I would be looking at a life sentence, as was Danny Boyle, one of my co-accused. Danny had finished his five-year sentence and was on remand, because the courts would not give him bail. My other co-accused, Billy Lewis, was doing two life sentences, so if he was found guilty, there was not much the courts could do to him.

The trial gave me the opportunity to see my friends for the first time in one whole year. Danny was looking fitter and healthier, whereas Billy, on the other hand, had put on nearly three stone in weight, which was a very big surprise, as I've never known Billy to be so heavy. He's now thirteen-and-a-half stone, but he looks good for it, all the same.

The night before the trial, I had a phone call with my old mother. I couldn't get her words out of my head, as they kept playing over and over in my head: 'James, son, I hope to God you get found not guilty of the crimes, as I want you out of that awful place before I die, son. I haven't got too much longer to live; I'm hanging on in the hope you get out soon. I can't eat or sleep, I pray to God every day for you to be set free.' I desperately wanted to tell my old mother that I loved her so much and wanted to be by her side and to taste her homemade cooking, but I couldn't because the screws around me would see that as a sign of weakness. When I heard my old mother crying down the line, there wasn't a thing I could say or do. That night, I lay in bed tossing and turning, not being able to sleep. I had so many things running through my head that I wanted to scream.

On the journey down to Edinburgh from Perth, I felt really pissed off, as I was in the cat-A van with a five-screw escort and my hands were double cuffed. Two sets of handcuffs for a little cherub like me! The cat-A van only had little windows, no more than 60cm wide and 30cm high, so I couldn't see anything. Scotland is so beautiful, people from all over the world come to see the landscapes and structures, whereas I was going over one of Scotland's most famous landscapes and couldn't see its magnificent beauty. That is what really pissed me off. I let my escort know how dirty and low-down they were for depriving me of a view, but as usual he blamed his boss for the security arrangements. They are all dirty cunts! That's why I hate the system so much.

7 JANUARY 2004: 4.47PM

So here I am, in the cell waiting to go up to court. It's 4.47am. I'll stop here to get the three-and-a-half hours sleep before I have to face the court like some kind of serial killer. My head is thumping. I've got a constant ringing in my ears, but I don't want to tell the prison nurses or doctors about it, as they'll only offer me Panadol, and then write in my notes that I'm going off my head or something to that effect. Instead, I will gather my strength from thinking about my family and friends. I want to thank Linda, Scott, Wee Jay, my mum, my brothers, Rose, Lynne, Lizzy, Steph, Sharon, Paul Green, Big Alan and his family Rebecca, Delia, Mick, Joe, Billy, Scouse Barry, Raymie and everyone else for helping me get through this. If it wasn't for all their words of support and kindness, then this would have been much harder to deal with.

8 JANUARY 2004: 6.23PM

I've just got back from court. The day was a complete disaster for me and my co-accused. It had however started well, when I got to meet my new lawyer for the first time. Once I had a private meeting with him, he came across really well, and talked my kind of lingo. The Crown offered us a deal, but one of us didn't think it was beneficial to our way of thinking, so the deal was rejected. Now we're supposed to be going to trial on Monday, 12 January. My new lawyer and QC have not got the paperwork concerning my defence. I don't know how much more I can take of it, as I'm starting to lose the plot. It's very nippy, building yourself up to have your day in court, hoping your defence team is better than the Crown's legal team.

On the trek back from Edinburgh High Court, the screws asked me what was happening, so I gave them some small talk. They all want to see you hammered with the worst possible outcome, even though they sit and look you in the eye and tell you 'the sentence was a bit steep'.

But I'm not the only one losing the plot. When I had my tea back in the solitary seg cells, one of the boys who I was speaking with cut his face open with a razor blade. He gave himself ten stitches on one side and thirteen on the other side. If that wasn't enough, he also shaved half his hair off down one side and shaved his eyebrows off. The boy had definitely lost the scheme of things, but this kind of thing is not uncommon in the solitary cells up and down the length of Scotland.

12 JANUARY 2004

I'm over the moon today, this fine day on God's earth. For once, I've nothing to complain about. My new legal team got a copy of the video evidence of the incident that I'm currently going through trial for. As expected, my heart was fluttering around in my chest like autumn leaves in the wind – not, though, with fright, but with excitement in anticipation of what lay ahead.

My co-accused and I were double cuffed at the wrists before they escorted us into the courtroom to watch the movie. My new lawyer, Mr Turnbull, sat just in front of the dock with paper and pen at the ready. He'd never seen the video nasty himself, so it was a first all-round. Without any warning, the state-of-the-art plasma TV screen burst into life. I didn't recognise any of the stars of this movie as it's very strange looking at yourself on TV and the people you know. I carried on watching, not even blinking, to see if I could see myself stabbing the four prison wardens, but I couldn't see myself. I never saw any of my co-accused stab any of the wardens either.

After the second viewing, we were escorted back down to our cage-like cells where fifty pairs of screws' eyes burned on to our backs. I kept my head held high, with a smile on my face, letting them all know what I really felt about them.

Once we were placed back into our cages and the screws left us to our own thoughts, I heard my two co-accused arguing amongst themselves in a heated manner. I didn't join in. I just listened to what they had to say to each other. I'll not impart what they said to each other, but best just to say that neither of them was happy. After some minutes, I joined in their conversation. Before I could say what I had on my mind, they wanted my point of view. I never gave them one, as I knew that whatever I said would make one of them unhappy. Instead, I told them that the Scottish prison system was going to set us up to be railroaded as a warning to anyone else that had stabbing screws on their minds.

'Take a minute to think what I'm telling you, troops,' I said.

After a few more minutes, they shouted to agree with me. I had opened their eyes as to what was really going on. That's why I stalled the court case for so long, as I knew it would make the court men panic. They knew that their case wasn't as strong as the courts and prison service had led us to believe.

I'm looking forward to a long lie-in, as we don't need to be in court for trial until 16 January.

16 JANUARY 2004

When I entered the dock on 16 January with Billy Lewis and Danny Boyle, things didn't feel right. After the jury were all seated to our left, the judge asked Billy's QC, Mr Edger Praise, to take the floor. What Mr Praise lacked in height, he more than made up for in vociferous volume. I knew Billy had picked the right QC for his defence. After Billy's QC had done the damage, my QC, Mr McKenzie, stood up. This man was much taller than Mr Praise, but his voice was much shallower, to the point that I had to strain my ears to listen intensely to what he had to say on my behalf. After he was finished, Danny's QC, Mr Hughes, took to the floor. I don't know if Danny's QC had been a QC for very long, as the old judge, Roderick Macdonald, kept interrupting Danny's QC to tell him he couldn't allow certain questions.

This intervention from the judge flummoxed and agitated the man to the point where he started looking at the jury in disgust at the judge's rulings. This hullabaloo went on for some two days before the first bombshell happened. Danny Boyle was offered a deal from the Crown. The Crown was willing to drop all of the four attempted murders, the hostage and the petrol bombing if he pleaded to vandalism. I was then called out to see my QC, who also offered me a deal from the Crown, which was to drop the four attempted murders if I pleaded guilty to chasing a screw about the special unit with a screwdriver.

I didn't even stop to ponder this deal. I said, 'No.' My QC was stunned. He told me Danny had taken his deal and he could get two or three years instead of the five or six years. So why didn't I want a deal from the Crown too?

Well, for starters, I was brought up to plead to nothing and, secondly, I wasn't going to leave Billy Lewis sitting in the dock by himself, charged with four attempted murders, a hostage taking and a petrol bombing. I couldn't do that to a man who, out of sheer loyalty, flung all caution to the wind to defend Danny Boyle and me and all the other prisoners in the unit. When I went back round and told Billy that the Crown had just offered me a deal, Danny told me to take it.

I told him, 'Fuck off.'

He replied, 'You're mad!'

I told him I wasn't mad. I said, 'I'm loyal to my friends, to the end, so be it! Whatever happens, I'm not jumping off a sinking ship.'

Danny Boyle was stunned when I told him this. Billy shouted and told me to take the deal if I wanted to. But, when I told Billy I was going back up there to fight the Crown's case against us, Billy couldn't have been happier.

All of us went back up after lunch. Danny Boyle's QC stood up and told the judge his client was taking the deal. The Crown accepted this and Boyle was taken downstairs. This left Billy and me. I am now facing all the charges on the indictment, but this doesn't bother me, not one little bit.

28 JANUARY

Much has been happening over the last few days. The screws stood in the witness box and said Billy stabbed them and alleged that I stabbed one screw called Wallace. It was so surreal to see these so-called tough-nut screws standing pointing their fingers at Billy and me. These contemptuous screws were caught red-handed by our lawyers, but still the judge never did anything about it, old prick that he is. If that wasn't enough, one of the screws who was stabbed stood in the box and told the court that Billy and I were animals.

Then another bombshell. One of the screws told the court that he'd received two letters from prisoners that were in the special unit with us telling him that Billy and I had planned the four stabbings some weeks beforehand. Our QCs stood up and asked the screw the names of these prisoners, but the judge ruled that the informers' names had to be kept secret from us under the Human Rights Act.

The trial went on for another two days before the Crown finished their case against us. That's when the third bombshell came out. My QC came down to see me to tell me one of the screwbirds that I wanted to put on the stand had breast cancer. As a result, he didn't want to ask her about the sex and drug allegations. So I had no option but to sack him and my full defence team, as I needed to ask this screwbird questions that were important to mine and Billy's defence.

The judge gave me two days to get all my papers in order to defend myself with the help of a lawyer, but this never happened, as no lawyer wanted to help. Give Billy his dues, he sacked his full team as well, so we had no one to help or point us in the right directions. The prosecutor must have thought it was his lucky day. Billy and I, instead, conducted our own defence. I now want to thank Scobbie Wilson, David Blavajeric and Geo McGeoch, who all stood up in court and told the truth. You all did Billy and I proud. I also want to thank Andrew Spooner from Irvine and his bird, Shirley, and daughter, Jade, for their help in this trial. You're one in a million, Spooner.

After Billy and I conducted our own defences, we went down to the cells to write our summing-up speech in pencil, as we weren't allowed pens. The two little screws escorting us were brand new: Jamie from Glenochil, a pro boxer, who had words of support, and Rab, who too was brand new with me. He played with Dundee United reserves a few years back. These two men may be screws, but I'm giving them a mention because they treated me like a human being, not some sort of fucking animal.

Once I'd written my speech that I was going to address to the jury, I read it out to Jamie and Rab, and they loved it.

29 JANUARY

My time had come to address the jury. I was going on about William Wallace and *Chewing The Fat*, a Scottish comedy show. I finished by wishing that Jordan wins *I'm A Celebrity Get Me Out Of Here*, which made the jury burst out laughing.

After that, I shouted, 'I'll sit on my arse.'

After Billy and I had finished our speeches, the judge went through the charges that Billy and I faced and summed up to the jury. They were then sent out to make a verdict.

When the jury came back at 3.12pm, I knew, for some reason, that I was walking. They convicted Billy of attempting to murder two screws and assaulting a third by stabbing him with a screwdriver. Me? Well, my trial was over. I was found Not Guilty of all charges, all off my own back. I now believe in God or someone higher up.

We were then put back down to the cells, then I went back up with Billy to get formerly cleared of all charges on the indictment. Before I left the court, I thanked the jury and told them they'd done justice. I then turned around and looked at all the governors and screws, gave them my middle finger salute, smiled and walked out.

But poor Billy got sentenced to life, with a recommendation that he serve twelve years minimum. But he's already doing two life sentences, poor cunt. Billy took it as if he was just sentenced to sixty days. I've never seen a man being so cool under pressure, and I certainly couldn't have acted the way my friend did. I'll always visit and look out for my friend Billy Lewis. He's one in a million. Watch out for his life story if it ever gets put into print, as it will blow your mind. This boy is one of the real bad-ass cons of the British penal system.

Remember earlier on when I asked you to remember what I said about 'dock identification' in court and that I would mention a happy ending in the last chapter? Well, here goes. Your man here has made legal history – I have won my appeal! On 11 May 2005, the Judicial Committee of the Privy Council in London overturned a decision made by the Scottish Law Lords. This is first time that this has happened. And guess what that means? A long story short ... my appeal on two robbery charges, which was turned down by the Scottish Law Lords on the strength of dock identification and non-disclosure by the prosecution, has been won. My winning of this appeal has massive implications too complicated for me to go into, but I am sure it will open the floodgates for those that have endured 'dock identification' and will change the ways Scottish courts use this outdated and unsafe way of helping to convict people.

The other two charges out of the four, for which I received a nine-year prison sentence, were not appealed against, but it means that sentence is now way over what it should have been. This means that I have now got an appeal in against the severity of the prison sentence for the two remaining softer charges.

My solicitor, Jack Brown of Brown's Solicitors in Glasgow said, 'This is the first time this happened. A Scottish conviction has been overturned outside of Scotland by the Privy Council in London. An interim liberation appeal has been set in motion and this will be heard in the next week or so and it could see Jimmy being released.'

14 JULY 2005

I have won freedom in an application to the courts by virtue of what is called 'interim liberation'.

So there you have it, I won and I beat the system. Now I just need to start putting my words about reform into action. Only time will tell.

Epilogue

A MOTHER'S LOST LOVE

1970 – 2005

I only found out that my mother, Liz, was still alive when I was doing research for this book. For twenty-eight-and-a-half years of my life, I was led to believe that my mother was dead. When I first found out that she was alive, I was totally gutted. All I wanted to do was phone her up and call her every name under the sun. At nights, I would lie in my bed and ask why she dumped me at a hospital instead of taking me with her to start a new life down in England. Why hadn't she once tried to come and find my brothers and me? But I'm not going to sit here and blame all my fuck-ups in life on my mother not being there for me. That's just a coward's way out of things.

I saw my mother for the first time in my adult life in Glasgow High Court when I got sentenced to the nine years for the robbery and gun charges. I didn't mind one little bit about my mother sitting at court watching her son taking another trip to prison; after all, what else was I brought on to this planet for?

But who is to blame? Well, the state certainly has a lot to answer for. Its many faceless children's homes, the foster families that were only in it for the extra money, being carted around like an animal, all these things have made me into the man I am. Now I'm not looking for pity, as I'll take the blame on my own chin for all my subsequent fuck-ups, but just stop and think how many people are in prison or mental hospitals through the things that have been dished out to them by the state. Is it any wonder that our children grow up to be mass murderers, rapists, robbers, junkies, homeless thugs and the like when they are treated no better than dogs?

My relationship with my mother has developed to the extent that I phoned her once a week but now that I have won my appeal I want to see her. She can't travel up to see me, as she is far too sick, but we have rather a good friendship over the phone. I've discovered that she has also lived a life of hardship. I've also discovered that I've got a half-brother called Ruben, who is half-Jamaican. I love him like my full brother.

For a long time I had to hope against all hope that I could win my appeal, as it was another criminal that grassed me up for something I didn't do. I've already done plenty, but it's double sore to accept it when you never did the crime in the first place. Anyhow, I intend going down to meet my mother and all my other family members that I've never seen. I don't know if my father's still alive just now; the last I knew or heard, he was in some homeless hostel, drinking himself to death. That's his fucking problem. I'm not going to shed any tears over him. I feel the same way about my two brothers, who have never done fuck all for me. I've told me dear mother how I feel towards them, and she keeps telling me to write or phone them, but I wouldn't even waste the price of a stamp on those two arseholes.

I didn't know that I had a hidden talent for books, but I now think I've found out who I really am and what I want to be. Please ask for my other books that I hope will follow, as I want to raise money for the homeless young children of Glasgow. I promise that I'll donate ten per cent of my earnings to help make children's lives better. I couldn't be one of those selfish people that wants money, money, money. Money has never changed my life.

I hate prison as much as the next man, but I've learned to adapt to my surroundings and make the best of a bad situation. After all, you don't need to go over to Africa to see poverty. No, sir, it's right here on your own doorstep, in every city, up and down Britain. Come on, this is Great Britain, not some Third World country! No child should need to stay on the streets committing crime and selling their body to sex predators for money to feed themselves.

Finally, there are some people I need to mention before I sign off. Rose, Lizzy and Lynn have stood by me through thick and thin, good or bad. I couldn't quite believe their love and friendship. They make sure I've changed my pants, had a shower and all the stuff any sister in the world asks their brother. My adopted sister, Lizzy, as I call her, has had her own little boy called Lee, who is a little star. I can't wait to take him out for walks and kick a ball about some park with him. Lynn is my youngest adopted sister and she is so bright and full of life that it was a joy to hear her little voice on the other end of the phone to cheer me up when was down.

I would also just like to say hello to Trish, Gordie, young Trish, young Gordie, Diane, Tottie and his lovely family. Also a big hello to my pal Alan and his family for showing me kindness over the years. And to uncle Macky, who sadly died during the writing of this book. The family and friends miss him dearly, but he's always there in our hearts. R.I.P., Mac the Hat.

Finally, to the man who helped me through every aspect of this book, Steve Richards, many, many thanks. If it weren't for Steve Richards, I'd still be sitting twiddling my thumbs, just another messed-up, burned-out criminal junkie with no future ahead of him. Thanks to his loyalty and respect and hard, hard work, we've managed to bring this story to life.

Other titles by Stephen Richards available from
John Blake Publishing

Insanity: My Mad Life
Charles Bronson with Stephen Richards
ISBN:1844540308

The Krays and Me
Charles Bronson with Stephen Richards
ISBN: 1844540421

The Good Prison Guide
Charles Bronson with Stephen Richards
ISBN: 1844540227

The Lost Girl
Caroline Roberts with Stephen Richards
ISBN: 1843581485

It's Criminal
James Crosbie with Stephen Richards
ISBN: 1844540596 (Hardback)

Born to Fight
Richy Horsley with Stephen Richards
ISBN: 1844540960

Street Warrior
Malcolm Price with Stephen Richards
ISBN: 1904034632

Crash 'n' Carry
Stephen Richards
ISBN: 1844541061

The Taxman
Brian Cockerill with Stephen Richards
ISBN: 184454134 7

Viv Graham, Britain's Most Feared Gangster
Stephen Richards
ISBN: 1844541274